IN THE CULTURE SOCIETY

How do different artistic and cultural practices develop in the contemporary consumer culture? What do we mean by the 'aestheticization of everyday life'? In this new collection of essays Angela McRobbie considers the social consequences of cultural proliferation and the social basis of aesthetic innovation.

In the wake of postmodernism, McRobbie offers a more grounded and even localized account of key cultural practices, from the new populism of young British artists, including Damien Hirst and Tracey Emin, to the underground London sounds of drum 'n' bass music; from the new sexualities in girls' and women's magazines, to the dynamics of fashion production and consumption. Throughout the essays the author returns to issues of livelihoods and earning a living in the cultural economy, while at the same time pressing the issue of cultural value.

Arguing for a new materialism in cultural studies, McRobbie also focuses attention on cultural producers including artists and musicians, designers, editors and journalists. *In the Culture Society* provides a new direction in cultural studies as well as a vigorous defence of the field.

Angela McRobbie is Professor of Communication at Goldsmiths College, London. She is the author of *Postmodernism and Popular Culture* and *British Fashion Design*.

IN THE CULTURE SOCIETY

Art, fashion and popular music

Angela McRobbie

London and New York

First published 1999
by Routledge
11 New Fetter Lane, London EC4P 4EE

Simultaneously published in the USA and Canada
by Routledge
29 West 35th Street, New York, NY 10001

Routledge is an imprint of the Taylor & Francis Group

© 1999 Angela McRobbie

Typeset in Galliard by
J&L Composition Ltd, Filey, North Yorkshire
Printed and bound in Great Britain by
Clays Ltd., St. Ives plc

British Library Cataloguing in Publication Data
A catalogue record for this book is available
from the British Library

Library of Congress Cataloguing in Publication Data
A catalogue record for this book has been requested

ISBN 0–415–13750–0 (pbk)
ISBN 0–415–13749–7 (hbk)

CONTENTS

ILLUSTRATIONS

ACKNOWLEDGEMENTS

The author and publishers would like to thank the following for kind permission to reproduce the articles in this collection.

Chapter 2 first appeared in *Media, Culture and Society*, vol. 18, 1996. Reproduced by permission of the publishers.

Chapter 3 first appeared in *Feminist Review*, no. 55, Spring 1997. Reproduced by permission of the publishers.

Chapter 4, revised and updated here, first appeared in J. Curran, D. Morley and V. Walkerdine (eds) *Cultural Studies and Communications*, London: Edward Arnold, 1996. Reproduced by permission of the publishers.

Chapter 5, edited here, first appeared in K.S. Chen and D. Morley (eds) *Stuart Hall: Critical Dialogues in Cultural Studies (Comedia)*, New York: Routledge Inc, 1996. Reproduced by permission of the publishers.

Chapter 6 first appeared in M. Ferguson and P. Golding (eds) *Cultural Studies in Question*, London: Sage, 1997. Reproduced by permission of the publishers.

Chapter 8 first appeared as a review article in *Media, Culture and Society*, vol. 17, 1995. Reproduced by permission of the publishers.

Chapter 9 first appeared in *Soundings: A Journal of Culture and Politics*, issue 3, 1996. Reproduced by permission of the publishers.

Chapter 10 first appeared in *Soundings: A Journal of Culture and Politics*, issue 9, 1998. Reproduced by permission of the publishers.

INTRODUCTION

The process of gathering together a collection of essays, published over the last two to three years in a diverse range of journals, is usually accompanied by a sense that there is, or ought to be, an underlying theme. These articles were all written while I was completing a study of young British fashion designers. Arranging them now into an order for publication, it is clear that many of them deal with the broader issues I was thinking about while focussing more specifically on fashion. The future of work in the creative sector has been a recurrent interest, as has the growth of self-employment, an increasing part of which is 'cultural work'. The social consequences of this shift towards a kind of work which appears to be particularly rewarding on the grounds of its emphasis on creativity, threads its way through many of these essays. Suggesting that in Britain by the late 1990s 'All the World's a Stage, Screen or Magazine' (Chapter 2), is not merely a polemical point. However, there is much more empirical work to be done in this area and several of my essays simply point the way forward.

If the 'aestheticisation of everyday life' provides an over-arching theme, so also does the idea of 'after postmodernism'. By this I do not mean some major current of thinking which has emerged to replace postmodernism. Instead I have found myself looking back at postmodernism as a body of writing which, despite its critique of the grand narratives of modernity, came to occupy the position of a meta-narrative itself. Postmodernism was expansive, it was a big picture. There remains a sharp sense now, some years later, that postmodernism was primarily a Western phenomena which latched onto notions of hybridity and movement, uncertainty and 'loss of faith', but which left relatively untouched and intact those people who remained behind. These were those who did not have the basic resources to become part of the cosmopolitan world, who could not travel, or who could not travel back to where they had come from, or whose relation to the flickering world of television images meant watching soap operas while engaging in homeworking, sewing parts of clothing together, night and day, for sweatshop wages, or working, again for low pay, in the new service sector, as security guards or petrol station attendants. This sense that the aesthetic force of postmodernism did not fully acknowledge the way in

ix

which these changes were registered at ground level has sent me back towards a new kind of materialism, one which attempts to connect the large scale changes with the small scale cultural economies and livelihoods upon which so many people now depend for a living.

There are four other things to be said about this collection of articles. First, that they came about because I was drawn by a sociological interest to phenomena like the new girls' and women's magazines, such as *Sugar* and *More!*, which seemed to go overboard to embrace an unprecedented degree of sexual frankness in their pages. It was sociological curiosity which drew me to these forms and encouraged me to ask what was going on here and how it could be explained within the framework of feminism and so-called post-feminism. Likewise, it was almost impossible for me not to be interested in the new forms of dance music which, from the early 1990s, began to resonate across the airwaves. I was interested in how music like that of Talvin Singh, Tricky and Goldie incorporated small slices of black and Asian social history, from across the 'black Atlantic', from Asia, the Caribbean, New York and Britain, into their distinctive sounds. They each did this in very different ways but in all three there was an extraordinary energy which seemed to emerge from the creative possibilities made available by new technology and its application to music.

The second strand which runs through the essays is the suggestion that subcultural or underground forms such as these are not just worthy of notice but are aesthetically innovative as well as politically significant. The rise of dance music and, in particular, the growth of drum 'n' bass and all its subsequent variations marks in my mind the single most important breakthrough in contemporary music since reggae. It is the British equivalent of American hip hop, it explores its own history back through reggae and dub and further back to bebop while at the same time leaping forwards into the age of computerized, sampled sound, introducing also a shot of dark, dystopian panic and anxiety. As several of the articles in this collection indicate, the musicians involved in this dance scene are predominantly male and are themselves heavily dependent upon this freelance, creative economy. The volume of releases, the variety of mixes and the sheer energy of the output also says something about the tension and the uncertainty of earning a living in this subcultural labour market. The breakneck speed of the music itself describes the frantic economic lifestyle of the musicians, producers and DJs.

In the past when writers like myself, from a cultural studies background, have described the importance of popular musical forms, we have often been accused of romanticism or of over-emphasizing the potential political dynamics of such forms. Here I am boldly suggesting that these are contemporary art forms of the highest order. In my opinion, there is nothing in contemporary British fiction, film-making or fine art which comes anywhere near the intensity and experimentalism, the energy, lyricism and inventiveness of some of the music I describe here. However, I want to distinguish between the sociological curiosity which leads me to *Sugar* and *More!* magazine and the questions of aesthetic value which encourage me to write enthusiastically about this new music. These are two separate things, only sometimes interconnected: I am not attributing the same cultural value to popular magazines as I am to specific musical forms. Magazines are by definition entertaining commercial forms, dependent upon advertising for revenue and focussed primarily towards sustaining and extending the consumer culture.

The music I write about here operates on a very different basis. Of course the record companies converge with lucrative deals. But there is another momentum which drives and creates a different kind of economy. This also incorporates a wide range of shady practices, from the outright criminal, to the merely informal economies of living off 'door takings'. Located at the bottom end of the cultural hierarchy where there are no grants or Arts Council funding, dance culture musicians and DJs have no alternative but to go for the best possible deal with a record company, but that does not negate the primary commitment to artistic values. Nor does it mean that the record companies underwrite these activities in any way. Indeed, there is as yet no accurate account of the particular economic space occupied by the DJs, although it is fair to say that their activity fits neither with the mainstream model of record company practices (the majors) described by Negus (1992) nor with the accounts of the 'indie' music scene provided by Dave Hesmondhalgh (1995). This suggests the need for more detailed, more local accounts of precisely these kinds of personal economies.

The third theme which runs through this book is that of cultural studies and its relation to feminism. On the question of cultural studies I have found myself repeatedly on the defensive, as this inter-disciplinary field is attacked from outside the academy, in the press and media, and also from within, indeed from certain strands in media and communications studies. Several of the chapters here continue to argue the case for cultural studies and its methodologies, against its detractors. On feminism, I find myself continually interested in how feminism has made its way downwards to a younger generation (where it is frequently repudiated) as well as into the popular media (where it undergoes a different kind of transformation). What remains certain is that, in whatever form, the ideas of feminism have become reference points for defining how we now live. In this respect the disdainful rebuke one male academic commentator recently made against cultural studies and, by implication, against its feminist dynamics, that it is 'flighty and opinionated' (see chapter 7), might also be taken as a signal of his exasperation. In that short comment it is as though what he is complaining about is the broad feminization of the academy. The peculiar inter-relationship between feminism as a particular political movement and as a source of intellectual critique, and the 'new femininity' as a wider cultural current, one which marks not just the presence but the impact of women in contemporary social life, has, to an extent, transformed the academic curriculum in the social sciences and in media and communication studies. Sometimes it feels as though the ambitious young women flooding into these areas in recent years, and the way in which they quite vociferously choose their options in the direction of gender-related topics, is too much for the old guard of the academy to deal with.

The final strand which runs through this book is the relation between teaching and writing. For academics today the spectre of the research assessment exercise dictates that priority is given to forms of writing which faithfully subscribe to the guidelines of assessment. In particular this emphasises the importance of publication in academic refereed journals. This means that academics, now more so than in the past, direct their work almost solely to the highly rated journals, the ones that count as being the leaders in the field. However, this can mean that individual contributions on related themes become scattered across a range of journals. This is one reason to bring articles like these together. But, despite the pressure to focus on the conventionally academic, it is often tempting and desirable to write in a more direct way. Two of the articles here (chapters 9 and 10) appeared in the more popular, left-wing journal, *Soundings*. They are, to an extent, more accessible versions of two of the chapters included in Part I ('Art, Fashion and Music in the Culture Society', and '*More!* New Sexualities in Girl's and Women's Magazines'). As the reader will see at several points these two articles cross-refer to issues also discussed in the *Soundings* pieces. I have included these shorter versions, despite the overlap, because students often describe how they need shorter, more topical, material like this to provide them with a framework for ideas. I would hope that the articles in Part II are useful in this respect. It is not so much the case that students nowadays simply want academic work watered down, but rather that their interest in the field is often, in a sense, secondary to their main academic work. If they are fine art students, or if their main subject is quite far removed from media or cultural studies, then it is not at all unusual to want more abbreviated material. For this reason the division in this collection between Part I and Part II is based upon the assumption that readers who are more involved in debates on cultural studies will be more interested in the first set of longer articles, while students like those described above will find more of use to them in Part II.

References

Hesmondhalgh, D. (1995) 'Independent Dance Labels', PhD Thesis, University of London.

Negus, K. (1992) *Performing Pop*, London: Edward Arnold.

Part I

1

ART, FASHION AND MUSIC IN THE CULTURE SOCIETY

'I'm classically trained, though I've since broken all that down. But the training was important, otherwise you don't really know why you are doing something and it's just gratuitous . . .' (who does he think he is, Picasso?).
(Interview with Guido, hairdresser, *Independent on Sunday* 15/3/98)

The intention here is to explore some consequences of the 'aestheticisation of everyday life' from the viewpoint of Britain in the late 1990s, which various cultural theorists including Jameson (1984), Featherstone (1991) and Lash and Urry (1994) have described. This broad social process raises a number of questions. These include the changing meaning of art in such a context; the further implications of the breakdown between 'high and low culture'; the growth of creative labour markets; and the challenge to judgement on questions of cultural value. All four of these dimensions have recently become prominent and are seen when we explore the new cultural triumvirate; fashion, art and popular music, currently the subject of political attention by the Creative Task Force set up in July 1997 by the newly elected Labour government.

It is now almost fifteen years since Jameson argued that culture was the logic of late capitalism. More recently the German sociologist, Herman Schwengell, has proposed that we now live in a *Kulturgesellschaft*, Culture-Society (Jameson 1984, Schwengell 1991). All the more reason then to consider what has happened to culture after postmodernism. If both these writers are right, and culture now fires the engine of economic growth, it is not surprising that it becomes a key issue for government. As cultural phenomena seek global markets on the back of home-grown creative energies, and with 'culture becoming strategically linked to inward investment' (Ford and Davies 1998: 2), New Labour proclaims its enthusiasm for art, fashion and pop flying the flag for Britain. The image of 1960s Swinging London updated to a 1997 picture on the cover of *Vanity Fair* magazine featuring Patsy Kensit and Liam Gallagher in bed, draped in the Union Jack, and Naomi Campbell on the catwalk in a Union

3

Jack dress designed by Alexander McQueen, shows what happens when cultural practices like fashion design and pop music get drawn upon a populist wave into promoting the national good abroad.

This kind of seemingly innocuous 'banal nationalism' (Billig 1995) strikes a discordant, uncomfortable note, especially for non-white people for whom ostentatious flying of the Union Jack in parts of London associated with racist activity signals a real threat to safety. The Union Jack flown outside Damien Hirst's *Quo Vadis* restaurant in Soho in London is a self-mocking signal that art nowadays is both commerce and tourism, and commerce itself is also art. It is a provocation to those he sees as part of the political correctness establishment and, as several writers have already pointed out, this gesture is in tune with the 'art offensive' of the young British artists. But seeing the world in terms of political correctness is in itself a mark of affiliation. It describes those who repudiate feminism, anti-racism and other similar movements as constraining, authoritative and almost bullying political practices (or else as simply dull and worthy).

The convergence of Damien Hirst's flag flying and New Labour's endorsement of the Cool Britannia initiative which emerged from the DEMOS report (the think tank with close links with new Labour) on re-branding Britain, represented an attempt to re-define culture and the arts away from their more traditional image as recipients of funding towards a more aggressively promotional and entrepreneurial ethos (Leonard 1998). They were to become 'more British', but for the international market. The rebranding was proposed on the basis of old Britain's image being out of date (John Major's 'warm beer and cricket') and in need of both modernisation and rejuvenation. But in this context Tony Blair's clumsy embracing of popular music, culminating in various photo-opportunities showing him shaking hands with Noel Gallagher, backfired when two months later, in April 1998, the *New Musical Express* ran a seven page special feature on how young musicians were disenchanted with New Labour policies. Gradually the media over-exposure of the ideal of Cool Britannia became unattractive to the kinds of figures which the government was hoping to use as examples of successful and creative British talent, and quietly the tag was dropped.

While the concerns of the Creative Task Force remain relatively opaque, a more detailed analysis of the culture industries is urgently required. Despite the interest in the cultural sector on the part of big business, the grassroots of cultural activity remains small scale. The upsurge of creative activity which has recently come to fruition on the art, fashion and music front has done so in the adverse economic circumstances of the Thatcher years. This may be the single most important feature which they share in common, that the designers, musicians and artists have all depended on Thatcher's Enterprise Allowance Scheme (EAS) and have all struggled to survive in the space between unemployment and self employment.[1] No records exist of the precise number of fashion designers, artists and musicians who were recipients of the EAS in the ten years of its existence from 1983 to 1993. However, various reports and studies all point to the important role it played in under-writing the early work of the young British artists (O'Brien, quoted in Harlow 1995), the expansion of the fashion design sector (McRobbie 1998) and the popular music industry. It is equally difficult to get a clear picture of how many people are employed in the culture industries as a whole, since that could embrace all communications workers, television and press, film, leisure and entertainment. Given this broad spectrum, figures vary wildly according to which categories of work are included although there is agreement on the expansion of the field and its overwhelming concentration in London (Garnham 1990; Pratt 1997).

Given the importance of the culture industries it is remarkable how under-researched they have been and it is the sparsity of research across the whole sector which accounts for the reported difficulties faced by the Creative Task Force in formulating policy. For example, with the introduction of the Job Seekers' Allowance in 1997, young musicians who depended upon the dole and eked out an impoverished existence for themselves while signing on until such a time as they might land a recording contract were, it appeared, now going to be forced into work. This, argued Alan McGee, a member of the Creative Task Force and owner of Creation Records, would mean the end of creative talent in Britain's music industry. Without the dole young musicians would not be able to write songs, rehearse, and hang about in the pub waiting for inspiration. Following a certain degree of uproar across the music press, the government surprisingly backed down. Behind the scenes a deal was set up which was intended to ensure that the talented would not be pushed out into work but would be placed on work experience placements in the music industry. With the fine details of this deal still to be published at the time of writing, the idea of young musicians having to perform to a panel of government-appointed experts as a sort of creative means-testing, to qualify for exemption from having to take a less creative job, seems somewhat unwieldy as social policy. Will there be enough placements to fill this demand? Is there not a stronger case to reintroduce some new version of the EAS for new recruits into the culture industries? After all, its track record is not so disastrous. Tricky was on an EAS scheme when he released his first record and there are plenty of other examples.

At present, policy is at best haphazard and cloaked in administrative mystery. At worst, it is publicity-led and seemingly thought up on the spur of the moment.[2] I would argue here that for policy makers some of the key issues will be: (a) how cultural activities which have historically depended upon state support can actually be capitalized. Is it possible to envisage a scenario where practising artists are not just self sufficient but are 'income generating'?; (b) how young people can be supported to create careers for themselves in these fields, where they move from poorly paid freelance work into sustainable careers, that is, how breadline existences can be turned into a business ethos; and (c) how public sector bodies which have traditionally supported artistic and creative activities can themselves be revamped in order to respond more directly and more imaginatively to changes in the cultural sector.

Sensation: Art as 'Cultural Populism'?

What exactly are these cultural changes? The *Sensation* exhibition held at the Royal Academy in London (18 September to 28 December 1997) demonstrates how the work of the 'young British artists' (including Damien Hirst, Rachel Whiteread, Mark Wallinger and the Chapman brothers, among others) is now phenomenally successful (300,000 visitors) and simultaneously less special. This new brand of art is no longer the prerogative of the élite, and this less special status warrants more attention. Not that we are witnessing a new democracy or a radicalization in the field of art. The young British artists distance themselves from all the art theory, the Marxism and post-structuralism which they may have come across at some point in their training. Tracey Emin's reported enjoyment of studying Marxism and feminism while at art college is touched with irony. The art work comprising the infamous tent in which she named everyone she had ever slept with owes more to the bawdy 'girls just wanna have fun' humour of *More!* magazine than it does to her feminist elders, Cindy Sherman or Mary Kelly.

There is, then, a rebuff to the seriousness of the political art and photography of the 1980s generation. A whole range of art magazines, galleries, cultural theorists and artists themselves are instantly forgotten. These include, for example, *Camerawork*, magazines like *Ten Eight*, influential cultural theorist Victor Burgin, and also the generation of black British artists whose work began to appear in galleries from the mid 1980s, such as Chila Burman, Mitra Tabrizian, Sonia Boyce, David Bailey, Keith Piper and film-maker Isaac Julien, all of whose worked engaged at some level with cultural theory, with questions of identity and with new ethnicities. In addition there is no sign of the whole wave of art work which developed in relation to the crisis of AIDS and HIV. Some critics, notably John Roberts, have argued that this disengagement with theory allows a new licentious and profane philistinism to emerge, particularly as the Jameson-inflected works of postmodern art have become over-institutionalized (Roberts 1998). The cynical, apolitical individualism, as well as the weary, not to say tawdry, disengagement of many of the pieces (Sarah Lucas' soiled mattress with phallic shaped fruit pieces casually thrown on top or, for that matter, Tracey Emin's tent) certainly says something about how art now perceives itself and where it also places itself. Acknowledging and even endorsing what Kobena Mercer has described as the 'vulgarity and stupidity of everyday life' (Mercer 1998), is casual, promiscuous, populist art which wishes to be repositioned inside the chat show world of celebrity culture, alongside the sponsorship deals, in the restaurants and at the very heart of consumer culture. This is art made for a prime-time society, where daytime television encourages the parading in public of private misfortunes ('My wife weighs 900 pounds' was the title of

Figure 1.1 Everyone I have ever slept with 1963–1995 by Tracey Emin
Source: Photograph by Stephen. White. Courtesy of Jay Jopling/White Cube, London

one Jerry Springer show broadcast on British television on 7 August 1998). Exposure and confession are recurrent themes in *Sensation*. The power of the popular media to penetrate every moment of our daily lives makes the tabloid-isation of art inevitable.

It is tempting, but not entirely satisfactory, to explain all this on the grounds that art nowadays is simply good business and that these artists are 'Thatcher's children'. Liz Ellis has suggested that in this context the new art has reneged on all feminist achievements and shorn itself of all recognisable ethics, it is art as part of the political backlash (Ellis 1998). Convincing as this account is I would argue for a rather different approach to the young British artists. Ensconced inside the consumer culture, less lonely and cut off, the new art simply becomes less important, it downgrades itself, as an act of conscious bad faith. The *Sensation* exhibition did not require the usual quantities of cultural capital to enjoy it. It did not invoke cathedral-like silence. It self-consciously staged itself as shocking but was also completely unintimidating. In this respect art has come down from its pedestal, it has relieved itself of the burden of distance and of being expected to embody deep and lasting values. But, if not all art can be great and if there are more and more people seeking to earn a living as an artist, then this is a realistic, not merely a cynical, strategy. The new 'lite' art also means the blurring of the boundaries between where art stops and where everyday life commences. The singularity of art begins to dissolve. Is it a sculpture or a dress by Hussein Chalayan? Is the video by Gillian Wearing entitled 'Dancing at Peckham' effective because it isn't real art, just a small slice of urban life? Given the 'Nikefication' of culture, are the artists (most of whom emerged from Goldsmiths College in the early 1990s) literally 'Just Doing It'? Maybe they are simply making things based on ideas. And, in so doing, they are deliberately challenging the art world with its patrician critics and its lofty standards. In the late 1990s, instead of demystifying art (the traditional strategy of the left) the yBas are redefining it, repositioning it and, to use the language of New Labour, 'rebranding art' in keeping with what it means to be an artist today and how that cannot mean being pure about sponsorship and, consequently, very poor.

As students from more diverse backgrounds enter art school, Bourdieu's notion of the artist being able to stay poor in the short term thanks to some small private income in order to achieve success on the longer term is no longer appropriate (Bourdieu 1993a). There has to be some way of being an artist and making a living. We must also take into account the historical moment of the yBas. They have been brought up with their peers to venerate and value the conspicuous consumption of the 1980s, they are part of what Beck has called the 'me first generation' (Beck 1998). Few of the generation educated through the 1960s within the full embrace of the welfare society have really come to grips with the power which money and consumerism has over a younger generation. This new love of money crosses the boundaries of gender, class and ethnicity and, as Beck has also described it, is not incompatible with strongly expressed views about social injustice, poverty, the environment and human rights (ibid., 1998). Rather than be startled by the new commercialism in contemporary art we should therefore recognise how slow an older genera-tion of social and cultural theorists have been to recognise this issue.

The experience of *Sensation*, the strangeness and the slightness, might there-fore be enough and perhaps we need not expect more of art than this. Challeng-ing, indeed confounding, critical judgement and thus freed from the burden of being classified in terms of great, good, mediocre or bad, there is a sense that there is nothing much to lose. (Some critics have referred to the self-conscious strategy of making bad art.) In an aestheticised culture art becomes another transferable skill. Train as an artist to become a DJ. Work nights in a club or bar and get a commission from the promoters to do an installation. Make a video, take photographs etc. Art can now be pursued less grandiosely. And considering that there are fewer traditional jobs to return to if all else fails, the yBas seem to be aware that ducking and diving is no longer the fate of unqualified working-class males but almost surrepticiously has crept up on us all. Sociologists have written extensively about the new world of work characterized by risk, uncer-tainty and temporary contracts. But their attention so far has not been focussed upon creative work. For this reason nobody has posed the question of how much art, music and fashion the culture society can actually accommodate. How many cultural workers can there be?

Although there is great diversity within the work of the yBas, there are a number of features which are common throughout. First, there is a generational revolt against the conviction and enthusiasm of their Marxist and feminist predecessors which has produced a marked anti-intellectualism in their work. Second, they relate to popular culture by simply adopting it wholesale, its gestures, language and identity, without attempting to explore it and then elevate it back into the art world and its circuits. Popular culture is staged 'post-ironically' as presentation rather than as representation, as if to reassure the viewer that there is absolutely nothing clever or complex going on here. These artists deliberately seek out the most downgraded forms, for example the 'Sod You Gits' headline of the 1990 piece of the same name by Sarah Lucas. This flat endorsement of popular culture and its transgressive pleasures describes a hedonism also connected with this particular 'tabloid loving' generation.

Even extreme or violent material remains devoid of social or political content or comment. *Sensation* exists in a generationally specific 'chill out' zone where, after the pleasure, thoughts of death and mortality make a seemingly inevitable appearance. But this is not marked by a sudden gravity. There is curiosity, a touch of morbidity (as in Ron Mueck's model of a miniature corpse carefully laid out, naked and still sprouting hair), but otherwise a casual interest in death and decay. This forges another link with the tradition of British youth cultures. Two pieces in *Sensation* reference the impact of punk. Marcus Harvey's *Myra Hindley* evokes Malcolm McLaren's 'God Save Myra Hindley' T-shirts, and Gavin Turk's *Pop* is, of course, a lifesize cross-breed of Sid Vicious and Elvis. While the explosive intensity of punk hurtled towards the violent deaths of Sid and Nancy, the yBas disavow such extremity. It is as if neither life nor death is really worth the effort of thinking about or reflecting upon.

The connection with youth culture leads to the third unifying feature which is the impact of rave and club culture and the effects of Ecstasy. The extension of bodily pleasures which underpins club culture also presents itself in the art, as does anti-intellectualism. The body is the focus of all attention and the mind is left to lag behind. There is something of the white, laddish 'off yer face' informality of rave lingo and the crude colouration of rave party flyers in a good deal of this work. The Chapman brothers' dolls have a drug-induced psychedelic and nightmarish quality about them and, inevitably, the DJ is the real artist and therefore the hero for the yBa generation.[3] But there is nothing novel in this, the veneration of the DJ is now subculturally the norm. As the title of the CD (August 1998) by the band Faithless indicates, 'God is a DJ'.

Fourth, and finally, there are the self-curating and promotional activities which the critics take as another mark of distinction of the yBas. From running their own shows to setting up shop (Tracey Emin and Sarah Lucas reportedly

9

lived off the profits of their second-hand shop for a year), critics have seen all these as commercial strategies, which indeed they are. But these are also ways of getting work seen and commented upon, and getting off the dole and away from unemployment. This also locates the new artists in the do-it-yourself tradition of punk and its aftermath and in the enterprise culture of Mrs Thatcher. The enormous promotional energy involved in rave culture also serves as a model. Putting on a show is pretty much like doing your own club night. None of the pieces on show at the *Sensation* exhibition would be out of place in a club setting, from Whiteread's sepulchural baths, to Hirst's rotting cow's head, from the fleshy hugeness of Jenny Saville's canvases, to the Chapman brothers' mannequins with their grotesquely positioned sexual organs. And this is conveyed in the manner in which they are set out in the exhibition. Casually strewn, or simply jammed up close to each other, the anti-intellectualism of the ethos pervades the spatial organization of the show.

Overall this exhibition confounds most theoretical insights on the post-modern condition not so much by showing a 'waning in affect' as suggesting that there is nothing beyond affect, nothing but affect. In this sense, the yBas expose postmodernism by revealing the trust in theory to be a trust in the world, ultimately a kind of humanism. However, there are costs and the shallow life preferred by the yBas produces a scanty repertoire of themes. The overall 'liteness' is countered only by the literal heaviness of the work of the two most sophisticated yBas, Hirst and Whiteread. They each bring some primal belief in the sheer weight and solidity of (even decaying) matter and, by extension, a belief in sculpture itself. For them art provides some minimal core of value, for the rest, in a further subversion of the Duchamp tradition, it is virtually indistinguishable from anything else. The key issue in the long term might well be how long the yBas can afford to dispense with politics, history and theory. It would be surprising if, in the near future, questions of gender or ethnicity for at least some of the artists did not test to the limits the abandonment of commitment.

Yet even if the critics are often in agreement about the promotional dynamic of the yBas taking priority over a deep commitment to art, the work is none-theless discussed. This may be the intention, to demonstrate (as did the holiday-making escapade staged by final year fine art students at Leeds University in June 1998)[4] that what art is depends upon what the critics and the media say it is. The key factor is the existence of taste groups, critical bodies who are all engaged in casting judgement and bringing the work into discourse, into language and into popular controversy. If this is then what really enervates art, the scale and volume of the talk is a sign of the privileged status of fine art. In fashion no such critical talk exists and in popular music, where it might be argued there is the greatest degree of creative activity occurring, there is also a less voluble and certainly less recognised set of intellectuals and critics whose judgement matters in the field of cultural capital.

Fashion dreams of art

An equally coherent story cannot be told about British fashion design as can be narrated about the yBas. If Bourdieu is right in his claim that words create things, then it is the absence of a substantial body of cultural intermediaries in fashion which accounts for its disembodied existence (Bourdieu 1993b). Despite individual designers becoming internationally famous there is nothing which binds them together as a movement other than their training in the British art schools, their commitment to conceptual rather than commercial fashion and their singular inability to stay in business. Unlike British trained artists or indeed pop musicians, fashion designers have never displayed a high degree of political engagement. Nor has there been any substantial theoretical tradition which has underwritten their practice. At best they have been seen outside the fashion media as an interesting part of popular culture, sometimes innovative or even revolutionary (as in the cast of Mary Quant) or as producing spectacular and theatrical displays of sartorial splendour (Galliano's shows). More often there is a kind of trivial image which reveals itself when, on occasion, mainstream broadsheet journalists make disparaging comments about the fashion design world. Despite this, the expansion of space given to fashion coverage in the national press, and the attention which figures like Galliano, McQueen, Westwood and McCartney attract, has boosted the self-image of this sector. If yBas are making art less special and more ordinary, fashion designers are insistent upon fashion being extraordinary. Their new confidence has allowed them to be even bolder in making claims for themselves as practising fine artists in the most conventional of 'art for art's sake' terms. They are encouraged in this respect by the fashion media who have also felt themselves to be the lesser partners in the world of the arts. But this coming of age, whereby fashion people now talk confidently in terms of minimalism, deconstruction and postmodernism, and fashion journalists proclaim figures like Galliano and McQueen as geniuses, is problematic for the very reason that there is no known standard of judgement or criteria against which these claims can be measured. Almost nobody knows why Galliano is a genius. This is because there is virtually no developed language of art criticism (in the art history tradition) which would introduce and comment upon the work of young British fashion designers. There is a new journal, *Fashion Theory*, and there is a tradition of dress (or costume) history and, of course, a number of interesting monographs on dress (Harvey 1995) as well as the various feminist accounts of fashion. But this is a field where biographies of the great designers (often in the style of coffee-table books) has taken precedence over scholarly analysis. Unlike subcultural style, fine art fashion has been considered by only a tiny handful of writers (Evans and Thornton 1989; Wollen 1993).

There is also no sociological analysis about the distinction of this sector. As a result, when so many designers are forced out of business, there is very little response other than from fashion journalists who bewail the lack of investment

Figure 1.2 The work of Antonio Berardi: Courtesy of Mike Russell

but who otherwise are so used to this that it is almost a *rite de passage*, something young designers might almost expect to happen to them. Fashion designers in Britain are trained in the fine art tradition. This informs their identities and explains why they see their work ideally as pieces to be hung on the wall, and more reluctantly as items of clothing (McRobbie 1998). But, unlike fine artists, fashion designers must be able to follow their work into production. They must be able to produce a run of jackets. It is this which accounts for the high rate of bankruptcies and business failures. Even successful designers (with a few exceptions) actually have very small businesses, most with a turnover of less than £2 million (for example, Betty Jackson and Ally Capellino), and all the well-known British designers are now being supported (and, in effect, rescued) by deals with bigger companies to produce in-house lines.

The designers' situation is further aggravated by the differential economies at work in the fashion system. There is a huge disparity between the consumption of the fashion image and the consumption of its object (that is, we look but do not buy). This means that designers can be international names while still signing on and working at the kitchen table. This mismatch produces a series of dislocations and unevenness. Fashion design is a highly disorganized and disintegrated economy (Lash and Urry 1994). It is not the case that there is no market for the goods in the shops but that the high street intervenes in the space between the image on the page and the designer items in the shops, producing lower quality cheaper ranges. The market for the genuine article remains tiny. And, as Baudrillard would see it, the image overall remains more real than its object. Fashion economies as a result are almost virtual, or deferred economies. This is a field where nobody really seems to get paid even at the image industry end where the stylists, photographers and even the supermodels all work for exposure. Magazines like *The Face, i-D, Dazed and Confused* and *Don't Tell It* rely on work which is in effect donated. The pay-off is the huge readership among the global image industry corporations who spot and then offer these underpaid British-trained cultural workers lucrative contracts, making the magazines function as job centres, or portfolios. Those working in this image industry are also products of the aestheticisation of society. Their priority is to make works of art. As the fashion editor of *i-D* says 'the page is art' (McRobbie 1998). Likewise, the stylists describe their work as 'image making'. The closeness of these fashion worlds, as well as the residual unconfidence on the part of its participants (including the fashion media) means that serious questions of cultural value and issues of judgement are sidestepped and replaced by euphoric assertions of greatness, genius and inspiration. These traditional vocabularies once again demonstrate the dislocated nature of fashion design as a cultural practice. While in almost every other part of the art world the boundaries appear to be breaking down and while, as various critics pointed out, *Sensation* marked a decisive shift for young artists into the field of popular culture, fashion in effect seeks a reconsolidation of the boundaries between

13

high and low with fashion recognized in its rightful place in the cultural hierarchy.

Only more engaged debate, argument and scholarship can ease fashion design of its status panic. The designers ought to be eligible for Arts Council grants while, at the same time, the sector as a whole needs a much more effective industrial strategy. Designers like Hussein Chalayan should be entitled to Arts Council funding to show their collections on the catwalk as performance art. At the same time clearer thinking is required about the production and manufacturing side. It is the need to put a range of clothes into production which distinguishes fashion design from sculpture or installation work. In fact the obstacles to turning this into a more successful cultural sector are less unsurmountable than they frequently seem. Collaborative strategies to share expensive facilities, equipment and promotional services between designers under the auspices of urban regeneration schemes, the reintroduction of fashion centres and the provision of incentives to employ local direct labour rather than rely on anonymous chains of sub-contracted labour, are all feasible under a New Labour commitment.

'Deep anonymous murmur'

When we turn our attention to the world of contemporary dance music (in particular, drum 'n' bass) the themes addressed in this book become particularly pronounced. Here is one of the clearest signs of the *Kulturgesellschaft* – the flow across the airwaves produces tracks that even the most avid listener is never likely to hear again (never mind write down who produced it so that he or she can actually buy it). So committed to experiment and improvisation are the 'junglist', or drum 'n' bass, musicians and DJs that they are frequently producing and playing tracks of which there is no record and no original. The commercial dynamics, the record deals and the whole political economy of this style of music remain elusive and undocumented. Only figures like Roni Size and Goldie have really registered in the public domain. This anonymous quality, where name DJs are known only to the various crowds who follow them around a number of different club locations, is connected with the music's primary identity as flow. Drum 'n' bass borrows from modern classical European, reggae, Hollywood and also Indian Bollywood soundtracks. Underneath all this is the dark and fast rumble of the distinctive booming drum and bass beat, across which echoes the intermittent scattergun, patois-influenced voice of the DJ (although often it is wholly instrumental). Whilst thudding out from specific points in the urban and domestic landscape, from car sound systems, black workmen's vans, the open windows of maisonnettes at four o'clock in the afternoon as 16 year olds get home from school, this is also a 'deep, anonymous, murmur' (Deleuze 1986).

Martin James defines drum 'n' bass as 'a combination of timestretched breakbeats played at approximately 160 beats per minute with bass lines lifted

Figure 1.3 Goldie: Courtesy of London Records

from reggae, running at 80 beats per minute and the metronomic 4/4 bass drum removed' (James 1996: xi). This is a speeded up reggae- and dub-influenced sound combined with frenetically fast drums from computer pro-grammed sequences (thus beyond the humanly possible in performance terms) which also carries elements of the techno style of 'white' rave music, in

15

particular stretches of swelling, deeply melodic sequences. However, live exposure to this music reveals its fully black aesthetic (McRobbie and Melville 1998). Listening to Grooverider, behind the decks, or to MC Nathan Haines it is possible to hear the full force of the improvised tradition of jazz, combined with the reggae sounds and toaster voiceover of the Jamaican dancehall, with the hip hop tradition of the rapper, now souped up by technological means to produce a thunderous and uniquely black and British underground sound. But there is no crude ethnic absolutism inscribed within this form, instead its openness and fluidity and serious, indeed scholarly, concern with the music celebrates the movement between the black, white and Asian mixes which is such a hallmark of this musical style. The DJs who form the inner circle around Goldie's *Metallheadz* label are young black and white Londoners. As Goldie said of fellow DJ Doc Scott, 'I seen niggers dance like they wouldn't ever dance before to this guy and nobody would believe that Scotty was blue eyes and long hair . . . He's got jet blue eyes and long hair to here.' (Goldie 1996: 41).

As 'Britart' flirts with the masses it could be argued that black British drum 'n' bass attempts to retain its own subcultural capital and underground exclusivity (Thornton 1996) by being forever ahead of the masses and the media. However, I argue that the relation maintained here between underground and mainstream is not so much a strategy of distinction, a game of culture, as a sign of aesthetic seriousness. It is about playing primarily for other musicians and DJs and also for the crowd which, in this case, is comprised not so much of fans as of fellow travellers. Such cerebral values are not typically associated with such a low culture form practised by otherwise unqualified young males ('inner city ghetto music' as Goldie has also called it). That is, the emphasis on what is special and unique about this music is not just a gesture of style, a pretence about not wanting to sell out, but a question of value. The elaboration of a distinctive artistic vocabulary is an expected bid for autonomy amongst any creative group but when it is from black culture and also a sector of black culture associated with poverty and social exclusion (Goldie grew up in care and in a series of foster homes) the complexity of this language is disregarded. So absorbed are these musicians, producers and DJs in what they are doing that, to an extent, the market and commercialization fades in importance.

The wild and noisy participative dynamics of the audience at 'jungle raves' of 1994, together with the extraodinary declarations of love, passion and commitment to the music from its followers, has produced a subcultural phenomena of exuberance and volume. As James writes 'the crowd would demand rewinds and when the MC shouted for them to make some noise the cacophony was deafening' (James 1996: 43). But the underground location and distinctive style and language means that only insiders from the DJ and dance music press comment upon it. On the part of Oxbridge-educated establishment critics drum 'n' bass remains a bewildering and confusing thing. In a recent two page profile of Goldie in the *Guardian*, Decca Aitkenhead failed to mention the music at all but was instead charmed by how 'he made up his own words' and 'claimed not to read' (Aitkenhead 1998: 3). This sense of being unable to place, locate or assess the artistic value of such work is both a mark of its otherness and also, as Bourdieu would say, of the unwillingness of the cultural legitimators to consider, never mind categorise as artists, those who exist at the far end of the social scale.

Of course there are boundaries which make access to this music difficult to outsiders. In particular there is a line that divides a generation of clubbers from those who dropped out in about 1986 when warehouse parties held in illegal spaces and hosted by DJs like Baz Fe Jazz or organised by anarcho-types like Mutoid Waste sowed the early seeds of rave. Now, in the late 1990s, it is striking how these new clubs also function as arts venues (rather like the old London Film-makers Co-operative). Most show films or slide shows during the course of the night. There is a real, tangible sense that what is happening inside these places is breaking new creative ground. For example, in one club, the 333 in London's Old Street, music evolves from week to week, from Jamaican-influenced drum 'n' bass to Asian tabla 'n' bass to Japanese taiko 'n' bass to 'eastern drum 'n' bass and, most recently (at least in my own experience), to something akin to drum 'n' drum. What is constant is the presence of rapturous audiences drawn from the entire metropolitan mix of London's young people.

I want, therefore, to invert the cultural hierarchy which still puts fine art at the top and this type of music at the bottom by suggesting a return to Gilroy's notion of 'black musical genius' (revised to take into account the more authorless nature of these particular musical forms), to the power of musical creativity as a lifeline of hope for black diasporic peoples, and to the complexity of this particular music whose own 'organic intellectuals' have forged an anti-essentialist aesthetic (black grooves on white rave–techno foundation) (Gilroy 1987, 1993). Contemporary dance music also tells us something about history and about the conditions of growing up and living in a mixed race urban culture and having some access to the creative potential of new technology in the form of the home or bedroom computer. This is cheap to produce music. It is a matter of 'taking the software and pushing the sound through the ringer backwards, just to see what it would do' (James 1996, p. 52) or again, to quote Goldie, 'We're joyriding technology, pushing it to the edge' (ibid: 53).

I am aware of the accusation of cultural studies romanticism and celebration or, worse, of 'middle youth voyeurism'. I am also aware of the dangers of returning to a mode which simply confers cultural value, but from a lower position, which says that this is great art. We need to ask, what it is we want or expect of art in a culturally saturated society? Is it possible to hold out for some idea of art when it is so thoroughly absorbed by, and integrated into, the field of popular culture? Does art simply become the new, serious, complex and interesting end of popular culture? Or is art the fiction which a particular form weaves around itself, its own distinctive 'rap'? Is it a matter of institutionalization and representation? Or am I arguing here that the art in dance music is also a type of politics, not in the overt sense, but in the sense that it writes and re-writes history in the collectivity of its style (The Roni Size Collective), and in its melting of the boundaries between black and white?

With the yBas we have seen a drift from the art world down towards the vulgar, cheap and tacky, a cynical, indifferent story about what I describe as merely liking pop, and doing self-consciously artistic things with it while avoiding the tedium of trying to be clever. The outcome is post-ironic. In contrast the music I have just described comprises a passionage, frenetic, quasi-private and urgent socio-historical dialogue, an equivalent to Afro-American hip hop, and an example of what Bhabha has called the 'uncontrollable innovations' of young black (and white) urban and disadvantaged populations (Bhabha 1998). However, the yBas still attract huge amounts of attention because what they do is still notionally art and supported by Saatchi. This makes it comprehensible to the middle-class critics who somehow create an appropriate vocabulary for debate (McCorquodale *et al.* 1998). As Bourdieu says, 'they create the creators' (1993a). Fashion exists as a weak shadow in comparison to both these voluble practices – it is hampered by its gendered, dressmaking history. However, instead of challenging this divide it has merely sought to emulate a fine art mode, as a kind of second best. It pays its respect to the street but needs the fine art tag to justify its presence. The only radical scholarship in the field of fashion comes from subcultural and feminist theory but the designers shy away from this type of connection as either too sociological or too political. This leaves its cultural intermediaries to be the journalists who for various reasons find themselves cloven to a vocabulary of approval (McRobbie 1998).

If academics and journalists have recently converged to write about yBas, and if fashion journalists have largely been responsible for the prominence and visibility of designers, the hidden and underground identity of drum 'n' bass music and its largely youthful following has meant that only a handful of writers, notably Sharma *et al.* (1996) and Melville (1997), have shown how it so clearly evokes the ideas of Stuart Hall and Paul Gilroy as an unwitting commentary upon and update of their work on 'new ethnicities' and the black Atlantic (Gilroy 1993; Hall 1992). There have been a few attempts to locate jungle and drum 'n' bass as Deleuzian forms 'Cubasing across bedroom studios . . . swerving through clubland . . . transmitting as cultural virus, pirate radio, illegal duplication . . .' (Ansell Pearson, quoted in McClure 1998: 184; see also Gilbert 1997; Hemmett 1997). But in none of the Deleuzian accounts is there any grounding in race and history, in the political economy of growing up at the edge of a de-industrial, post-employment society. Nor is there an engagement with the micro-economies of being a DJ or with what Harvey describes as the 'survival strategies of the unemployed' (Harvey 1989).

We are left then with a curious scenario in the 'Culture Society', with the breakdown of high and low culture being more apparent than real. Even when fine artists think they are not doing art, the critics, collectors and academics bring their own professional vocabularies to bear on the work and confirm that, yes, it is art. Fashion designers, in contrast, think that they are fine artists, giving rise to more than a few sniggers on the part of the culture critics (Glancey 1997; Johnson 1997). More generally they are seen as providing enjoyable visual spectacles, good copy for the front page. A touch of English eccentricity[5]. Meanwhile, the drum 'n' bass musicians are producing the most innovative and dynamic aesthetic in music since reggae, but there are so few black scholars, intellectuals and critics who have made their way up through the ranks of the academy or into journalism that there are virtually no voices of representation, never mind debate, except those that come from other, largely hidden, spaces.

Likewise, the economies underpinning these activities are more apparent, indeed virtual, than real. Apart from a few stars and celebrities at the top these are casualized, insecure occupations, more so than ever before. Yet increasingly there are no 'day jobs' to fall back on, especially for young black males. While this music can be seen as a soundtrack to the work of black intellectuals like Hall and Gilroy, it also describes a significant distance between the world of the black intellectual and that of the DJs running around London trying to make a living by creating clubs, setting up small labels and immersing themselves in creating new sounds from old sources. Should there be a dialogue between these musicians and people like Paul Gilroy, and on what lines would such a dialogue proceed? What would Goldie have to say to Gilroy? This is not to invoke some happy idea of intellectual and artistic community. Indeed, the small chance of such an encounter merely dramatizes the political reality where the resources of the university and art school system, made generously available to art students and fashion designers, remain foreign territory and an unknown and untapped resource for those who might derive the greatest benefit (despite living and working in the same city). The utopian space of the university as Edward Said has described it has not provided the haven for musicians like those mentioned above as it has done for generations of practising artists and also for fashion designers (in the guise of visiting teacher posts). This in itself is a clear sign of continuing inequalities reproduced through the rigidity of the cultural hierarchies of taste.

This music functions as a record of the lives of its producers. It is extra-ordinarily self-reflexive, continually redressing itself, telling and re-telling its own story. It combines elements of improvisation, uplift and utopia inscribed within its practice and performance (and described by Gilroy as part of a black Atlantic musical aesthetic) and also something newer, darker and different. A shot of fear, even terror, runs through the core of drum 'n' bass music. Virtually without voice or lyrics, except for the commands and commentary from the MC, there is also the underside of racial memory where there is no community, no protection, no security – only paranoia. Speed, physical force and vibration replace heart and soul. The energy and the danger also tells us something simple and direct about the sheer effort needed to make a living and forge some kind of future being black in the culture society.

19

Notes

1 The Enterprise Allowance Scheme helped get people off the dole and into self employment by providing forty pounds a week for the duration of a year.
2 The operations of the Creative Task Force have remained obscure. At the time of writing no further documents or statements have followed press reports of a U-turn on the Job Seekers' Allowance.
3 During the summer of 1997 the ICA in London held a series of club nights hosted by artists-turned-DJs Jake and Dinos Chapman, Tracey Emin and Gillian Wearing.
4 In June 1998 as part of the final year degree shows a group of fine art students from Leeds University staged an elaborate hoax. The group work comprised an announced trip to Spain followed by a public return at the airport. The media predictably reported these events as a waste of taxpayers' money, at which point the students revealed that the trip had been to a local holiday resort. The 'art' was the media reaction.
5 English Eccentrics is the name of a London-based fashion label.

This article was first delivered as a lecture to students of the Fine Art Department, Glasgow School of Art, in December 1997.

References

Aitkenhead, D. (1998) 'Dances With Wolverhampton', *Guardian*, 23 January 1998.

Beck, U. (1998) 'Cosmopolitan World', *New Statesman*, April 1998.

Bhabha, H. (1998) Lecture delivered at Stuart Hall Conference, the Open University, Milton Keynes, 14/15 May.

Billig, M. (1995) *Banal Nationalism*, London: Sage.

Blair, T, the Rt. Hon. PM (1997) 'Can Britain Remake It?', *Guardian*, 21 July 1997.

Bourdieu, P. (1993a) *The Field of Cultural Production*, Cambridge: Polity Press.

—— (1993b) *Sociology in Question*, London: Sage.

Deleuze, G. (1986) *Foucault*, Minneapolis: University of Minnesota Press.

Ellis, L. (1998) 'Do You Want To Be in My Gang?', *nParadoxa: An International Feminist Arts Journal*, vol. 1, pp. 6–14.

Evans, C. and Thornton, M. (1989) *Women and Fashion: A New Look*, London: Quartet.

Featherstone, M. (1991) *Consumer Culture and Postmodernism*, London: Sage.

Ford, S. and Davies, J. (1998) 'Art Capital', *Art Monthly*, no. 213, February, pp. 1–4.

Ford, S. (1998) 'The Myth of the Young British Artist', in D. McCorquodale *et al.* (eds) *Occupational Hazard: Critical Writing on Recent British Art*, London: Black Dog Publishing, pp. 130–42.

Garnham, N. (1990) *Capitalism and Communication: Global Culture and the Economics of Information*, London: Sage.

Gilbert, J. (1997) 'Soundtrack For an Uncivil Society: Rave Culture, the Criminal Justice Act and the Politics of Modernity', *New Formations*, no. 31, Summer, pp. 5–23.

Gilroy, P. (1987) *There Ain't No Black In the Union Jack*, London: Hutchinson.

—— (1993) *The Black Atlantic*, London: Verso.

Glancey, J. (1997) 'All Dressed up by the Queen of Frock 'n' Roll', *Guardian*, 18 July 1997, p. 18.

Goldie (1996) 'Goldie's Jukebox', *The Wire*, Issue 144, February 1996.

Hall, S. (1992) 'New ethnicities', in J. Donald and A. Rattansi (eds) *'Race', Culture and Difference*, London: Sage.

Harlow, J. (1995) 'Home is Where the Art is', *Sunday Times*, 17 December: 3.

Harvey, D. (1989) *The Condition of Postmodernity*, Oxford: Blackwell.

Harvey, J. (1995) *Men in Black*, London: Reaktion Books.

Hemmett, D. (1997) 'E is for Ekstasis', *New Formations*, no. 31, Summer, pp. 23–39.

James, M. (1996) *State of Bass: Jungle, the Story So Far*, Basingstoke: Boxtree Press.

Jameson, F. (1984) 'Postmodernism or The Logic of Late Capitalism', *New Left Review* 146, London.

Johnson B. (1997) 'Was Versace Really a Genius?', *Daily Telegraph*, 17 July, p. 21.

Lash, S. and Urry, J. (1994) *The Economy of Signs and Spaces*, London: Sage.

Leonard, M. (1998) 'Re Branding Britain', London: DEMOS.

McClure, B. (1998) 'Machinic Philosophy', *Theory, Culture and Society*, May, vol. 15, no. 2, pp. 175–85.

McCorquodale, D. Siderfin, N. and Stallabrass, J. (eds) (1998) *Occupational Hazard: Critical Writing on Recent British Art*, London: Black Dog Publishing.

McRobbie, A. (1998) *British Fashion Design: Rag Trade or Image Industry?*, London: Routledge.

McRobbie, A. and Melville C. (1998) 'Amblyssical Chords: Goldie's Saturnz Returns', *Village .Voice*, 17 February, p. 68, New York.

Melville, C. (1997) 'Breakbeats and Metallheadz', MA Dissertation, unpublished, Goldsmiths College, London.

Mercer, K. (1998) Lecture delivered at Stuart Hall Conference, The Open University, Milton Keynes, May 14/15.

Roberts, J. (1998) 'Pop Art, the Popular and British Art of the 1990s', D. McCorquodale *et al.* (eds) *Occupational Hazard: Critical Writing on Recent British Art*, London: Black Dog Publishing, pp. 52–80.

Pratt, A. (1997) 'The Cultural Industries Sector: its definition and character from secondary sources on employment and trade, Britain 1984–91', Research Papers in Environmental and Spatial Analysis, no. 41, London School of Economics.

Schwengell, H. (1991) 'British Enterprise Culture and German *Kulturgesellschaft*', R. Keat and N. Abercrombie (eds), *Enterprise Culture*, pp. 136–51, London: Routledge.

Sharma, S., Sharma, A., and Hutnyk J. (1996) *Dis-orienting Rhythms: The Politics of New Asian Dance Music*, London: Zed Brooks.

Thornton, S. (1996) *Club Culture: Music, Media and Subcultural Capital*, Cambridge: Polity Press.

Wollen, P. (1993) *Raiding the Icebox: Reflections on Twentieth Century Culture*, London: Verso.

2

ALL THE WORLD'S A STAGE, SCREEN OR MAGAZINE

When culture is the logic of late capitalism*

Cultural policy, the missing agenda

Some time ago the *New Left Review* ran a cultural studies intervention by Simon Frith and Jon Savage. This was in fact a denunciation of what had happened to cultural studies in the 1980s. A whole bunch of left academics, it seemed, had, during the long Thatcher years, taken leave of their senses by abandoning the critique of capitalist culture in favour of celebrating popular culture and the values of commerce and retail. As they put it, cultural studies now seemed to comprise 'cheerful populism' on the part of academics possessed by a 'new found respect for sales figures, by the theoretical pursuit of the joys of consumption' (Frith and Savage 1993: 107). The authors then link this development to the growth of a new brash form of cultural journalism, from the *Modern Review* to BBC2's *The Late Show*. More media in the 1980s also meant more media and cultural coverage and this, in turn, coincided with the increasingly blurred line between high culture and low culture, with *The Late Show*, treating 'popular artists, quite inappropriately . . . with all the awed attention of high art appreciation' (ibid.: 113). In addition, they attribute the disappearance of sharp and consistently critical voices from the cultural field to the emergence of the new right in journalism, which of course was emboldened by the success of Mrs Thatcher. Frith and Savage then connect these new right style-led journalists who, as they put it, 'surely understand shopping' not only with the cultural studies academics who write about shopping but also with the cultural studies courses, '. . . and indeed, cultural studies courses were a spawning ground for eighties style journalism' (ibid.: 113).

I have argued elsewhere the extent to which this is both a simplification and a real distortion of cultural studies writing, pedagogy and even of so-called style journalism (McRobbie 1996a). The authors conflate cultural studies into an undifferentiated and uncritical monolith so as to be able to blame it for an equally conflated version of cultural journalism. They do this to be able to argue

*Note: This is an edited version of a lecture presented at the Raymond Williams Memorial Conference in London, June 1995.

22

for 'a new language of pop culture . . . derived from anthropology, archetypal psychology, musicology . . .' (Frith and Savage 1993: 115). If this does not seem like laying a claim to the corpse of cultural studies, so as to resurrect it in their own image, then it is difficult to imagine what would. However, it is not my intention here to revisit the site of this debate, nor to settle scores over what is or is not cultural studies but, rather, in the light of the recent demise of both *The Late Show* and the *Modern Review*, to raise some questions about the production of culture, including cultural television programmes and magazines and also about cultural policy in general. My concern then will be the sort of people who now work in culture, or who aspire to work in culture. It is my contention that they are by no means homogenously 'new right'. However, their precarious position as cultural producers urgently needs to be taken account of. It is not that cultural studies has failed them but rather that it has not spent sufficient time thinking about policy and about the human products of its own pedagogy.

What is needed is a new space of political intervention with a view to contributing to policy debates but from a different vantage point than in the past. Policy has often prompted a great yawn in cultural and media studies. The exception has been in television broadcasting where policy debates have retained both a topicality (deregulation, censorship, etc.) and a platform where broadcasters and academics are quite regularly brought together. But otherwise policy has been almost abandoned, with the exception of Tony Bennett's work (see Bennett 1992) through sheer frustration at the endless rounds of cuts to the arts, culture and media. These cuts remind us of our own marginality, requiring of us at the same time that we step inside a sponsorship or lottery culture. Why participate in sponsored support, when it is more often a warranty to industry to flag their own products in cultural locations where the incoming level of support falls well below the costs that industry would have paid for such expansive advertising? Involvement at this level makes culture policy makers little more than unwitting agents to marketing professionals.

Not surprisingly, cultural studies people are more likely to analyse what is going on in cultural forms which emerge fully formed from outside the field of sponsorship and subsidy. I am thinking here of Tricia Rose's rhapsodic accounts of 'rap as urban renewal' (Rose 1994). Rose does not suggest that rap represents the pure, unmediated and authentic voice of experience. She is not promulgating the old celebratory account of innovative popular culture emerging from the people uncontaminated only to be destroyed by predatory capitalist forces. Nonetheless, the emphasis is still on the finished product in all its hybridic, hi-tech complexity. Here and in most other responses to the emergence of rap and hip hop culture (see Lipsitz 1994) there is little attention paid to the precise practices of cultural production or to the micro-economics of club promotion and performance (i.e. who gets paid, how much, how do new rap artists get started, etc.?). Now, whether we call this the business of culture or the production of art or, indeed, cultural entrepreneurialism or all three, is not the point. The point is that this is a missing dimension in cultural debate and until we know more about it we cannot speak with much authority on anything other than the cultural meaning, significance and consumption of these forms once they are already in circulation.

Thinking more about the subsidized forms of art and culture it is clear that, by pulling back from policy issues, the precise scale of the transition to a market economy has remained undocumented, nor do we have any idea of what it is like working in this sector, as a performer, artist, administrator or freelance. The whole arts and cultural landscape is becoming so transformed that there is now a substantial backlog of cultural policy matters urgently in need of an imaginative response from the left beyond the uninspired ideas occasionally issuing from the Labour Party. What prevails instead is either desperation or weary cynicism: 'Let's try and get some Laura Ashley money', or else some instinctive assessment about some sponsors or business partners being more ethically acceptable than others. Those on the left with a more finely tuned entrepreneurial outlook also seem to forget too easily how unstable and volatile so many of the businesses with whom they seek partnership are. How many businesses and consultancies have been temporarily bailed out by contracts from the public sector including the arts and education? A good deal of sponsorship culture is actually a two-way process. If a company sponsors a fashion degree show by providing textiles and fabrics (often material they are happy to get rid of), they frequently expect more than publicity in return. Under the guise of setting a 'live brief' they also get ideas and designs provided by talented students which they then put into production at no cost whatsoever.

The practices of the labour market for cultural workers across the whole sector ought to attract a good deal more attention than they do. Instead, cultural policy remains confined with a traditional framework. Writers like Ken Worpole are more aware than many other policy-led cultural researchers on the need for reconceptualizing how the arts, media and culture now exist in new and different relationships with 'the people', or with the socially diverse and fragmented populations for whom class is no longer a primary or exclusive mark of identity. But there still remain large gaps between how culture is understood in policy and how it is theorized in cultural and media studies. Cultural policy remains based on an image of culture either being indigenously produced and worthy of support or else of it being something which needs to be more generously and efficiently delivered to those who cannot afford the full market price. This model reproduces a fairly conventional divide between 'worthy' cultural production being community based and 'high' cultural consumption as being subsidized. Cultural theory has not been very helpful in moving policy out of this binary divide since it has been so preoccupied with either the politics of meaning in film or television studies or else, as in the work of Jameson (Jameson 1991), with the meaning of global cultural totalities (i.e. postmodernism). Despite the dazzling range of his scholarship, Jameson sidesteps the question of the institutional, commercial and educational conditions of cultural production in favour of a trenchant critique of postmodern forms. Slick, knowing (and this is a word I will come back to), superficial and depthless, Jameson sees only reason to decry the politics of postmodern culture. There is no concern in his writing with who produces these forms and under what socio-economic conditions.

Social intervention drawing on a cultural studies framework would be easier if even some of the theoretical work carried out in the 1980s had been backed up by more substantial concrete research. Although a good deal of cultural theory did open itself up to this as a possibility, the overall absence of funding had the effect of over-theorizing cultural studies and confining it to the world of the text. In addition, the overwhelming impact of psychoanalysis and post-structuralism posed fairly damning critiques of what I have recently labelled 'the three E's: empiricism, ethnography and the category of experience (McRobbie 1996b). The efforts given over to exposing these sites of 'truth' and 'knowledge' as artificially coherent narrative fictions made it difficult for media and cultural studies to participate in facts and figures-oriented policy debates, or indeed in relation to the social problems whose roots seemed to lie in innovative cultural practices, for example, the rise of rave and dance cultures and the consumption among young people of 'Es' (i.e. ecstasy). It has instead been left to sociologists like Jason Ditton in Glasgow to do the dirtier work of developing policies on youth cultures like rave, which necessitate having access to reliable facts, figures and even ethnographic accounts to be able to argue with angry councillors, police and assorted moral guardians (Ditton *et al.* 1995). So, I am not suggesting that those 'raves from the grave', the three Es are simply exhumed, but rather that they are reconceptualized in the light of the anti-Es (anti-essentialism, post-structuralism, psychoanalysis) so that one strand of cultural and media studies is at least better able to position itself in the field of policy. This would mean doing more empirical research, it would also mean re-instating ethnography despite and in response to Clifford's testimony to its poetic character (Clifford 1992). In this respect it should be noted, perhaps, that in the UK the recent ethnographic work of Phil Cohen, which looks at the racist narratives of white, working-class primary-school children in south east London goes some way in making concrete post-structuralist thinking in applied cultural studies, as does Valerie Walkerdine's imaginative drawing together of psychoanalysis and empirical work with girls and young women (Cohen 1992; Walkerdine 1990).

The subjects of cultural studies?

Cultural policy has been concerned with either supporting culture as a kind of amateur or indigenous activity, or else with providing culture, or access to it. The assumed social relations which underpin the first of these is now anachronistic. Where substantial numbers of people produce their own cultural forms using, for example, camcorders, with skill and expertise, and where broadcast

TV like *Video Nation* or *Video Diaries* taps into the home video market, it is inappropriate to cast ordinary people in a purely recipient category or amateur role. Not everybody is a cultural producer, but those who are involved in this way ought to be at least recognized as participants. There are also problems with the support and access model even in its most facilitative guise. The problem is that the market often seems to do this work of delivery more effectively than the public sector. It is easier for a busy mother to buy a paperback on the way home from work than to get to the library after work, borrow a number of books and then remember to return them on time. Likewise it is easier and less exhausting to wait for a good film to come out on video at the local Blockbusters store than it is to get and pay for a babysitter, go out to the cinema and then arrange for the babysitter to get home safely.

Overall, these kinds of changes mean that culture has to be considered not only as a practice of consumption but as a substantial sector of the economy, a sizable mode of production, and also a field of employment, increasingly of self-employment. The market for cultural goods has been swollen by the number of new producers entering the field. We also have to consider cultural practice for profit or merely for a livelihood or as a supplement to the dole, as now taking over that space in people's lives which we once would have called hobbies or activities. In the context of unemployment these frequently become 'gainful activities' i.e. cooking, gardening, sports, rambling, 'internetting', producing fanzines etc. The interesting and sociologically fascinating point here is that in a situation of virtually no external economy, hobbies are being transformed with the help of the Small Business Support Scheme into new forms of cottage industry. How sustainable these activites are, what kinds of margins of profit or loss they operate with and what their long-term viability is, remains purely a matter of speculation at this stage, but it certainly should be the subject of research and analysis. We should also be looking at the social processes which underpin shifts of this sort. How do people become DJs? How do gardeners become such experts that they get featured in magazines or even get to write a magazine column? What does it take to become a television cook? What are the micro-economies which support these new working identities? How connected are they with the hidden economy? In the context of the larger media institutions like magazines we would also have to ask more particular questions about the practices of production. What kinds of debates and discussions go on behind the scenes in magazines like *More!* or *Just Seventeen*? Who are the new cultural producers, what kind of career pathways do they follow? Some of my own recent research has been on precisely the field of cultural activity referred to by Frith and Savage, that is, fashion design and style-led journalism. The picture which this current research reveals offers a useful counterpoint to Frith and Savage. The respondents certainly do not conform to their neo-Thatcherite image of media producers. Indeed, it seems that we on the cultural left have an altogether monolithic and outmoded notion of who makes culture. Media workers are no longer exclusively Oxbridge élites nor are they necessarily supporters of the new right. Indeed, it would even be difficult to cast them as shining examples of 'enterprise culture'. What we should be talking about instead is a sprawling sector of micro-economies of culture which now traverses the boundaries of social class, ethnicity and gender. Many young working-class people now become self-employed in the cultural field (as 'stylists', make-up artists, or by setting up club nights, or making dance tracks at home in their bedrooms) as an escape from the inevitability of unemployment, or in preference to an unrewarding job in the service sector. In some cases, a desire for and commitment to producing culture in the form of music coincides with a criminal career, as the life histories of so many talented rap artists show. Not that culture necessarily brings the rewards that it may have to the likes of Snoop Doggy Dogg. The majority of the young fashion designers I have interviewed would earn more as temps or secretaries but their commitment to notions of personal creativity provides them with a utopian idea of breaking down the distinction between dull work and enjoyable leisure. If paid employment is no longer secure, then self-employed but 'creative' insecurity is often more appealing than uncreative job insecurity in a large company or corporation. The culture industries themselves now comprise a huge but still undocumented sea of freelance workers, funding one more creative project from the proceeds of another more commercial one, and relying on Small Business Support grants to pay for the business cards, plans and some of the equipment and overheads.

Some sociologists have seen the emergence of this sector as the legacy of Mrs Thatcher's enterprise culture. Pollert, for example, is particularly scathing, and sees the emergence of freelance and flexible jobs as being forced to live with insecurity and then 'learning to love it' (Pollert 1988). Alternatively, self-disciplining for new kinds of work is given a Foucauldian gloss by Paul Du Gay, who analyses this whole restructuring of the labour force through the language of self-enhancement and creativity as a means of producing new social subjects (Du Gay 1996). The redefinition of work as creative proves all the more successful at producing 'docile bodies'. Bourdieu, in contrast, would presumably ask for a more empirical analysis of the jobs and those who do them. He would possibly argue that the production of culture is internally differentiated by class and by those who possess different levels of cultural capital (Bourdieu 1993). He would see the middle classes being especially anxious to assert a reasonably secure place for themselves in this new economy of culture.

Whichever account proves most useful would partly depend on doing the practical work of researching this sector. Despite all the problems of dealing with personal accounts as evidence, testimony or simply data, it still seems worthwhile to me to ask how these cultural workers experience this form of economic activity. My own current work reveals young fashion designers to be well aware of the precariousness of their work and of their own capacity for self-exploitation. They worry about getting sick and many put off having children because they could not keep up the frenetic level of activity necessary to function and survive in this sector. Almost all the people I have interviewed tend politically towards the left, and this also is significant since fashion designers typically have an image as being apolitical if not apathetic. My research on young women magazine journalists also shows them to be political subjects, continually embroiled in debates on the sexual politics of magazine production. Several of these journalists and editors have described at length the battles they fight to balance the input of feminist ideas with the need to keep sales high and circulation figures healthy. Most of these young women, working on magazines like *Just Seventeen, More!* and *19* have done media, cultural studies, sociology or women's studies at some level in their education and, in addition, they see this as providing them with a framework or reference point for the debates and discussions in which they participate with other magazine professionals, such as designers, advertising managers and art directors. So, drawing on Foucault, we could argue that these are also the subjects of cultural and media studies, recognizing this too as having a regulative, constraining force. This would be to locate cultural and media studies not as counter-discourses (which implies a starkly oppositional relation) but rather one set of competing discourses within a professional field of others. Thus the institutionalization of these still relatively new academic practices (media and cultural studies, gender studies) means that us academics are also employed in the business of producing new social subjects. It is possible to take this even further, and suggest that the existence of these cultural studies discourses allows the new cultural workers to rearticulate enterprise culture so that it can be compatible with a more democratic, more co-operative, less individualistic cultural practice. To be self-employed as a graphic designer need not mean being simply the subject of Thatcherism or the new vocationalism in higher education. Indeed, we can re-inflect Jameson's post-modern category of knowingness (Jameson 1991) to describe the purposeful reliance on irony and pastiche in magazine journalism, as producing a space of critical distance and reflection for the reader. The ironic and even camp language now accompanying and in some ways overdetermining the conventional commercial texts of male pin-ups, heart throbs, romance and 'fellas' in magazines like *Just Seventeen*, produces a shared sense of knowingness. The editors and journalists, through this self-consciously superficial style of writing, signal the existence of a space of knowing that it is not to be taken seriously and that girls are no longer passive female subjects, the victims of romance. This degree of knowingness or self-reflection now pervades a multiplicity of cultural forms, from the drag act of Lily Savage to the rap tracks which quote black intellectuals like Paul Gilroy (and in the US, bell hooks). In the former case, a young South London follower of the Nation of Islam slams Gilroy for his stand against ethnic absolutism in *There Ain't No Black In The Union Jack* (Gilroy 1987) while in the latter the 'rapper's delight' is in bell hooks' potent analysis of sex and race.

How can we connect these social processes and transformations with cultural policy? How can we begin to develop a strategy for employment in this sector where, in some parts of the country such as Liverpool or the North East, being a musician means more or less being on the 'rock and roll' for life, while in London it can mean being made redundant from a full time job at ITN only to be re-employed by the same company in the same job as a freelance? We would also have to be able to track the employment practices inside different cultural and media institutions, in glossy magazines, for example, where the number of full-timers now frequently dwindles to less than a handful, and where pages are 'looked after' by freelancers, free also to work simultaneously for other magazines or newspapers. At the very least, surveys of these forms of cultural employment would force the Labour Party to take this kind of work seriously and stop thinking about small businesses solely in terms of fish and chip shops or road haulage companies.

The Small Business Support scheme would need to be revised and extended, culture industry centres could provide shared computerized equipment and freelance workers might be encouraged into forming associations for pooling jobs and resources. The DTI would need to be persuaded that, for example, fashion design is real work and needs proper support and investment to produce for international markets. Social policies would also need to be introduced alongside cultural initiatives. Better links could be forged between universities and cultural industries, particularly with access to research and technology. Finally, welfare and social security would need to be reconsidered in the light of the prevalence and inevitability of the temporary contract. As freelance, short-term or temporary becomes the norm across whole sectors of work, housing associations would need to be reinvigorated, indeed, there might even need to be a return to 'council housing'. Likewise, the system for paying national insurance contributions would need to be reassessed with a view to easing the means of paying for low-earning freelance or self-employed workers. For a Labour government, the current pitfalls of private pension insurance schemes would also need to be confronted more directly.

The deep pessimism on the left about the future of welfare and the stark recognition that there will be no prospect for reindustrializing the economy need not lead only to resignation or despair. Even where all the odds are stacked against them we do not find this level of hopelessness among those constituencies where culture is a resource (i.e. among the black and Asian communities). Indeed, as many black commentators have pointed out, cultural forms such as rap and hip hop are not just brilliant and haunting political aesthetics rising from the ruins of deindustrialized cities, they are also global communicative forms. Culture may be commodification but it is also communication.

What is needed now is a better, more reliable set of cultural maps. We need to be able to do more than analyse the texts, we need data, graphs, ethnographies, facts and figures. It is unfortunate that debates on these kinds of questions have been so bifurcated along the lines of those on the side of political economy against those on the side of meaning and consumption (Garnham 1995; Grossberg 1995). There are in fact many points of intervention and analysis which neither of these approaches has as yet fully explored. The complex appeal of work in the cultural field, the utopian and transformative aspiration which resides alongside what might more typically be understood as individualizing cultural and economic practices, needs to be considered in the context of contemporary historical realities. The so-called aestheticization of culture has opened up desires for social transformation which can be seen in those forms of work and economic activity which have been too easily dismissed as marginal, merely cultural and politically insignificant.

References

Bennett, T. (1992) 'Putting Policy into Cultural Studies', in L. Grossberg, C. Nelson and P. Treichler (eds) *Cultural Studies*, London and New York: Routledge, pp. 23–38.

Bourdieu, P. (1993) *The Field of Cultural Production*, Cambridge: Polity Press.

Clifford, J. (1992) 'Travelling Cultures', L. Grossberg *et al.* (eds) *Cultural Studies*, London and New York: Routledge, pp. 96–117.

Cohen, P. (1992) 'It's Racism what Dunnit: Hidden Narratives in Theories of Racism', in J. Donald and A. Rattansi (eds) *'Race', Culture and Difference*, London: Sage, pp. 62–104.

Ditton, J. *et al.* (1995) 'Dance, Drugs and the Information Needs of Young People', Report from the Scottish Centre for Criminology for the Health Education Board of Scotland.

Du Gay, P. (1996) *Consumption and Identity at Work*, London: Sage.

Frith, S. and Savage, J. (1993) 'Pearls and Swine: The Intellectuals and the Mass Media', *New Left Review*, 198: 107–16.

Garnham, N. (1995) 'Political Economy and Cultural Studies: Reconciliation or Divorce?', *Critical Studies in Mass Communications*, March: 62–71.

Gilroy, P. (1987) *There Ain't No Black In The Union Jack: The Cultural Politics of Race and Nation*, London: Hutchinson.

Grossberg, L. (1995) 'Cultural Studies vs Political Economy: Is Anyone Else Bored with this Debate?', *Critical Studies in Mass Communications*, 12(1): 72–81.

Jameson, F. (1991), *Postmodernism, Or, The Cultural Logic of Late Capitalism*, London: Verso.

Lipsitz, G. (1994) *Dangerous Crossroads*, London: Verso.

McRobbie, A. (1996a) 'Looking Back at New Times and Its Enemies', in K.H. Chen and D. Morley (eds) *Stuart Hall: Critical Dialogues in Cultural Studies*, London: Routledge.

McRobbie, A. (1996b) 'The E's and the Anti-E's; Questions for Feminism and Cultural Studies', in M. Ferguson and P. Golding (eds) *Beyond Cultural Studies*, London: Sage.

Pollert, A. (1988) 'Dismantling Flexibility', *Capital and Class*, 34: 42–75.

Rose, T. (1994) *Black Noise*, New York: Routledge.

Walkerdine, V. (1990) *Schoolgirl Fictions*, London: Verso.

3

BRIDGING THE GAP
Feminism, fashion and consumption

The social relations of consumption

This chapter was written partly out of a sense of frustration that so much recent writing on women and consumption has been flawed by an inattention to the processes of exclusion which structure and limit access to consumption. These of course are largely to do with disposable income. But there are additional absences in this work which have to do with specificities and particularities in regard to consumption, that is with how different groups of women, from different class and ethnic backgrounds, actually experience this thing called consumption. Indeed there often seems to be a wilful avoidance of questions of poverty and hardship. Nor is there any emphasis on those who work at producing consumption. Both of these omissions contribute to a sense that 'we' can indeed all consume and that this process gives rise in our minds to no awkward questions about how much the shop assistant is being paid, or how, having purchased the weekly shopping, we will get through to the end of the month. Consumer culture is instead an arena of female participation and enjoyment. This runs the risk of inducing a sense of political complacency.

When feminist writers and cultural historians attempt to re-investigate the neglected field of consumption by showing how women were produced as the ideal subjects of consumption in early twentieth century America, or with the new role they were given following the growth of advertising and marketing in the inter-war years, or with how women flocked to the department stores, my own reaction is to require some qualifications in this respect. They did not flock equally to consume. Nor was the invitation to consume extended to all women independent of means and status. On both sides of the Atlantic the imagined female consumer was invariably white and almost always middle class. And as we know from the direct experience of being treated with condescension or dismissal in upmarket department stores, shopping may be nominally open to all but this does not stop department stores from screening out 'unwanted customers'.[1] The status of the shop assistant is indicative in this respect. She is typically low-paid but is trained in accent and demeanour, with her job depending on her successful demonstration of these skills, to reflect the high-class quality of the goods. This practice dates back to the early days of the department store when wealthy customers complained of being put off the products by the unhealthy, poor-looking shop girls who were serving them.

For many, if not most, women throughout the periods described by authors such as Pumphrey (1987), Felski (1995), Nava (1996), Bowlby (1985) and Reekie (1995) i.e. from the mid-nineteenth century through the early years of this century, consumption has been an aggravated activity. It has most certainly been linked with the necessity of both paid work and also with unpaid work in the home. If women consumed fabrics, for example, it was to take home and make clothes for themselves and their children, unless of course they could pay other women to do this for them. So the act of consumption was merely the precursor for further domestic labour. While some of the above writers (e.g. Pumphrey and Reekie *en passant*) note the unevenness of women's ability to participate in consumption, the structures which produce and reproduce these divisions and the consequences these have for relations of power and powerlessness tend to be marginalized. Consumption is extrapolated from the broader sociological context in which purchasing is only one small part of a whole chain of productive activity.

As the academic interest in this field gains ground through the 1980s it is also surprising that instead of re-conceptualizing the traditional division between production and consumption to take into account the multiple levels of social and cultural as well as economic practices which traverse this divide, there is instead, in academic feminism over the last fifteen years, almost imperceptibly, a new division of labour which has emerged. Such a division suggests quite major political differences within feminism, though there is no space here to explore the fine nuances of disagreement and emphasis. Those who engage with issues of consumption (e.g. fashion), but from the viewpoint of production, could be described as 'materialist feminists', while those who are associated with the politics of meaning and with the world of texts and representations could be described as 'cultural feminists'.[2] In the former group figures including Rowbotham and Mitter (1994), Tate (1994) Phizacklea (1990) and others approach the world of goods from the viewpoint of the highly exploitative conditions under which these goods, usually items of fashion or clothing, have been produced by Third World women and children, often in sweat-shop conditions, or else by very poor First World women employed as homeworkers or in the small workshop units of North London and the West Midlands. Meanwhile feminists working in cultural and literary studies often tend to discount or overlook the material context of the production of consumption as indicative of a crudely economistic and reductionist approach, untuned to the level and meaning of female popular desires for consumer goods. In fact it is the concept of desire and with it pleasure which partly fuels this approach. It is worth briefly rehearsing that trajectory, as it is aspects of this that I now want to challenge.

The original argument was that the academic left including feminists too often felt the need to disavow their own participation in some of the pleasures of the consumer culture for the reason that these were the very epitome of capitalism and also one of the sources of women's oppression. This produced a culture of puritanism giving rise only to guilty pleasures. The study of popular culture in its most expanded sense allowed feminists to revise this traditional stance. The fact that many of these forms were also enjoyed by ordinary women allowed us to at least re-interrogate this terrain rather than to merely understand it as a site of 'false consciousness'. In addition through the 1980s the growth of a new kind of left and feminist cultural politics which involved exploring how more popular broad-based alliances could be forged made it possible to acknowledge the enjoyment people got from consumption (Hall 1989; Mort 1989, 1996). The issue here was of broadening out the political constituency to which the left could legitimately speak by including for example the newly affluent upper working and lower middle classes i.e. the '*Daily Mail*' terrain of support for Thatcherism. What seemed to happen, however, was that this momentum, combined as it was with speaking to other social identities and movements, resulted in the bottom end (whatever that might mean in economic terms) of the social hierarchy being dropped from the political and intellectual agenda. This raises the question of the terms and limits of popular left and feminist politics. Is it possible to address the very poor and the pretty affluent in the same political language? At any rate the interest in the practices of consumption was only rarely put to the test in the field of empirical investigation. Instead it was used to flag the conceptual autonomy of consumption away from the more problematic field of production. In effect it was about symbolic complexity, i.e. with all the unexpected things people do with items of consumption (Fiske 1989). My argument now is that the emphasis has swung too far in this direction with little attempt being made to ask whether it is 'as much fun on the other side of the counter'.[3]

This writing suggests the far distance between contemporary consumer culture and the world of long hours, unrewarding work, drudgery and brutal exploitation. Celia Lury writes, for example, in the introduction to her recent volume, that there is a 'relative independence of practices of consumption from those of production', this giving, she continues, 'growing power and authority . . . to (at least some) consumers' (Lury 1996: 4). Clearly this independence is a matter of where you look and where you stand in the labour market. In my own case the reality of homeworking was literally on my front doorstep. Neighbours on both sides of my last home in North London were up all night sewing, the lights were on and the gentle whirring of the sewing machines could be heard through the walls on either side. One was a Greek Cypriot woman whose 'bags' would be delivered early one morning and collected in exchange for finished work the next. On the other side of the wall an Asian grandmother also worked through the night and would then child-mind during the day having deposited her finished goods with her sons for delivery to the various street-markets of North and East London.

While there might be a case to argue that if the materialist feminists like

Annie Phizacklea fail to look at what happens to the clothes once they leave the shops and enter the field of symbolic value then it is unfair to accuse the cultural feminists of ignoring questions of production and manufacture. The answer to this has got to be that while ideally both sides might be brought into dialogue with each other, there are more glaring political problems in the cultural feminists' avoidance of all questions of pain and suffering. This means that the whole basis of feminist scholarship, founded as it is upon interrogating issues of gender inequality and subordination, is somewhat jeopardized. Lury, for example, mentions poverty in the opening pages of her book and only returns to it once, fleetingly. 'Deprivation in contemporary Britain is widespread . . . it extends throughout the bottom half of society, becoming particularly acute in the bottom 30–40 per cent' (ibid.: 5). These are hardly insignificant figures for any discussion of consumer culture, especially if we are concerned with how relations of inequality and of power and powerlessness are reproduced in society. Lury's 'bottom 30–40 per cent' would also doubtless include Phizacklea's Asian women homeworkers. Indeed if we take into account the feminization of poverty, the 'top half' of society with which Lury is primarily concerned becomes top heavy with men, and with white, wealthy middle England married couples. In effect she is talking about the privileged social classes.

The emphasis in the new consumerist studies is on what women and girls do with consumer goods and with how commodities give rise to meaning-making processes which are frequently at odds with the intended meaning or usage. Thus the 'world of goods' offers certain types of 'freedom' or even 'authority' to women as consumers with these taking on overtones of sexual freedoms or transgressive pleasures (Fiske 1989; Nava 1992). The strength of the historical case argued by Nava (1996), Felski (1995), Bowlby (1985) and Reekie (1995) hinges around the social reaction to the growth and popularity of female consumption in the late nineteenth century and into the twentieth century. However, the scale of the scandal of feminine pleasures in consumption was as double-edged and ambivalent in Victorian Britain, in America and in Australia, as moral panics are today. What can be read into the titillated, exaggerated over-reactions of the male moral guardians is as much a projection of their fears and fantasies of female sexuality as it is any accurate reflection of what women are doing or thinking about as they walked around the department stores. In other words, fascinating though these accounts may be (and this includes the novels upon which many of these authors are also reliant as evidence), it is historically and sociologically debateable to construct an argument about female consumption in nineteenth-century society by relying on such limited source material.

Women's new public freedom in the new department stores, to browse and wander, to feel the luxurious textures of the silks and laces on display and to linger in the restaurants, described as it is in this context, gives us only the merest hint of the social relations entailed in these leisure practices. Shopping in the grand sense described by these authors was, at that time, for ladies of leisure.

Reekie acknowledges this point without further problematizing it: 'the typical drapery store customer in the nineteenth century was a middle-class or wealthy woman' (ibid.: 7). The precise history of how and where working-class women and girls did their shopping is yet to be written. And who is to say that these same middle-class women were not possibly the sort of customers for whom class antagonism was waged over the counter. Shop assistants played the same sort of role as servants. Theirs was a position of servitude (Benson 1986). They could be sacked on the spot for not treating the customers with the correct degree of deference. In these circumstances empowerment and authority can be (and certainly was) as much about power and authority over those deemed socially subordinate as it is (or was) about new female freedoms. This treatment by women who consider themselves socially superior is the sort of experience which anybody who has ever served in a shop has direct experience of and to have this important, indeed even formative, moment of social interaction written out of feminist histories of shopping is strange to say the least. In some respects it is a way of avoiding the issue which is that these relations are not just about the neutral-sounding term class difference between women, but are actually about class antagonism. If 'we' feminists now recognize diversity within the category of women, then we must also recognize the consequences of this in terms of both class and ethnicity. Middle-class women can be as much the perpetrators of class inequalities as their male counterparts. The privileges of their social position will inevitably be manifest in those spheres in which they play a key role. Not to acknowledge this as an ongoing issue in feminist scholarship is to exculpate whole social categories of women from responsibility and agency in history on the grounds of their sex. Vron Ware has charted white women's role in the construction of empire and imperialism (Ware 1992). But we cannot talk about middle-class women 'at home' during the same period unless we are willing to confront some of the social consequences of their status in their everyday environment.

So keen to foreground female pleasures, this work studiously ignores the production of consumption as though it did not exist. This is as true in the historical work on modernity as it is in the recent work on consumer culture. It is as though no women were employed in the low paid retail sector, as though no women worked through the night to 'finish' off the dresses and ball gowns which only a tiny few could afford, and as though no women were employed to service the consumer goods in the home as domestic servants, washing and laundering, repairing and mending, 'dressing' the mistress, looking after her wardrobe and picking her discarded clothes from the floor, i.e. providing the human service needed to allow the consumer goods to function as such.

Feminist critics argue that women as a category have been left out of the great accounts of modernity (e.g. Berman 1982). But instead of tackling some of the more politically problematic aspects which emerge precisely from all these exclusions from modernity, exclusions without which it could not have constructed its marvellous edifices (see Braidotti 1992; Gilroy 1993a), some feminists have chosen to write women back into this history through a focus on consumption and the urban experience and in so doing reproduce these same evasive strategies around class and inequality. As a result at points they portray a social scenario of delights, pleasures and achievements rather than miseries and exclusions.

In retrieving a presence for middle-class women in the city and arguing this to play a role in the formation of modernity, these authors miss the opportunity of developing a fuller argument which might suggest that it was partly through the various forced exclusions of women into the domestic sphere, into the household world of shopping and into the internalized world of the sexualized body and femininity and maternity that modernity allowed itself to emerge triumphant in the public sphere as a space of white, male, reason, rationality and bureaucracy. While some strata of young middle-class women could be drafted into carrying out the regulatory social work of the city, in the form of philanthropic visiting, their services were quite quickly dispensed of when it came to developing the great infrastructures of state and government.

Mica Nava suggests that Janet Wolff's (1990) argument, that women in the modernity of the late nineteenth century were not able to be 'flâneurs' because they were in the process of being removed from the public sphere of work and the urban environment into the safety of the home and the suburbs, needs to be revised to take into account the new freedom women had to browse and spend time in the department stores. (Wolff actually quite carefully qualifies her claims by emphasizing that she is concerned very much with the literary and poetic accounts which configured the flâneur as observer of modernity. She also notes the inevitable discrepancy between the ideology of domesticity and the reality of working women's lives (Wolff 1990: 35).) Nava then reminds us of the busy lives of 'middle-class women' who 'travelled with increasing freedom through the streets and open spaces of the city' (Nava 1996: 43). She also notes how these women 'also visited less salubrious neighbourhoods as part of the pro-liferation of philanthropic schemes' (ibid.: 44). She continues, 'Indeed in their pursuit of "adventure, self-discovery and meaningful work" many [women] would have ventured into slum territory unfamiliar even to their husbands or brothers' (ibid.: 44). While Nava does then note that 'the visionary element in their activities was perhaps somewhat compromised by the fact that their personal freedom . . . was gained in the process of trying to enforce it else-where, on the women of the poorer classes' (ibid.: 44), my own response to this can only be polemical. If the streets were 'notorious' and full of 'disreputable strangers', who were the degraded and impoverished bodies who constituted these social categories? How was their experience of modernity? The power and privilege which allowed this minority of women such 'freedom' cannot in short be understood without taking into account the experience of those many women and girls who were the object of these concerned gazes and for whom the city was a place of work and livelihood, who lived in 'slum territory' and who travelled about the city not because they had gained some new found freedom but as part of their everyday gainful activities. How else did working women through the centuries get to their work, run errands for their masters and mistresses, take some time for pleasure and enjoyment, and indeed escape the overcrowded conditions of their homes, but by walking about and by hanging about on the streets? Judging by some recent accounts it is as though until middle-class women tested the waters of danger by stepping foot inside a department store or by visiting the poor, the streets of the great cities like London were populated only by men. Apart from anything else this contradicts the historical evidence put forward in Sally Alexander's account of women workers in nineteenth-century London. Alexander quotes Arthur Mumby describing the flow of female labour over London Bridge in 1861 as follows:

> One meets them at every step; young women carrying large bundles of umbrella frames home to be covered; young women carrying cages full of hats, which yet want the silk and the binding, coster girls often dirty and sordid, going to fill their empty baskets, and above all female sack-makers.
>
> (Mumby quoted in Alexander 1976: 73)

What I am arguing is that it makes no sense at all to correct the gender blindness of writers like Berman by writing middle-class women into modernity as consumers or indeed as philanthropists (who were in the privileged position of being able to work unpaid) without also recognizing that the majority of young and old working-class women at this time had to get up at ungodly hours in the morning and walk unchaperoned to their places of work in shops, factories as well as in private homes thus making a remarkable contribution to the *workforce of modernity*. In summary it might be more useful to consider one manifestation of the productivity of power in the late nineteenth century as residing in the complex ways in which some degree of female freedom could be permitted by exacting from these women knowledge of the more dangerous classes obtained through practices of urban surveillance in the form of visiting, etc. At the same time some of these women might well have been so shocked by the poverty and suffering which they witnessed that they indeed became deeply committed to campaigning for political action and reform.

These new consumerist perspectives have emerged out of debates in media and cultural studies which have disputed the image of consumers as manipulable, passive dupes. In the analysis of contemporary consumer society, it has grown out of an awareness that the categories of social class and the traditional place occupied by the working class has undergone rapid and irreversible change in Britain over the last twenty-five years. The focus then is on how attachments to goods and to the 'social life of things' can in fact be productive of new social identities. On occasion this has allowed contemporary social and cultural theorists to leave class behind. But such social changes along with the intensification of consumption and the apparent access of ordinary people to wide ranges of consumer goods should not be used as an excuse to ignore the limits of consumption and to dismiss the work and wage needed to be able to participate in consumption. Nor should it lead to the abandonment of class as a primary concept for understanding social structure. Class, gender and ethnicity have to be continually re-interrogated for their meaning and they also have to be 'thought together'. The same goes for discussions of consumption. Since women's place in contemporary society has undergone such rapid changes it is also necessary to take these into account. If, for example, 25 per cent of the labour force in Britain now works part-time, and if 65 per cent of these workers are female, and if 42 per cent of births are to unmarried women and 1 in 3 (soon to be 1 in 2) marriages fail, and if 20 per cent of all households are currently headed by an unsupported single mother, and finally if 60 per cent of part-time workers need to rely on income support to bring their weekly income up to a so-called living wage (all figures from *Social Trends*, March 1996), then to talk in uncomplicated terms about women comprising the bulk of consumers without considering the consequences these factors have for participation in consumption, is neither politically nor intellectually viable. These figures make Lury's a conservative estimate of poverty and suggest that most women in contemporary Britain are struggling and making sacrifices to make ends meet.

Perhaps the real issue is that a good deal of the new consumerist studies remain sociologically ungrounded. With the exception of Lunt and Livingstone's social psychological study of attitudes to money and goods, savings and debt (Lunt and Livingstone 1992), there are few detailed accounts of consumption and I am unaware of any feminist work which is looking at how women actually shop and what sort of issues influence their choices. The only material on this subject comes, not surprisingly, from the poverty lobby and from those concerned with the feminization of poverty (see Brannen and Wilson 1987). What scanty work there is shows that women most often consume with their family's or their children's needs uppermost in their minds. Women frequently consume on behalf of others. They make personal sacrifices as a matter of course to be able to afford treats and birthday presents for their children and grandchildren. Single mothers often find themselves put under enormous pressures to compensate to their children for not having a father and hence not fulfilling the real family image which prevails in consumer culture by giving into their demands for the latest pair of trainers (Middleton, Ashworth and Walker 1994). Indeed the phrase 'giving in' is indicative of all the conflicts and anxieties around consumption.

There is also a complete absence of the position of black and Asian women as consumers. Were this to be done it would surely point to other variables, other clusters of meaning coming into play, many of which would once again tell of memories of poverty, domestic service and of being 'on the other side of the counter'. This is not to suggest that Asian and black women only engage with consumption from the perspective of exclusion, far from it. It is simply more likely that, as with women of working-class origin, it is difficult to embrace the language of the new consumerist studies without questioning the terms of participation. Many women would not want to be understood as participating in the consumer culture with the same casual confidence as their white, middle-class counterparts. Many are (and were) not permitted to, through the subtle grids of classification and distinction which define how and where we consume. Modes of consumption thus become marks of social and cultural difference. Likewise the frustrated experience of exclusions from consumption can be a profoundly politicizing process which forces young people to confront the meaning of class, gender and ethnicity in their own homes, neighbourhoods, schools and shopping centres.

While every young black or Asian women I have interviewed or spoken to in relation to my research on the fashion industry (McRobbie 1998) has described their relation to fashion in terms of pleasure and enjoyment they have also all referenced this interest through the language of work and labour.[4] Many of their mothers and grandmothers learnt to sew as a way of avoiding having to clean white people's houses (Wallace 1996). Sewing and dressmaking were handed down to their daughters as useful skills which would also allow them to produce their own beautiful clothes when they could not possibly have afforded to buy them. This is borne out by the fact that most young women and men of so-called ethnic origin studying fashion design in the art schools and as far as I can ascertain all well-known black fashion designers currently working in the UK come from families where the mother and other women in the house sewed and where the kitchen and living room floors were continually covered in fabric and paper patterns and where sewing and dressmaking (whether here in the UK or else in Jamaica, in Africa or in Asia) was an ongoing household activity. Although much of this kind of domestic work is now being replaced with new cultures of consumption in the form of ready-made clothing purchasable on a global basis, it functions nonetheless as an important, even formative memory.[5]

Having described some of the problems with the new consumerist studies I want to conclude this section by pointing in turn to some of the political weaknesses of the labour economists and sociologists whose concern is with how low paid work and exploitation provide the cheap goods for western consumers. Feminist writers like Rowbotham, Phizacklea, Tate and others have concerned themselves with the endless relocation of capital to off-shore sites and Free Trade Zones and then back to on-shore even cheaper and local sites offering low cost labour provided typically by immigrant women. They have shown how the opportunity to exploit this powerless labour force of women and children has produced the apparent buoyancy of consumer culture in fashion and in domestic goods in the west from the late 1970s. The problem lies in their reluctance to cross the divide and engage with feminists who are working at other locations in the field of consumer culture. Cultural questions including the symbolic role played by consumer goods cut no ice with these writers. In their work there can be no suggestion that the women and child labourers of these exploitative systems are or can also be participants at some level in consumption. There is certainly no hint of the fact that consumption might also bring some degree of enjoyment beyond the grim reality of earning enough to feed a family. In this respect these writers 'culturally deprive' women workers by so emphasizing 'dignity and daily bread' (Rowbotham and Mitter 1994). As Stuart Hall has reminded us 'Everybody, including people in very poor societies whom we in the West frequently speak about as though they inhabit a world outside culture, knows that today's "goods" double up as social signs and produce meanings as well as energy' (Hall 1989: 131).

The message which comes across from this political and intellectual lobby is to boycott all goods found to be produced in low wage, non-union factories or sweatshops. The eventual success of the recent 'anti-Gap' campaign initiated by the Labour Co-ordinating Committee of the US in 1995 was the result of intense struggle and extensive publicity drawing attention to the child labourers used to produce the cheap but high-quality cotton shirts we have come to associate with The Gap. In the end The Gap signed an agreement guaranteeing the protection of human rights to all its employees along with regular inspection of factories. However The Gap is one of thousands of successful retailers and bad publicity does not always lead to manufacturers signing agreements to introduce better working conditions. A recent documentary programme accused Marks & Spencer of exploiting child labour in South East Asia and the response of M&S was to take out a libel action against the TV company on the grounds that it never 'knowingly' employed under-age workers. In Britain, where trade unionism has been more or less decimated (with unions like USDAW barely holding onto any membership whatsoever, and that only in food retail and not at all in fashion and clothing), and where most fashion manufacturers now run strictly non-union shops, and where anyway most fashion producers work as part of a long and anonymous sub-contracting chain, dispersed across country and city, the prospect of re-unionization and even of a decent battle for a minimum wage is bleak.

There are also limits to the politics of the boycott. Hard pressed consumers will frequently return to the cheap retail outlet when the fuss has died down. This means that in broad political terms the campaigns can only play on people's consciences and as we all know battling against povery on a global basis is an exhausting and demoralizing struggle. However, the inattention to cultural questions by the materialists and the excessive concern with culture and meaning by those in feminist cultural studies means that an opportunity for dialogue is continually averted. In addition where the materialists look in depth at the scale of exploitation with all the facts and figures at their fingertips, they remain unimpressed it seems by the arguments emerging from the field of post-colonial writing where consumer culture in the form of global communications offers new possibilities for hybridic political alliances (Gilroy 1993b; Hall 1996). Meanwhile cultural studies remain relatively oblivious to facts and figures and to the political role they can and do play. But even if these facts and figures are 'fictions', they are useful fictions and the extent to which current talk about consumer cultures is ungrounded by sustained historical or sociological research seriously weakens the case of those who suggest the political mobilization that can be done around consumption.

Fashion production, fashion consumption

My argument has been to re-integrate the study of production and consumption and to foreground not just work and employment in the production of consumption but also to take into account the changing nature of work and employment. Given that I have also been arguing for specificity and particularity it makes some sense to end this piece by making some comments about how the British fashion industry looks if we approach it from this more integrative perspective. Given that there has been a concern with political change in this piece I will also argue that indeed the only hope for both the fashion industry per se and for those women employed at each rung on the low pay ladder is to be able to think across the currently unbridgeable gap between textile production (i.e. weaving, fabric-making, etc.), manufacture and design, between sewing and sketching, between serving and being served and between working and wearing.

Fashion is of course an almost wholly feminized industry. Apart from a few men at the top, including manufacturers and retailers, celebrity designers and magazine publishers, it is and has been a female sphere of production and consumption. For this reason alone fashion *is* a feminist issue. It comprises of six component parts: manufacture and production; design; retail and distribution; education and training; the magazine and fashion media; and the practices of consumption. If we consider these one at a time, demonstrating their mutual dependence as well as their apparent distance from each other, it is possible to see a set of tensions and anxieties which in turn provide opportunities for political debate and social change. Thinking across the fashion sector in this way also has the advantage of disaggregating what often seem like a series of starkly monolithic institutions. Given the scale and the power of the huge multinationals which create the conditions for consumer culture in the west it is often difficult to see a political light at the end of the tunnel, and perhaps it is for this reason that the new consumerist writers place so much emphasis on the subversive things people can do with consumer goods.

Let us look then, briefly, at manufacture and production. Phizacklea has already shown that factory production in this country is a sunset industry and the only on-shore activity of any significance comprises the small sub-contracted units of production often headed by small-scale ethnic entrepreneurs themselves seeking a livelihood in fashion manufacture as an alternative to unemployment (Phizacklea 1990). The women workers in this sector receive very low pay and are often also homeworkers. There is no significant union recognition nor any likelihood of it. However gloomy though this may seem, self-organization of homeworkers is not unimaginable, as Tate has shown (Tate

41

1994). There is no reason why the highly skilled knitters described recently in *The Independent* as supplying the top fashion designers should not find ways of improving their working conditions and their wages (*The Independent*, 24 February 1996). Publicity, lobbying and support from other sectors of the industry including the powerful fashion magazines (and so-called celebrity politics) could achieve a lot in a short space of time. The recent Oxfam Clothes Code campaign has, for example, drawn on figures like comedienne Jo Brand to persuade all retailers to adhere to a code of conduct guaranteeing decent working conditions in all their factories across the world. This sector could also put pressure on government to support further training and education which would allow women to move into better paid and more highly skilled work, as pattern cutters, for example (where there is a skill shortage) and it would also allow them to cut out the middlemen and subcontractors who currently negotiate all costs and take comfortable percentages. Finally this strategy would also allow the low paid women to get closer to the designers and retailers who at present they never see and often don't even know they are working for. British fashion designers typically work on a small scale self-employed basis. Even well-known names frequently employ fewer than twenty people direct. There is no inherent reason why closer collaboration of this sort could not take place to the mutual advantage of all parties.

Education and training would also have a role to play in this more collaborative strategy. At present fashion design education is too committed to defending the fine art status of fashion to be interested at all in manufacture and production. As a feminine field in the high culture-oriented world of the art schools, fashion design educators have looked up towards the fine arts for legitimation. But this is helpful neither to the industry as a whole nor to the young fashion design students themselves for whom it is often a mark of professional pride *not* to know how to put in a zip (astonishing though this may be to the outside world; see McRobbie 1998). The vast majority of fashion students never visit a factory throughout their degree. In some ways it is convenient to them not to have to know about how orders are actually put into production and who actually makes them since this would raise the unpleasant question of what sort of wages they are being paid and what sort of working conditions they are being expected to put up with. As one fashion academic said to me, 'It would take all the romance out of it for them.' But not knowing about production and manufacture is also unhelpful to the graduates in the longer term. It leaves them open to exploitation by unscrupulous suppliers and middlemen who over-charge them while massively under-paying their sub-contracted women workers. It means in short that fashion designers don't have the kind of grasp of the industry as a whole that they should have. It is not inconceivable however that at some point with more realistic education and training, young designers might work on a more equal basis with the women who do the sewing and finishing. All it would take would be more open public debate on the fashion industry and also on the unviability of designers making a livelihood for themselves without thoroughly involving themselves at every stage in production and manufacture. Fashion educators, the great majority of whom are women, would also have a clear role to play in this respect.

The designers themselves, most of whom are working in the shadow of unemployment and are or have been dependent on government sponsored schemes like the Enterprise Allowance Scheme and other benefits, might also recognize what they have in common with other women working throughout the industry. The class divide between them and the machinists is not as great as it might seem. Many have mothers who have worked in the industry. In addition fashion designers are as likely to exploit themselves as they are to employ an exploited workforce, so there is a good deal of work of de-mystification and de-glamorization to be done in this respect.

The final three parts of the industry, the magazines, retail and consumption, would also need to be re-conceptualized along the same lines. Fashion magazines at present have a foolish and unnecessary commitment to avoiding serious or political issues. But this might change. Young women fashion journalists might at some point be willing to persuade their editors that a piece on the exploited labour that goes into a designer dress might be worthy of a few pages. Instead of supporting the fashion industry by producing gushy pages of praise for the work of the new crop of British designers, the magazines could take this kind of risk. Likewise retail workers might recognize themselves to have more in common with other workers in the fashion industry than with those employed in selling food or furniture or whatever. Anyway, given the virtually non-existent rate of trade unionization in this sector, new forms of organization and collaboration would need to be established. Fashion retail staff identify strongly with fashion and less with retail, but they are now employed on short-term, part-time contracts, often they are working largely for commission. Their self-image as working in the glamorous fashion industry must surely be undercut by the reality of knowing that in a few years time possibly with children to support it is unlikely that they would hold onto the job of decorating the shopfloor at Donna Karan. What sort of long-term career is there in fashion retail? At present nobody knows because no research has been done on this side of shopping. Research and public debate would be a useful way of beginning to improve the conditions of women who work in this sector.

This leaves us with the practices of consumption. If consumers were to be thoroughly alerted to the inhumane activities which eventually bring clothes to the rails of many of the department stores in the way that the politics of food production has made some impact on food consumption then pressure might also be brought to bear by consumer organizations for changes in the fashion industry. Many women and girls already deeply object to the 200 per cent (at least) mark up on items of fashion. They know how little the women who produce the clothes get paid and frequently the consumers vote with their feet and look but don't buy, even if they could afford to. The fashion industry knows this to be the case but is at present incapable of thinking reflexively about its own practices. A (New) Labour policy which realistically recognized the British fashion industry as a place of many people's livelihoods and also as a potential site for providing more work on a more secure basis on the longer term, instead of seeing it as a piece of light entertainment, might be better able to translate the desires of many women, including young women, to make a good living in fashion. Often it is through consuming that women want to become producers. The energetic enthusiasm of women across the boundaries of class and ethnicity for fashion could be used to transform it into a better place of work rather than allowing it to remain a space of exploited production and guilty consumption.

Notes

1 Some upmarket fashion shops in London now employ doormen/security guards who can stop people from entering if they do not look as though they have the money to buy. They do this by saying that 'the shop is too busy right now', even though it is quite clear to the would-be customers that the shop is in fact relatively empty.
2 These political positions could be broadly characterized as traditional socialist-feminism in contrast to variations of the new post-feminism which also embrace so-called identity politics.
3 The same argument could be made in relation to recent discussions of the 'pink pound'. What is missing here are the working conditions (i.e. behind the bar) of those mostly young gay men who service this industry. What sort of career is it? What are the pay and conditions?
4 This research has involved extensive interviews with young British fashion designers with a view to building up a picture of employment in the creative and cultural sectors.
5 I count myself in this category since my own grandmother was a skilled tailoress from Dublin who emigrated to Glasgow in 1915.

References

Alexander, S. (1976) 'Women's work in 19thC London', in Mitchell and Oakley (eds), *The Rights and Wrongs of Women*, Harmondsworth: Penguin.

Benson, S. (1986) *Counter Cultures: Saleswomen, Managers and Customers in American Department Stores 1890–1940*, Urbana: University of Illinois Press.

Berman, M. (1982) *'All That Is Solid Melts Into Air': The Experience of Modernity*, London: Verso.

Bowlby, R. (1985) *Just Looking: Consumer Culture in Dreiser, Gissing and Zola*, London: Methuen.

Braidotti, R. (1992) 'On the feminist female subject or from she-self to she-other', in G. Bock and S. James (eds), *Beyond Equality and Difference: Citizenship, Feminist Politics and Female Subjectivity*, London: Routledge.

Brannen, J. and Wilson, G. (eds) (1987) *Give and Take in Families*, London: Allen & Unwin.

Felski, R. (1995) *The Gender of Modernity*, London and Cambridge, MA: Harvard University Press.

Fiske, J. (1989) *Understanding Popular Culture*, London: Unwin Hyman.

Gilroy, P. (1993a) *The Black Atlantic: Modernity and Double Consciousness*, London: Verso.

—— (1993b) *Small Acts*, London: Serpents Tail.

Hall, S. (1989) 'The meaning of new times', in S. Hall and M. Jacques (eds) *New Times: The Changing Face of Politics in the 1990s*, London: Lawrence & Wishart.

—— (1996) 'New ethnicities', in D. Morley and H.-S. Chen (eds), *Stuart Hall: Critical Dialogues in Cultural Studies*, London: Routledge.

Lunt, P. and Livingstone, S. (1992) *Mass Consumption and Personal Identity: Everyday Economic Experience*, Buckingham: Open University Press.

Lury, C. (1996) *Consumer Culture*, Oxford: Polity Press.

McRobbie, A. (1998) *British Fashion Design: Rag Trade or Image Industry?*, London: Routledge.

Middleton, S., Ashworth, K. and Walker, R. (1994) *Family Fortunes: The Pressures on Parents and Children in the 1990s*, London: Child Poverty Action Group.

Mort, F. (1989) 'The politics of consumption', in Hall and Jacques (eds) *New Times: The Changing Face of Politics in the 1990s*, London: Lawrence & Wishart.

—— (1996) *Cultures of Consumption*, London: Routledge.

Nava, M. (1992) *Changing Cultures: Feminism, Youth and Consumerism*, London: Sage.

—— (1996) 'Modernity's disavowal: women, the city, and the department store', in M. Nava and A. O'Shea (eds) *Modern Times, Reflections on a Century of English Modernity*, London: Routledge.

Phizacklea, A. (1990) *Unpacking the Fashion Industry: Gender, Racism and Class in Production*, London: Routledge.

Pumphrey, M. (1987) 'The flapper, the housewife and the making of modernity', *Cultural Studies*, Vol. 1, No. 2: 179–93.

Reekie, G. (1995) *Temptations: Sex, Selling and the Department Store*, Sydney: Allen & Unwin.

Rowbotham, S. and Mitter, S. (eds) (1994) *Dignity and Daily Bread: New Forms of Economic Organising Among Poor Women in the Third World and the First*, London: Routledge.

Social Trends (1996) London: HMSO.

Tate, J. (1994) 'Homework in West Yorkshire', in Rowbotham and Mitter (eds) *Dignity and Daily Bread: New Forms of Economic Organising Among Poor Women in the Third World and the First*, London: Routledge.

Williams, S. (1996) 'The designer jumper you're wearing: where did it come from?', *The Independent*, 24 February.

Wallace, M. (1996) 'Fashion consumption', paper delivered at Fashion Victims Conference, New York University, March.

Ware, V. (1992) *Beyond the Pale: White Women, Racism and History*, London: Verso.

Wolff, J. (1990) *Feminine Sentences: Essays on Women and Culture*, Cambridge: Polity Press.

4

MORE!

New sexualities in girls' and women's magazines

Feminist scholarship and women's magazines

For over twenty years feminists have singled out girls' and women's magazines as commercial sites of intensified femininity and hence rich fields of analysis and critique. So established is this interest that it can be read in its own right as part of the history and development of feminism in the academy. The purpose of this chapter is to offer an account of these changes in feminist analysis in conjunction with the equally visible, indeed quite dramatic changes which have taken place across the landscape of the magazines over the same period.

In the mid-1970s feminist attention to girls' and women's magazines saw the magazines as exemplifying oppression. The glossy advertisements did nothing but convince readers of their own inadequacies while drawing them into the consumer culture on the promise that they could buy their way out of bodily dissatisfactions and low self-esteem. The magazines promoted romance as the means by which women should interpret and practice their sexuality. Inevitably this required submissive and compliant behaviour in relation to men, and as I argued in my early work about *Jackie* magazine (McRobbie 2000, new edition), it also produced a neurotic femininity. Since men could never be trusted to remain faithful, women were inevitably placed in competitive relationships with each other. The problem pages repeated and confirmed this narrow field of feminine interests. Even the enjoyment of fashion and pop music seemed to be defined in terms of the presence or absence of a boyfriend. It was a completely claustrophobic world. There was no interest in changes in women's position in society, only with the already established parameters of conventional femininity. The *Cosmopolitan* brand of liberation throughout the 1970s and into the 1980s only meant better or more sex for women. And from the mid-1980s onwards the whole field of magazines shifted towards self-improvement.

By failing to depart from the proven old formulae of commercial femininity the magazines could be accused of deep conservatism. On the other hand, if we read them closely, there are degrees of change within the genre-bound format of what constitutes the women's world. For example, there is an energy and vitality in magazines like *Just Seventeen*, a self-confidence and openness to the world rather than a retreat from it. At any rate this is what I (and some other feminists) have been arguing over the last few years in relation to magazines like *Elle, Marie Claire, Just Seventeen, Mizz* and many of the other new titles (see Driscoll 1995; McRobbie 1994; Stuart 1990; Winship 1987). There are as many other feminists, however, for whom commercial magazines remain quite unacceptably and irrevocably sexist. Condemned for, among other things, the assumption of heterosexuality as normative, the magazines are more or less dismissed by writers like Jackson (1996). Women and girls, she implies, would be much better off without them.

Stuart (1990) and Brunsdon (1991) have both characterized the early critical relation between academic feminism and commercial women's genres as an opposition between feminism and femininity. The argument in this chapter is that there remains an important relation between feminism and the world of girls' and women's magazines, the new intersections between them need to be examined in more depth. The stark opposition between feminism and femininity, as Brunsdon and Stuart both show, has given way in recent years to something more fluid. To feminists like Jackson commercial magazines function like a red rag to a bull. Responses to these cultural forms still have the ability to regenerate polarities and oppositions within feminism (as this chapter itself reflects), while at the same time the magazines themselves demonstrate an ongoing engagement with many feminist themes and issues.

In the pages that follow these dynamics will be explored more fully. The magazines in a sense provoke 'us' feminists into asking urgent questions not just about the changes we can see around us, but also about the changes we want to see. What sort of magazines would we like girls and women to read? While that was a relatively easy question to answer in the 1970s, it is almost impossible to conceive of an answer now in the 1990s. The popularity of magazines like *More!* also prompts us to consider our own political effectiveness as feminists. Have we managed to have any impact in redefining gender relations and sexual politics? How do we now stand in relation to the outside world of 'ordinary women' and commercial culture?

In media and cultural studies, scholarship on magazines has occupied a less central and prestigious place than academic research on other media partly because magazines remain a narrow sector of the global communications industry. In addition, because the focus has until recently been on women's magazines (although there is now a literature on men's magazines (see Nixon 1996)), the debate has been conducted more rigidly along the lines of gender than in other areas of study. It has remained, more or less, a debate among women. We can characterize the feminist critique of magazines as having taking place in four stages. First, there was the 'angry repudiation' stage. Second, the 'theory of ideology' replaced this earlier more polemical approach. This then gave way to the third stage, the focus on 'women's pleasure', which in turn led to a 'return of the reader'. I want to suggest in this chapter a further three stages of analysis to more fully update our understanding of the magazine form. These are the 'new sexualities' of the 1990s, the relation to feminism and, finally, through this relation to feminism, the reconceptualization of the social relations of production and consumption.

The 'angry repudiation' stage is self-evidently that formative moment in feminism when it was necessary to condemn the false and objectified images of women in the mass media. Not only were these images designed to make women attractive for male consumption, they also did this by pulling women into consumer culture since to achieve this ideal it was necessary to buy an endless stream of gadgets, devices, and artificial aids (as they were then seen). The overall message to women by feminists at this point was to stop buying magazines and therefore free themselves from this kind of pressure. This is exactly what liberation meant, to be free of the paraphenalia of oppression.

The second more academic stage of analysis drew on Althusser's theory of ideology (Althusser 1971). This argued that ideology was the key means by which dominant social groups retained their power and influence. Ideology worked by naturalizing and universalizing meanings and values which were in fact socially constructed. Ideology also ensured the smooth reproduction of existing social and sexual relations. By pointing to the pervasive force of ideology, feminists moved beyond the earlier and élitist assumption that 'ordinary women' were fooled by capitalist society into a kind of false consciousness, unlike their feminist counterparts who had managed to break free. Instead 'we' were all implicated in the spider's web of ideology, not least because it was this that gave us our identity. It 'interpellated' us, giving us a name, a place and a gender in society. It was through these means that our inner selves, our sense of self and our 'subjectivities' were also constructed.

Magazines were important because it was here that this work was carried out, this is where what it meant to be a woman was endlessly dissected. Feminist studies of magazines and of advertising aimed at women took us into the heartland of sexual difference. By the mid-1980s, the interest in poststructuralism meant the gradual displacement of the concept of ideology while retaining a focus on the politics of meaning. Ideology suggested that beneath the social construction and the power of interpellative fixing there was the possibility of an eventual and superior truth of womanhood. The dislodging of this model, under the influence of Foucault's writing gave way to a concern with the different discursive means by which the category 'woman' or 'girl' came to be understood. Magazines played a regulative, normalizing role. Located in the field of commercial culture they nonetheless spoke with authority on these matters. Failure to abide by their rulings also carried consequences. As Driscoll has said, the teenage magazine 'as a source of advice and a site of information exchange, sells its own necessity by emphasizing the unavoidable, all-important difficulty of unguided feminine adolescence and the untrained adolescent feminine body' (Driscoll 1995: 189).

Magazines are therefore discursive forms whose primary focus is on the representation of women. Their business is, in effect, the nature of womanhood.

48

But this is also the concern of feminism. It, too, is a discursive formation, a series of spoken and written engagements with the political question of what it is to be a woman. It, too, is concerned to represent women. Post-structuralist feminism has argued that there is and can be no truth of womanhood, just as there can be no single or true feminism. Power resides in and through the currents of meaning which exist at key cultural locations in society, in this case inside the pages of the magazines. Hence one important task for feminism is to show how magazines compete to construct the subjectivities of their readers by producing these great bundles of meaning each week. So familiar are these that they enter our unconsciousnesses producing desires and pleasures even when consciously we might not want them to. The convergence between feminist political discourse and feminine commercial discourse lies in the significance of the personal world of emotions, relationships, family and domestic life. Through this shared interest, feminism and popular femininity are locked together, most often with the one despairing of the other.

Feminist psychoanalysis can be seen as ushering in the third stage in this field of study (although these stages do not follow a strictly chronological order). The question of female pleasure coincides with an admission on the part of a few feminist writers that they have something of a love–hate relationship with these comics and magazines. The fantasies of the perfect body, the wonderful relationship, the glamorous lifestyle continue to have a presence in our daily lives. This admission begins to break down the lines of opposition between feminism and femininity. The fact that reason and political analysis tells us that femininity is bad, while the unconscious continues to produce guilty pleasures revolving round the practices of conventional femininity, evokes at least a complexity when it comes to thinking about how we consume commercial culture.

Feminist psychoanalysis also demonstrated the difficulty of psychic change and the complicity of feminists with their own desires even when these were understood as harmful. Rose's work showed how femininity as a normative structure of gender identity was never as assured as patriarchy required it to be (Rose 1987). This then accounts for the repetitive anxiety in commercial culture to continue trying to tie it down, to secure this otherwise meandering sexual identity to its correct place in the symbolic order. Hence the same old stories, the same problems, the same kinds of visual images. The perceived insecurity at the heart of culture, about how women ought to be, allowed feminists to prise open contradictory dynamics within a field which had hitherto been seen as a seamless web of oppression and objectification. It was obsessive and repetitive precisely because it was less sure of itself. Women could be other than what was normatively required of them. The magazines were engaged in deep, psychic work making sure that the sexual status quo remained in place. Far from being frivolous distractions, they plugged into fundamental social processes. As Driscoll has said of teenage magazines, 'It does not do justice to the complexity of adolescent women, or these magazines, to discuss their production only in terms of her commodifiction' (Driscoll 1995: 194).

The pleasure question had a resounding impact in the feminist academy. First, it put feminists on a more equal footing with 'ordinary women' once it was recognised that most of us seem to share many of the same pleasures. This also allowed feminists to feel more connected to the outside world of women. During the austere stages of feminism this had seemed impossible and so it was with a sigh of relief that it was now once again possible to be part of a women's culture rather than just a feminist subculture. There were two immediate effects. First, feminists began to rescue popular cultural forms from their low status as trivial and insignificant, not even worth of study in media or cultural studies and, second, they also described the opportunities that seemed to arise in gaining pleasure from, for example, autonomous, even clandestine, readings of romantic novels. Radway's study (1984) shows how this private reading gave her female respondents not just an escape from housework but also a kind of alternative to their perceived dissatisfactions in their real-life sexual relations. In short, it produced an openness to thinking about or imagining change from within the isolated conditions of being a housewife.

In magazine scholarship female readers were now also granted more power. Frazer (1987) demonstrated (as did Beezer *et al.* 1986) that my own earlier work about *Jackie* magazine wrongly assumed that ideology actually worked in a mechanical, even automatic kind of way. By carrying out interviews with groups of *Jackie* readers, Frazer showed that instead of accepting the meanings, the girls actually negotiated them, arguing with the magazines and taking issue with what they were saying. Walkerdine (1990) countered this by bringing herself in as reader and arguing forcibly and compellingly that the power of the text over the working-class girl/reader remained overwhelming. For Walkerdine, young girls' comics do nothing but encourage submissiveness and feminine passivity. All sorts of miseries and injustices are to be tolerated for the prize of being a 'good girl'. In contrast, my own argument (1991, 1994) has been that magazines for slightly older girls have, by the late 1980s and early 1990s, shifted decisively away from this kind of docile sensibility, replacing it instead with a much more assertive and 'fun-seeking' female subjectivity. This is signalled in the disappearance of romance. The magazines have also absorbed a sprinkling of feminist ideas, especially on the problem pages. There is a loosening of the opposition between feminism and femininity. The question is, what do we make of this process of detachment, how do we critically navigate the new spaces within which female subjectivity now finds itself being constructed?

'In yer face': the new politics of femininity

The 'new sexualities' refers to images and texts which break decisively with the conventions of feminine behaviour by representing girls as crudely lustful young women. For this new kind of (typically heterosexual) girl, frank information, advice and knowledge about sex is a prerequisite for her adventures. And so the first task to consider here is what is going on when oral sex and the quality of orgasm are the cover stories in magazines read by girls as young as thirteen years old ('Blissed Out: Treat Yourself to the 0 to Mmm of Orgasm', *19*). In a few scattered articles and chapters published in the last year or so there has been a sense that young women have dramatically changed in their attitudes and behaviour, especially in leisure. Sheila Henderson, for example, writing in *Druglink*, describes how young women have participated fully in the Ecstasy culture of recent years, dealing it, taking it and, as we know from the death of Leah Betts, also dying from it (Henderson 1993). Girls seem to have thrown off the old notions of ladylike behaviour and talk frankly about wanting to 'get out of it' or to 'get off their heads' on drink or drugs. Likewise, Beatrix Campbell reports in the *Guardian* (Campbell 1996) how girlfriends arrange their evenings of drinking or drug consumption to allow one person in the group to remain sober and in control and so able to deal with unwanted male attention or drink or drug-related accidents. These kinds of reports have led some feminist journalists to suggest that girls have simply become 'loutish and laddish'. If this is so, the question is why? Where does the encouragement to act in this way come from and what kind of confidence and enjoyment does it give to girls to have won the freedom to act like boys? If we look back to the magazines, especially *More!* and *19* (both read by girls much younger than the officially targeted age), we find an exact replica of this kind of talk. The new girls' magazines are all about 'shagging, snogging and having a good time'. The magazines are not alone in this respect. Late night television shows for young people, in particular Channel Four's *The Girlie Show*, or ITV's *God's Gift*, relish what happens when girls turn the tables on men. Usually this involves subjecting male victims from the audience to the same kind of scrutiny and lascivious comment as has been the norm for women. School toilet humour provides the entertainment for live audiences who join the leering, mocking female presenters in the ritual humiliation of young males.

However, it is magazines rather than late night television which have attracted the critical attention of politicians and moral guardians. In February 1996 Tory MP Peter Luff presented a private member's bill to Parliament (which subsequently failed) requiring that girls' magazines carry age-specification warning stickers on their front covers.[1] This was because he had inadvertently come across what he described as obscene material in *Sugar*, the magazine read by his thirteen-year-old daughter. Information about oral sex (i.e. how to do it), which was what he complained about, was also carried in a number of publications at the same time, including the popular family magazine, *TV Hits*. Luff was worried about the fact that this aggressively promoted material was being read by much younger girls than the publishers were willing to admit. Actually teenage magazines are always read by an age range below the target readership the editors officially aim at, for the simple reason that they perform the teasing role of guides to girls as to what is in store for them at the next

Figure 4.1 More!: Courtesy of EMAP

stage of growing up. So magazines like *More!* are indeed consumed most avidly by fourteen year olds. What the moral guardians found inside the pages of these publications were features like the now notorious 'position of the fortnight' showing a line drawing of a couple experimenting with different ways of having sex. The accompanying text gives more precise directions. The magazines carry explicit information about masturbation (male and female), sex games, sex toys, and an endless supply of sexual advice. Most of these features carry the logo of condom manufacturers in the bottom corner of the page and editorially they are presented in the context of safe sex. Most of the magazines borrow their editorial style from the downmarket tabloids, especially those which, like the *News of the World*, specialise in gossip and sex scandals. Typical *More!* headlines include, for example, 'Revealed! Claudia's Sexy Secrets' or 'I Read His Diary and Discovered His Dirty Secret' or 'Nanny, With Knobs On'. *Marie Claire*, despite being targeted at an older audience, also uses this tabloid style of journalism. Some of its lead stores include 'I Know He Has A Mistress', 'My Brother is My Lover and We Have a Child' and 'The Married Man with Sixty Eight Other Women'. This kind of shock-horror headline has now become the staple of the girls' and women's magazine market. Like so many other forms of the youth-oriented media this quoting of the sleazy tabloids, this borrowing from the downmarket 'true confession' kind of publication, is presented in a vaguely ironic way.

There is an assumption that we are not so naïve as to imagine that these captions are not a parody of vulgar or downmarket literature. The housestyle of the magazines draws upon the rhetoric of the silly tabloids and the sleazy porn magazines. This is clearly signalled through the use of exaggerated and 'over the top' headlines. The assumption is that readers know and recognise the element of pastiche. Everything in magazines like *More!*, *Sugar*, *19* and *Just Seventeen* has a staged feel about it. Irony is pervasive. Every individual who appears in the magazine, from the well-known star or celebrity, to the unknown reader having a makeover, is performing a role, or 'acting up'. The dominant editorial style is ironic and this produces a kind of licensed silliness with headlines for features presenting male pin-ups including 'Yabba Dabba Drool: Men to Make Your Bed Rock' (*Looks*). Underlying this is the idea that 'we' can all participate in the fun of the 'Snogger of the Week' competition because 'we' all know that none of us takes it seriously.

This new form of ironic femininity allows readers to participate in all the conventional and gender stereotypical rituals of femininity without finding themselves trapped into traditional gender-subordinate positions. Irony gives them some room to move. It says 'let's enjoy drooling over Noel or Liam Gallagher, or Boyzone. This is after all what girls' magazines are all about.' The act of 'being a fan' is now conducted self-consciously. There is a clear element of self-parody which allows the girls to be fans without being simply 'stupid girls'. The magazines also mock themselves, and the whole culture of femininity becomes more transparently self-reflexive. Feminism has played some role in this, by having put girls' and women's magazines under the microscope, and made them the object of political attention. However, while it may be possible to account for the popularity of the magazines in these terms, this still does not

Figure 4.2 More!: Courtesy of EMAP

fully explain the provocative new sexualities. Why the abandonment of romance in favour of foreplay, condoms and sexual pleasure?

I have elsewhere argued at some length why romance has withered away, as a now outdated code for constructing the dominant narrative of female sexuality

(McRobbie 1994). Where this has now been replaced by much more overtly sexual material, the usual explanation provided by publishers and academics alike is that sex on the covers and on the inside pages sells more copies and that in the competitive world of magazine publishing circulations, profits and advertising revenue are what keep editors in their jobs. But the fact that sex sells tells us nothing about the new or emergent social relations of sexuality which underpin this field of representation. To understand the distinctiveness of this new regime of representation we need to take into account two factors, first AIDS and its consequences and, second, the impact of feminism. AIDS and HIV have produced a new, more explicit, sexual culture which is itself the product of government-approved awareness and prevention programmes. Whether magazine publishers and editors act responsibly by speaking to readers in their own language even though, as the Luff case demonstrates, this might be too uncomfortable for many parents, or whether they merely exploit the freedom to publish what some might see as semi-pornographic material for young female readers and thereby reap the profits, is open to question. However, we do know that it is now widely accepted by professionals in adolescent health education that magazines of this sort provide a highly effective environment, much more so than sex education lessons, in which to get the message across about safe sex.[2]

The second factor which needs to be more fully explored is the impact of feminism itself on these publications. The approval by women (most of whom would define themselves as feminists) working in health education indicates that the contents are recognised as having some value by professional feminists. In the days running up to and following the Luff Bill, various women (including mothers, teachers, family planning counsellors, doctors and other health workers) who, although they did not speak as feminists, nonetheless spoke in the language of feminism, strongly defended the magazines in public. That is, an older generation of women entered the public sphere to defend the pleasure-seeking sexual identities of a younger generation of girls. At the same time the place of feminism inside the magazines remains ambiguous. It has presence mostly in the advice columns and in the overall message to girls to be assertive, confident and supportive of each other. It is also present in how girls are encouraged to insist on being treated as equals by men and boyfriends, and on being able to say no when they want to. For writers like Stevi Jackson the magazines only provide girls with the same old staples of heterosexual sex, body anxieties and 'the old idea that girls' sexuality is being attractive and alluring' (Jackson 1996: 57). So she is saying that there are no great advances here. What I would say in contrast is that feminism exists as a productive tension in these pages. As Brunsdon has argued in relation to a number of Hollywood films including *Working Girl* (directed by Mike Nicholls, 1988) and *Pretty Woman* (directed by Garry Marshall, 1990), there is both a dependence upon feminism and a disavowal of it (Brunsdon 1997). In the new 'girlie' culture this is taken further and there is also a desire to be provocative to feminism especially since it has become both common sense and a sign of female, adult authority. Generation proves itself to be a stronger and more divisive force than might have been expected. Young women want to prove that they can do without feminism as a political movement while enjoying the rewards of its success in culture and in everyday life.

Feminism and *More!*

Jackson's short commentary, in the light of the Luff Bill, follows a conventional feminist pathway. This avoids the challenge posed by the magazines by treating them as more or less the same and almost equally as bad as their predecessors, and also by understanding them as coherent texts, without contradictions, disruptions or uncertainties. The main problem with the conventional feminist attack is that it avoids reflecting on the relationship that feminism might have with the girls who read these publications and indeed with the female journalists and editors who produce the magazines. This, in turn, generates an enormous polarization between 'the feminists', as one critical mass, and the magazines and their readers.

The problem with this is that feminism gets let off the hook. This kind of approach does not ask what feminism actually wants young women to be like these days, nor does it hint at what women's magazines would look like if they corresponded more to a feminist agenda. It offers almost no opportunities for intervention or even dialogue with either the female producers of magazines or the consumers. But in the ideal feminist world of feminist magazines, what would go and what would stay? Who would make these decisions? This authoritative feminism seems to have no interest in interrogating its own foundations, its assumptions and its categories of both 'woman' and 'girl'. And yet it is obviously driven by such assumptions and such categories. Nor does it have any sense of feminism itself representing a field of power or regulation. It shows no interest in the consequences for feminism when feminists occupy positions of relative power and influence, in education, in the academy and elsewhere. It certainly never imagines that the editors of magazines like these might also think of themselves as feminists. Perish the thought! But 'we' feminists are many and diverse, and who is to say who the real feminist is? Many of us are now probably seen by younger women as figures of authority. And is it any wonder then that younger generations of women and their magazines join forces in rebelling against us too, as well as the moral guardians who condemn their reading material?

My instinct is to see this as healthy and interesting. It forces us feminists to at least think about what it is we expect of young women. Do we really want them to be like us, do we want to reproduce ourselves? Surely this would be a narrow, dangerous and historically unviable ambition? In fact Jackson finds it hard to present her negative case against the magazines unequivocally. She admits that the 'advice given on heterosexual sex in the problem pages is often sensible'

(Jackson 1996: 58). She also concedes that there are 'more serious articles about both sexuality and other aspects of life. . . . The readers of these magazines certainly know far more about coercive sex, sexual exploitation, rape and incest than previous generations.' Is this not exactly what feminism has argued for? In which case it would seem that the magazines are doing a good job. Indeed one could go further and suggest that even within the narrow, almost exclusive focus on sexuality there are strong signs of the influence of feminism. The idea that sexual pleasure is learnt, not automatically discovered with the right partner, the importance of being able to identify and articulate what you want sexually and what you do not want, the importance of learning about the body and being able to make the right decisions about abortion and contraception, the different ways of getting pleasure and so on, each one of these figured high in the early feminist agenda. This was the sort of material found in books like *Our Bodies, Our Selves* (Boston Women's Health Collective 1973), the volume which started as a feminist handbook and went on to sell millions of copies across the world.

The real issue upon which Jackson's case rests is the place of lesbianism in the sexual content of the magazines. Lesbian issues are now addressed much more directly by the magazines. Indeed *Just Seventeen* recently ran a three-page feature on 'Girls Who Fancy Girls', the first time as far as I can see that the idea of lesbian desire has actually been acknowledged in younger girls' magazines. However, Jackson is right to point out that heterosexuality is still the norm. The whole cultural field of the magazines takes heterosexual desire as constituting a framework of normality. There is no explicit information about the finer details of lesbian sex, no position of the fortnight for lesbian lovers. This point then marks the limits of permissible sexualities within the field of the magazines. Lesbianism remains, for younger readers, a social issue rather than a sexual desire. But does this mean we turn away from the magazines, dismissing them entirely on these grounds? Surely this too is an issue that has to be thought through more seriously. What would it take for a commercial magazine to promote lesbian desire alongside and equal to heterosexual desire? And what then might be the relation between feminist critics and the version of lesbianism now presented as normative? That is to say, what kind of lesbianism does Jackson have in mind when she points to its marginalization? What if it found a place for itself as normative on the pages of the magazines through the currency of gay and lesbian consumption, i.e. the 'pink pound'? Is so-called lesbian chic compatible or incompatible with feminism?

There is no underestimating the harm done and the injury caused by the endless invocation of femininities which violently excludes the desires and the identities of young lesbian women. But this very act of exclusion also poses important political questions. Does it produce and reproduce lines of division within feminism; that is, between heterosexual feminists and lesbian feminists? Or is it even more complicated than this? How, for example, do lesbian feminist mothers feel about their daughters avidly reading these magazines? How would a feminist like Stevi Jackson deal with female students, gay and straight, defending the magazines against her criticism? These seem important questions to me and the only way they will be answered is by opening up the magazines to a wider debate. One way of initiating such a debate is to explore how the magazines are produced and by whom, and also to consider how different groups of young women consume them.

Re-conceptualizing the relations of magazine production and consumption

Where has feminism, over the period I have described here, found a field of intervention, if not in education? Possibly the only direct channel for the wider dissemination of feminist debates on women's and girls' magazines is actually through the process of teaching. It is rare to find students who have never bought or read at least some of these publications. How they respond to this encounter between feminism and their own cultural forms now appearing in the more formal environment of the university curriculum is something of a litmus test for feminism, in much the same way as Brunsdon has argued that female students responding to the feminist analysis of popular Hollywood films (including women's genres) often represent a force of challenge to feminist scholarship (Brunsdon 1991).

However, the question of how we teach the media goes beyond simply arguing the feminist case in relation to particular cultural forms or genres. Not only do effective pedagogics depend upon listening to and responding to students, they also mean recognising the many differences between them and us. I will put this more concretely. Over a period of thirteen years in two London institutions I taught students for whom working on a magazine was not an unrealistic ambition. These were hard-working and motivated art students, graphic design students, fashion students and media studies students. I could not have done my job effectively and certainly not established a good rapport with them had my approach to the magazines been that of a blanket feminist critique or condemnation. I could certainly be critical, but I had to work with the principle that the magazines would not transform themselves suddenly one day into feminist magazines bereft of advertising, beauty products, pictures of pin-ups and problem pages, i.e. they would remain bound by the genre. I also had to start with the principle that a job on a magazine is a perfectly reasonable goal for young women being trained in media studies today, and that indeed by working inside the institutions opportunities might well arise for 'changing them from within' (as it used to be put). Over this period dozens of graduates from these courses have found work in big publishing companies. I cannot think of a single women's or girls' magazine whose (full-time or freelance) staff does not include some of my ex-students.

Building bridges with women working in the magazine field also gives us insight into how feminist and, more broadly, women's issues are negotiated outside the academy. It allows us to see the obstacles which editors and journalists come up against when they try to introduce material which the management considers inappropriate or unsuitable. This is not to suggest that the new women's and girls' magazines now serve as an alternative to the old feminist magazines like *Spare Rib*, or that all women journalists and editors are self-proclaimed feminists. But many are, and many well-known feminists write regularly for the magazines. Even those women who conform more to the career feminist image generally have more interesting views about the experience of women working in the commercial field than most of us public-sector feminists imagine. However, where feminism is viewed as moralistic and condemning of young women having fun and enjoying heterosexuality, it is true that the magazines adopt a more aggressively anti-feminist tone. One tension, therefore, is that between the magazines and a certain image or representation of feminism.

Overall this calls for more research on women journalists and editors as cultural intermediaries (Bourdieu 1984). There is still almost no information or analysis available about magazine journalism as a career for women, although there are many accounts of the textual meaning of images found on the pages of the magazines. Nobody, it seems, has thought to study the people who put these pages together, who argue about lay-out, captions and emphasis, who make decisions about how to 'do' a story on young lesbians, who challenge the senior editors and management (usually male) by giving frank information to readers about oral sex and who, at the same time, emphasize the fun element in magazines. To explore more fully the representation of the new sexuality and to really engage with the ironic style of the magazines it would also be necessary to ask the writers and designers what it is they think they are doing. What is their relationship to feminism? How aware are they of its influence? My own recent research on the British fashion industry has only touched on these themes. But it does show the editors to be feminist-inclined and committed to covering all issues relevant to their readers' lives despite opposition from chief executives and advertisers. Indeed it was this kind of adventurous brief which forced one of the early editors of the newly launched *Just Seventeen* to make a direct appeal to the readers to enable her to produce a magazine which, as she put it, 'no longer spoke down to its readers':

> We commissioned a large market research survey and we got thousands of girls to fill in a questionnaire and we were then able to deliver this material into the hands of the cynics and show them that girls didn't want romance and love stories any more. We could create a more up-to-the-moment magazine by getting rid of all the slushy stuff.
>
> (Editor, 1990)

Who the reader is and what she wants is part of the professional knowledge and expertise of the editorial team. Intimate knowledge of the reader is the means by which editorial autonomy is conserved. Thus 'readers' exist as much as concepts and strategies as they do as active consumers. This also suggests some re-conceptualization of the idea of magazine consumption. Instead of being at the far end of the chain which begins with production, the practices of consumption are built into the 'front end' processes of production. Cultural expertise of readers, as Sean Nixon has also argued in relation to the launch of the new men's magazines, is one of the means by which power struggles among various professionals are waged in the field of magazine production (Nixon 1996). The reader is in a sense a cultural, as well as an economic, category.

But if the traditional feminist critique of this field of mass media sets itself up in stark opposition to the magazines, there is no straightforward way in which feminists like myself can simply endorse the magazines because they or their editors might claim to have taken feminism on board. For a start this kind of feminism is narrow and restricted. It is the sort of feminism that benefits white First World women without having very much to say to women who live in poverty and who produce many of the luxury goods, including fashion, for the consumption of women in the affluent West. As Vron Ware has shown, this is also a feminism which allows white women to find sexual freedom and self-expression through global tourism and having sex with impoverished Third World men (Ware 1997).

There can be no comfortable reconciliation between feminism as a political discourse and the cultures of commercial femininity which define the terrain of the magazine form. In the various dialogues conducted across the pages of the commercial magazines, feminists find themselves embodying the role of mother or agony aunt. This is the most legitimate role for feminism. The feminist voice in magazines like *More!* is maternal and professional. It guides its wayward daughters, tolerating their rebelliousness and, by necessity, allowing itself to be the target of anger and rejection. Feminism has won this slot by redefining itself as persuasive, professional and 'common sense' and by more or less abandoning its polemical and campaigning identity as a political movement. While this might seem like a concession and a compromise it also remains an opportunity, one means of maintaining a channel of popular communication among different women across the boundaries of age, class and ethnicity.

Notes

1 Although the Bill failed, the magazine industry was called upon to be more vigilant in regulating itself in this respect. A forum was set up to provide guidelines for such material. It remains uncertain however how this has influenced editorial policy. Two years later there are still periodic complaints in the media about the sexually explicit contents of the magazines.

2 In spring 1998, the government indicated the influence that teenage girls' magazines had on their readers by deciding to involve the editors in a campaign to reduce the numbers of teenage pregnancies.

References

Althusser, L. (1971) 'Ideology and ideological state apparatuses', *Lenin and Philosophy and Other Essays*, London: New Left Books.

Beezer, A., Grimshaw, J. and Barker, M. (1986) 'Methods for cultural studies students', D. Punter (ed.) *Introduction to Contemporary Cultural Studies*, London: Longman.

Boston Women's Health Collective (1973) *Our Bodies, Our Selves*, New York: Simon and Schuster.

Bourdieu, P. (1984) *Distinction: Towards a Critical Judgement of Taste*, London: Routledge.

Brunsdon, C. (1991) 'Pedogogies of the feminine: feminist teaching and women's genres', *Screen*, Vol. 32, pp. 364–82.

—— (1997) *Screen Tastes: From Soap Opera to Satellite Dishes*, London: Routledge.

Campbell, B. (1996) 'Girls on Safari', *Guardian*, 15 July.

Driscoll, C. (1995) 'Who needs a boyfriend? The homoerotic virgin in adolescent women's magazines', P. van Toorn and D. English (eds) *Speaking Positions: Aboriginality, Gender and Ethnicity* in *Australian Cultural Studies*, Department of Humanities, Victoria University of Technology, Melbourne, Australia, pp. 188–98.

Frazer, E. (1987) 'Teenage girls reading *Jackie*', *Media, Culture and Society*, Vol. 9, No. 4, pp. 407–25.

Henderson, S. (1993) 'Time for a make-over' and 'Keep your bra and burn your brain?', *Druglink*, Sept–Oct, Nov–Dec, pp. 14–16 and 10–12.

Jackson, S. (1996) 'Ignorance is bliss: when you are Just Seventeen', *Trouble and Strife*, No. 33, pp. 50–60.

McRobbie, A. (1994) *Postmodernism and Popular Culture*, London: Routledge.

—— (2000) *Feminism and Youth Culture*, second edition, Basingstoke: Macmillan.

Nixon, S. (1996) *Hard Looks*, London: University of London.

Radway, J. (1984) *Reading and Romance: Women, Patriarchy and Popular Literature*, North Carolina: University of North Carolina Press.

Rose, J. (ed.) (1987) 'Femininity and its discontents', *Feminist Review, Sexuality: A Reader*, London: Virago, pp. 177–201.

Stuart, A. (1990) 'Feminism: dead or alive?', J. Rutherford (ed.) *Identity: Community, Culture, Difference*, London: Lawrence and Wishart, pp. 28–43.

Walkerdine, V. (1990) *Schoolgirl Fictions*, London: Verso.

Ware, V. (1997) 'Purity and danger: race, gender and tales of sex tourism', A. McRobbie (ed.) *Back to Reality? Social Experience and Cultural Studies*, Manchester: MUP, pp. 133–52.

Winship, J. (1987) *Inside Women's Magazines*, London: Pandora.

5

LOOKING BACK AT *NEW TIMES*
AND ITS CRITICS

New Times and in particular the volume entitled *New Times: The Changing Face of Politics in the 1990s* (edited by S. Hall and M. Jacques 1989) marked a controversial turning point for the left and for those concerned with the politics of culture. The work of the *New Times* drew on the Regulation School of economists to consider new patterns of work and leisure, the global media and cultural identity. In addition, there was a strong interest in the politics of identity and the 'return of the subject'. This latter term indicated a concern with questions of subjectivity, with how people are produced as subjects by a whole range of practices, including those emerging from the state and benefit system (e.g. the single mother), the consumer culture (e.g. 'yuppies') and also the emergent discourses of racialized identity (e.g. Black British) and so on. However, for the mainstream left the question of subjectivity remained awkward. There was a degree of hostility to the legacy of the term through Lacanian psychoanalysis, and also through the work of the Foucauldians on 'subjectivising discourses'. By drawing on elements of these theorists and attempting to construct a more popular and accessible political vocabulary with them, the *New Times* writers were bound to raise the hackles of left traditionalists. Even more so when they were seen to embrace a kind of eclecticism and open mindedness and a willingness to recognise the autonomy of social movements, the new politics of sexuality, pressure group politics, and the politics of difference. For sectors of the left this reeked too much of pluralism through the influence on the *New Times* writers of Laclau and Mouffe, who argued that radical social democracy could only be extended by these means (Laclau 1990, Laclau and Mouffe 1985).

From *New Left Review* to *Capital and Class*, from the *New Socialist* to the *New Statesman*, from *New Formations* to *Feminist Review*, *New Times* was either denounced for its disavowal of politics altogether, or for its virtual embracing of the language of Thatcherism (and more recently Majorism) as a desperate attempt to tune into what it was that made Thatcher click with ordinary people in the hope that if her lessons could be learnt then the left might be able to construct for itself a more electable platform. (McGuigan characterizes Stuart Hall's question baldly as 'Why did Thatcherism become so popular?' [McGuigan

1992]). There was a more muted response from Mike Rustin (also published in *New Times*), who argued that the project of change and transformation being described by the *New Times* writers was indeed part of the absolute logic of Thatcher's radical restructuring of the whole fabric of British society: 'Thatcherism may be understood as a strategy of post-Fordism initiated from the perspective of the Right' (Rustin 1989: 319). Rustin therefore secures the *New Times* analysis to a more familiar political anchor. He is saying that market forces, enterprise culture and the whole programme of privatization are what have effected the other shifts at the level of culture and everyday life. This is a somewhat nuanced account of *New Times* and it chooses to all but ignore the political challenge it begins to pose to old 'New Left' thinking. Instead it is seen purely as a new complicity: 'The positive emphases given to modernisation, consumption and individualism are instances of the tacit accommodation to the values of resurgent capitalism' (ibid.: 313).

The various writers closely linked with the journal *Capital and Class* are even more scathing in their condemnation of *New Times*. In a string of articles published over a period of five years they take the kind of writing found in the *New Times* collection to task for its capitulation to the rhetoric of the right and for its abandonment of a left programme in favour of an alliance-based politics of accommodation with Capital, on the excuse that flexible specialization is somehow progressive. Anna Pollert's 'Dismantling Flexibility' argues that post-Fordism is much less extensive as a new practice of production than the New Timers suggest (Pollert 1988). Where it does exist it offers secure jobs only to a small minority of highly skilled middle-aged men. 'The quality craft work that Sabel discovers is work for middle aged Emilian men' writes Pollert on the economic miracle of the so-called 'third Italy'. And it relies, she continues, on the insecurity of those forced onto the periphery to play the role of buffer against the instabilities of the marketplace. More than this, the shift to post-Fordism represents a long-term strategy developed on the part of Capital to circumscribe and sidestep the established strength and radicalism of the workers. Pollert also argues that where labour has cooperated and has won some concessions, such as participation in decision-making, these have also been the result of long years of struggle. And within the post-Fordist factories the establishment of work teams and the introduction of flexibility in the working day have to be set alongside the disappearance of space for autonomy and resistance. There is no longer the possibility of shopfloor culture where an integrated and less overtly hierarchical workforce watch each other in the workshop, and over the dinner table. And the consequences of post-Fordism for those excluded from the secure jobs is to consolidate the casualization of work for the rest and in the longer term to create a more divisive society, one with a real rather than simply an imagined underclass. Post-Fordism in its more alluring guise is, according to Pollert, nothing more than an ideology which conceals the radical restructuring which capital has found necessary to undertake as the older post-war economic and social settlement fails to produce the profit levels necessary to shield off international competition. As she puts it, 'the "discovery" of the flexible workforce is part of an ideological offensive which celebrates pliability and casualisation, and makes them seem inevitable'. She continues to argue that this is nothing more than telling people 'how to live with insecurity and unemployment and learn to love it' (ibid.: 72).

In Simon Clarke's response to *New Times* this argument is extended to include a strong critique of the emphasis on the market (Clarke 1990). He sees the seriousness with which the New Timers take the market as either a theoretical flaw or else as a sign of capitulation to the language of Thatcherism and thus an abandonment of socialism or indeed Marxism. Clarke and Pollert refuse to engage with Hall's earlier reformulation of the social meaning of the market. In *The Hard Road to Renewal* Hall argues that 'the left has never understood the capacity of the market to become identified in the minds of the mass of ordinary people, not as fair and decent and socially responsible (it never was), but as an expansive popular system' (Hall 1988: 215, quoted in McGuigan 1992: 38). In this way the market is opened up to incorporate some of the active cultural concerns of those who participate. Contrary to this position, for Clarke and Pollert the market remains nothing other than the outcome of the process of accumulation. The market is ideological in that it suggests a field of choice and expression but in reality it is a determined space, the point at which the rate of profit is managed, often through a complex set of controls and manoeuvrings involving the state in the form of subsidies, investments and welfare, all of which are means of ensuring the sustainability of profits for capital. Clarke's argument is that post-Fordism represents little more than a strategy developed from within Capital for dealing with the falling rate of profit which the old interventionist state can no longer prop up. It is the threat to profits which requires Capital to reorganize itself along the lines of flexible specialization.

In fact, between these writers there is less disagreement on post-Fordism emerging from the crisis of Capital following the break-up of the old postwar settlement than they themselves seem to imagine. It is more a question of the political analysis which follows. Needless to say there is no mention of the word 'culture' in the *Capital and Class* writing. The nearest Clarke comes to engaging with what people might look for or find in the commodities of consumer capitalism lies in a fleeting reference to the old postwar settlement responding to 'rising working-class aspirations'. My point is precisely that the refusal to unpack the world of meanings in the idea of 'rising aspirations' is a much greater flaw in the otherwise sophisticated arguments of both Pollert and Clarke than the difficult and sometimes uncertain attempts by the *New Times* writers to revise orthodox left thinking on the market, to bring the economy back into cultural theory and at the same time to engage with the politics of theory.

The *Capital and Class* position in contrast means being left with Capital lurching from one crisis to another but always with a set of strategies tucked up its sleeve for further exploiting the working class and also for pre-empting any possibility of class politics. It is here that ideology comes into play. It manipulates and controls the working classes, end of story. (*Capital and Class* have little to say about women or black people and even less to say about cultural or identity-based politics.) This is in my mind a deeply anachronistic model. While no single account can hope to embrace the entire sweep of social changes which leave their mark across the whole landscape of everyday life, the real value of the *New Times* writers is that they recognize the importance of understanding social change. Thus they take the emergence of new forms of work and new kinds of workers seriously. This is the first account for example to acknowledge the existence of substantial numbers of design professionals whose job it is to decide the economies of scope rather than scale and who develop an anthropology of consumption as they attempt to get to the heart of what people seem to want.

To writers like Pollert and Clarke such workers would be seen as either so small in number to be insignificant or else to be mere instruments of the big multinational companies who employ them to fend off competition by providing 'added value' in the form of design or unnecessary packaging of their commodities. In this respect they are mistaken. Any analysis of work which does not attempt to come to grips with the dramatic transformations which have created huge numbers of self-employed units or small businesses across the spectrum of class, gender and ethnicity, is simply not alert to the realities of working life in Britain today. To ignore these fields of economic activity (for example, the production of culture and the image industries) is to see only a void or a vacuum in that space opened up by the decline of heavy industry. This is not the place to engage in a debate about the sustainability of self-employment or semi-employment in Majorist (and post-Thatcherist) Britain but it is important to signal that these are patterns which are establishing themselves among young and not so young workers with astonishing rapidity. John Urry in the *New Times* reader says 'There have been a number of inter-related changes in Britain; sizeable increases in the number of self-employed people; the growth in the size of the secondary labour force so that one third of the labour force now consists of part-time temporary and home workers . . .' (Urry 1989: 98). As shown in my own work on British fashion designers, to have one's own label is simultaneously an overwhelming desire on the part of the many fashion graduates leaving art school each year and also a realistic response to the alternative of unemployment (McRobbie 1998). It is also a dream made possible by the Enterprise Allowance Scheme which provides £40 a week to help young people to move from unemployment into self-employment. However, there is much more to enterprise culture than simply numbers of young people on the EAS. This choice rarely coincides with an approval for Mrs Thatcher's idea of enterprise; it is an altogether more complex and even a more radical response. These young workers come closer to what Sean Nixon, talking about the people who launched *The Face* magazine in the early 1980s, describes as 'committed

65

entrepreneurs' (Nixon 1993). So, just as there is more to the market than the manipulation of needs, so also is there more to new work than the intensification of labour. It is in both these spaces that lived culture, social agents, and the categories of experience and desire come into play. All these remain, however, resolutely outwith the vocabulary of the *Capital and Class* journal. To these writers this is all ideology.

The problem of ideology

In one rather narrow respect the *Capital and Class* theorists present a convincing analysis of what it is that capital is doing as it shifts into a mode which is less centralized, less homogenized and more highly computerized, thus dispensing with substantial sectors of the workforce on the way. This is, they argue, managed through the successful deployment of a huge ideological offensive which was held together in Britain through the figure of Thatcher and through the ideas which came to be associated with Thatcherism. In this way the class struggle continues unabated as the workforce is beaten from pillar to post. The problem is, however, that there is little talk of the workers and the struggles they are engaged in throughout the *Capital and Class* writing. There is a large silence here. And the only assumption that can be drawn is that in the light of this offensive the working classes have been, temporarily perhaps, quietened. But this silence also means that the analysis itself is weakened because we have absolutely no sense of what this totalizing model of economic restructuring and ideological attack comes up against, or of what it encounters in its journey from factory floor, to dole office, to home, street and family.

In short, there is no sense of what the social field itself looks like, how it is occupied, what forms of social and cultural activity accompany changes in the workplace. The only conclusion that can be drawn is that the working class in whatever form it continues to exist (and this is also a question not raised by the *Capital and Class* writers) is won over by ideology, it is in effect made passive, it is the victim of Capital. It is precisely against this kind of manipulation thesis that *New Times* writers make a clear attempt to rethink ideology. From their point of view the lofty correctness of the left in relation to how the masses are simply duped, tricked or conned by the gloss and the glow of Thatcherism has a tinge of arrogance and élitism. In what is perhaps an urgent piece of pleading Hall asks that the left stops for a moment and thinks about what it is that makes the language of the new radical right sufficiently attractive to the electorate to keep the Conservatives in government for so long that the idea of Labour in office is now a hazy memory.

This is to return to those aspects of ordinary everyday life which connect people to the ideas of the right rather than those of the left, it is to show how questions of choice, how the 'right to buy', how the address to parents, and to citizens, had a resonance which the left were not able to match, even when they were able to demonstrate the shallowness and the dishonesty of many of these promises. Partly of course this had to do with the simultaneous negating of all ideas associated with the left which the Thatcher government also embarked upon and maintained through the heady days of gold cards and huge mortgages. It is ironic to say the least that Stuart Hall's account in *Policing the Crisis* (Hall *et al.* 1978) of the management of consent undertaken by the radical right, and the way in which that entailed the total discrediting of the ideas associated with the radical left from the late 1960s onwards, still leaves him open to scorn for adopting what is described as a new realist or accommodationist position today. It is as though 'letting the people in' to the field of analysis rocks the boat of left consensus. The people are too difficult in their diversity, too unpredictable in their tastes, too likely to stray from the path of class politics, that it is better and perhaps safer to run the risk of being seen as élitist and have them safely suffering from either false consciousness or ideological seduction.

Part of the *New Times* project was therefore to write into the analysis of the field of social and cultural life, not just the noticeable changes on the landscape of new towns and new shopping-centres and theme parks and heritage museums, but also the experience of these phenomena. As men of the left this perhaps did not come too easy and the suggestion of a personal voice in the account of walking around IKEA sometimes struck an awkward note. What is more, for feminists who had for some time been arguing for the inclusion of the category of experience in political analysis and in theory and who had with some difficulty also striven to find the right kind of voice, this new evocation of experience was maybe a little overdue. But that did not mean it was not welcome, the alternative assumption being that the austere writers of *Capital and Class* could not consider stooping so low as to express some degree of enjoyment in taking a stroll down South Molton Street or through Covent Garden or, as Frith and Savage do, remove themselves from such a discourse except when they write journalistically as rock critics in which case they come out as fans. Otherwise they see the current interest in popular culture as 'a method of uncritical celebration' or more aggressively they see in 'Contemporary cultural studies' cheerful populism' academics with 'new found respect for sales figures' (Frith and Savage 1992: 107).

My own critique of *New Times* was certainly not made in this rather spiteful spirit (McRobbie 1994). It was more of a reminder that for women a good deal of the construction of femininity, ideology or not, has focused around consumption, from the smallest item of beauty product to the perfect pair of shoes. Feminist theory has for many years grappled with the question of pleasure and complicity in the ideology of femininity and most importantly has shown women not to be simply taken in by consumer culture but to be engaged in everyday life neither as dupes nor simply and unproblematically as feminists and socialists waiting patiently for the great day when their sisters denounce Clinique or Next or Donna Karan and channel their efforts into something different and better.

What might have weakened the case of the *New Times* writers is that, while open to the question of experience, there were few spoken voices of ordinary people in the book as a whole. How such voices would have found their way into this kind of analysis raises a number of questions. David Morley's recent review of the current debate in cultural studies on ethnography, and on recording, documenting and analysing the accounts of 'other people(s)' is useful in that it reminds us of the inevitability and indeed necessity of authorial mediation in such work (Morley 1997). In the case of *New Times* and in relation to the importance of developing a nexus of institutional, ethnographic and empirical work, the obvious question is how and why? There is a tendency, when the question of experience is raised for it to act as a kind of touchstone of truth or authenticity. Only through a re-conceptualization of the category of experience, and with this a good deal of new thinking on how to use experience fruitfully whether in an ethnographic context or not, can we move towards a more integrative mode of analysis which overcomes this idea that ordinary people and lived reality are out there and somehow not in here. In fact the real attempt in the position pieces in *New Times* to articulate the shared enjoyments and small pleasures of everyday life mark one way of identifying oneself as part of that community of ordinary people, without shifting too decisively into the language of personal experience or autobiography. However, this remains very much an undercurrent. It leaves unresolved how spoken voices might be brought back into the distinctive kind of work which *New Times* represents.

Only in Bea Campbell's analysis of three new towns as viewed from the perspective of some of their female inhabitants, is there any sense of the lived, dense, textured quality of experience. Work like this, drawn up into a much fuller study, would indeed accomplish the move towards the kind of empirical and experiential realities, the absence of which leaves cultural theory open to attack for an overemphasis on representations, texts and meaning. If the key issue for *New Times* remains, however, that of how to make sense of social phenomena without unduly relying on ideology, then writers like Morley, whose sociological sense disallows attributing to the audience the enormous powers of opposition which some new cultural studies work permits, have also played an important role in disputing the totalizing power of ideology. Here attention is paid to the significant slippages which occur in the spaces which intervene in the passage of reading, watching or consuming. McGuigan, Frith and others conflate the careful attention to the interactive surface of texts with experience seen in the work of Morley (1992) and Ang (1991) with the more ambitious claims of others to find resistance in the act of turning the television on. The two terms of abuse from McGuigan *et al.* that keep reappearing are 'fashionable' and 'celebration'. McGuigan sees in Hall's *New Times* work and in all the authors cited above (in addition to myself) a kind of 'cultural populism'. By this he means a stretching out on the part of the theorist to understand that the popular pleasures experienced by ordinary people in the space of leisure or consumption or indeed in family life can contain elements untarnished by or unanticipated by capital or even provided by capital but at least reworked by the consumer in the practice of consumption. McGuigan mistakenly interprets Stuart Hall as pursuing this kind of analysis even further. He claims Hall sees ordinary people as 'active pleasure-seekers' and 'trusts in the good sense of their judgement' (McGuigan 1992: 38).

This suggestion, discounting for a moment the scale of misrepresentation here of Hall's writing, allows McGuigan and others, in particular Frith and Savage, to argue that cultural studies has abandoned all commitment to understanding relations of power and powerlessness, dominance and subordination as they are expressed in culture. For them the *New Times* writing is the ultimate example of recantation. The simple existence of clear signs of opposition and resistance in the heartland of consumer culture means that politics is happening anyway. This, argue Frith and Savage, allows the *New Times* writers to feel obliged to do no more than mention it and otherwise sit back and enjoy the sound of the tills ringing up more sales. Frith and Savage are even more aggressive than McGuigan in their account of this new kind of cultural studies, as the title of their polemic suggests. 'The pearls and the swine' sets a new and unwelcome standard in male intellectual-left combat. In the light of such antagonism let us stand back for a moment and absorb and reflect on the charges now being laid at the doorstep not just of *New Times* but of the whole field of cultural studies.

What is at stake?

First, I would suggest that in all emergent theoretical position-taking there are margins of provocation, there is an imaginative (perhaps too highly imaginative) staking out of new terrains. If that counts as being too fashionable, as McGuigan puts it, then it might be worth reminding that writer that the trivial pursuits which count for him as too fashionable, and thus lacking in substance, are precisely what cultural studies insisted on taking seriously in the first place. If this is too much for the critics then why do they too spend so much time on cultural studies itself? Are they somehow in possession of the real political agenda? If so, it might be useful to have an opportunity to look at it. Meanwhile the profound distrust of fashion and the charge laid against these writers as being merely fashionable, betrays the voice of the male critic for whom fashion is disquieting, uncomfortable, and thus best regarded as superficial and unimportant.

The same kind of dismissive (bordering on contemptuous) tone creeps into the language of another recent critic of cultural studies in what in this case is a defence of political economy. Writing against what he perceives as an excessive concern for cultural politics in black writing Garnham (1995) argues that 'it is hard to argue that much dent will be made in domination if black is recognised as beautiful but nothing is done about processes of economic development . . . and exclusions from and marginalisation in labour markets.' The same goes, he continues, for gender. As though all that has emerged from the extensive writing on race and ethnicity in cultural studies by Stuart Hall, Kobena Mercer and Paul Gilroy can be condensed into the idea that 'black is beautiful'. The scale of this reductionism is as revealing as it is extraordinary.

There is a world of difference between the few wilder voices who see self-expression and resistance residing in the actions of those who loiter in shopping malls (something for which Garnham also holds me responsible) and those who insist that we listen to how people interpret and make sense of their own experience. And that this experience points to something quite different from happy capitulation to New Right rhetoric is also interesting and important. But even where it does articulate a solid embracing of neo-conservative values, that too is something which has to be addressed. It goes some way in helping us to understand precisely what made Thatcherism so popular. Phil Cohen's recent and exhaustive work on the racism of white working-class children and young people in South-East London is an excellent example of work of this sort (Cohen 1992).

Christopher Norris is as critical in his response to *New Times* as McGuigan, Frith and Savage are to 'cultural populism'. In his reading of Stuart Hall's apparent shift to the outer reaches of apolitical postmodernism he inadvertently, at least from the point of view of this discussion, hits the nail on the head when he says 'What Hall cannot countenance is any hint of a return to notions like "ideology" or "false consciousness", terms that might provide the beginning of an answer to the questions posed by his article' (Norris 1992: 5). The challenge which *New Times* represents is exactly how to understand agency without relying on either ideology or false consciousness.

The difficulty in doing this is, as I suggested in 'New Times in cultural studies' (McRobbie 1991), also one of how to approach so vast a field as 'the social' or indeed the category of experience without a more reduced and more refined object of enquiry, and without seeing such a project as a kind of return, or even a retreat, to 'the local' or the 'micrological' (Morley 1997). Nor is it a question of defending empiricism or ethnography or indeed institutional research as good things in themselves. It is more a matter of turning attention to the daily practices of institutions, the ways of making sense which exist inside these structures and which have some effect on how they operate. To conclude, and to continue in this track, I will make some observations and raise some suggestions about why the *New Times* project seems still valuable and why the cultural studies strand in it indicates an area of academic work which it is important to defend.

In a sense it is, as usual, unfortunate that so heated a debate on the left should produce such high levels of hostility. While ideology in its tight version, that is as a distinctive unity, might no longer be such a useful way of under-standing the flows and crossovers and inter-textual connections which have become such a noticeable feature of the global culture of mass communications today (and ideology always seemed to work best when it was applied to the mass media), this does not mean, as Andrew Goodwin, using ideology in the more forceful sense, has usefully reminded us, that there is no such thing as market manipulation.

> One does not however have to agree that manipulation is always successful, or believe that it cannot be subverted or resisted, to see that it is attempted, routinely. Thus, in coming to terms with the construction of star images in music television it is impossible to avoid the conclusion that theories of manipulation should not be abandoned altogether.
>
> (Goodwin 1993: 105)

The argument is not therefore that institutional analysis of the sort being recommended here abandons the role ideology might play in the process of marketing new products, for example. It is more that attention must be drawn to the various levels of activity and the relations of power played out in the decision-making processes which produce the marketing campaign and the product itself. This allows us to open up what otherwise remains in political economy a fairly closed and monolithic notion of large organizations and of huge multinational complexes, particularly in the field of mass communications. Letting the people who work in them into the picture not only allows lived social relations to reappear in cultural studies, it also gives to the politics of theory a sharper sense of how these organizations actually work. The political value of this kind of project is more clearly indicated in *New Times* than elsewhere. For example, there is room in *New Times* for reconsidering the new politics of work. This would involve taking more seriously the kinds of employment which in the past might have been seen as having little intrinsic interest to the left because of their middle-class connotations. But working with design students who with few exceptions moved into either self-employment (as graphic designers, fashion designers, advertising copy-artists) or into working for small design studios employing a handful of freelancers, was enough to convince me that this sort of work was increasingly at the very heart of the new production processes. These were not highly paid middle-class professionals. They were inevitably doing real donkey work for the new culture industries (mock-ups for brochures, brochure-writing, corporate video production, styling for cookbook photography, etc.). Such young workers aimed high but were realistically reconciled to keeping their heads above water financially. The left needs to know precisely about the politics of work in this new kind of sector. It is completely possible to be 'fashionable', to embrace an ethos of 'expressive individualism' in work and indeed to seek great pleasure and satisfaction in creative work of this sort, and *also* to adhere to socialist values of equality, social justice, economic redistribution, the value of the public sector, anti-sexism, anti-racism, etc. If this is partly what was meant by 'designer socialism' then at least it was an analysis which took seriously where many thousands of young people (black and white, working class and middle class, female and male) were at and wanted to be, where they chose to work, not for huge financial gain but for the power of being able to redefine the working day, to bring together work and leisure, and to integrate their own often radical or, to quote Nixon again, 'committed' ideas into a kind of craft entrepreneurialism. This sector shows itself to be rising in number and poses therefore a real challenge to how we think about work and the politics of the composition of the workforce. Donzelot and others have poured scorn on those who have seen in post-Fordism the possibility of 'pleasure in work', preferring to interpret such promises as part of the new managerial reorganization of the experience of work. To encourage pleasure in work is to create a new more enthusiastic kind of worker who willingly gives his or her everything in the expectation of having this creative commitment rewarded (Donzelot 1991). This utopia is a 'shelter for the reign of imagination, extraverting the subject towards a world of possibilities that exhaust imagination' (ibid.: 276). But we could just as well re-inflect Foucault in another direction to recognize that the 'stylistics of existence' and the 'technologies of the self' manifest in this kind of choice of existence, far from signalling a retreat into narcissism, excessive self-regard or 'blind ambition', are in fact founded on real understanding of how changed the world of work is (Foucault 1988). In this sense there is a kind of pre-emptive opportunism in opting for the cultural or creative economy, one which is also protective, realistic and potentially rewarding. We cannot automatically read from this cultural response, accommodationism or a retreat into Thatcherite-influenced 'expressive individualism' as some have labelled it. Nor is it necessarily incompatible with the pursuit of what Laclau labels 'radical social democracy' (Laclau 1990).

A good deal seems to be at stake in the intensification of debate and even antagonism which has developed around the question of cultural studies, its so-called populist project and the kind of politics found in *New Times*. This stems partly from the popularity of cultural studies among students (and in this sense market forces increasingly matter in the funding of higher education). The hostility also is focused on the journalistic versions of *New Times* and cultural studies now found in magazines, newspapers and on the occasional television programme. It is as though the popularity of the subject forces those who would otherwise prefer to ignore it and continue with what they perceive as more conventional and rigorous programmes of study in fact to stake some claim to the field and in so doing redefine it again in the direction of some more manageable body of knowledge. There is nothing unusual or surprising about this since it is quite apparent that what emerged as cultural studies in the first place was always an open-ended and potentially redefinable field. To try to protect cultural studies from either the contamination of the culture industries (the *Modern Review*, for example) or from the old disciplines which feel themselves slipping from the centre of intellectual life, and therefore willing to redefine themselves as cultural studies too, would be a pointless task. There are also more immediate political issues to engage with than the charge that *New Times* is synonymous with a simple celebration of consumer culture. And yet it is because there is more at stake in these claims, that makes it important to indicate just how mistaken it is for critics to dismiss the necessity of the pleasures which happen to come to us in the commodity form, as a cultural lifeline, a way of allowing rather than disallowing critique and analysis and understanding. The real point seems to be that as more people (including young semi-employed people, black people, women) lay a claim to culture in diverse ways, in music, in politics and in theory, in images, in language, in pulp romance, in 'lesbian detective fiction', and as more people want to talk about culture at home, in the classroom, or even in the field of politics, and do so articulately and with increasing confidence, the old guard of cultural legislators including those from the left feel called upon to pull things into line, to impose some degree of order on a situation which they feel is sliding beyond their control. Hence the antagonism, hence the talk of 'skewering' the postmodernists (Frith and Savage 1992). Gilroy's brief comments on records and on record sleeves stand as a useful and poignant counterpoint to such academic posturing:

> 'Consumption' is a vague word that trips far too easily off the dismissive tongue. People *use* these images and the music that they enclose for a variety of reasons. For the black user of these images and products, multivariant processes of 'consumption' may express the need to belong, the desire to make the beauty of blackness intelligible and somehow to fix that beauty and the pleasures it creates so that they achieve . . . at least a longevity that retrieves them from the world of . . . racial dispossession. However trivial the black music record sleeve may seem to the outsider, it points to a fund of aesthetic and philosophical folk knowledge which the record as a commodity has been made to contain *in addition* to its reified pleasures.
>
> (Gilroy 1993: 256)

References

Ang, I. (1991) *Desperately Seeking the Audience*, London: Routledge.

Campbell, B. (1989) 'New Times towns', in S. Hall and M. Jacques (eds) *New Times: The Changing Face of Politics in the 1990s*, London: Lawrence & Wishart, 279–303.

Clarke, S. (1990) 'Overaccumulation, class struggle and the regulation approach', *Capital and Class*, 42 (Winter), 59–93.

Cohen, P. (1992) '"It's racism what dunnit": hidden narratives in theories of racism', in J. Donald and A. Rattansi (eds) *'Race' Culture and Difference*, London: Sage, 62–104.

Donzelot, J. (1991) 'Pleasure in work', in G. Burchell, C. Gordon and P. Miller (eds), London: Harvester Wheatsheaf, 251–81.

Foucault, M. (1988) *Techologies of the Self*, L.H. Martin, H. Gutman, P.H. Hutton (eds), London: Tavistock.

Frith, S. and Savage, J. (1992) 'Pearls and swine: the intellectuals and the mass media', *New Left Review* 198, 107–16.

Garnham, N. (1995) 'Political economy and cultural studies: reconciliation or divorce?', *Critical Studies in Mass Communications*, March, 62–71.

Gilroy, P. (1993) *Small Acts: Thoughts on the Politics of Black Cultures*, London: Serpents Tail.

Goodwin, A. (1993) *Dancing in the Distraction Factory: Music Television and Popular Culture*, London: Routledge.

Hall, S. (1988) *The Hard Road to Renewal*, London: Verso.

Hall, S., Critcher, C., Jefferson, T., Clarke, J. and Roberts, B. (1978) *Policing the Crisis: 'Mugging', the State and Law and Order*, London: Macmillan.

Hall, S. and Jacques, M. (eds) (1989) *New Times: The Changing Face of Politics in the 1990s*, London: Lawrence & Wishart.

Laclau, E. (1990) *New Reflections on the Revolutions of Our Time*, London: Verso.

Laclau, E. and Mouffe, C. (1985) *Hegemony and Socialist Strategy: Towards a Radical Democratic Politics*, London: Verso.

McGuigan, J. (1992) *Cultural Populism*, London: Routledge.

McRobbie, A. (1991) 'New Times in cultural studies', *New Formations* 13, London: Routledge, 1–18.

—— (1994) *Postmodernism and Popular Culture*, London: Routledge.

—— (1998) *Fashion and the Image Industries*, London: Routledge.

Morley, D. (1992) *Television, Audiences and Cultural Studies*, London: Routledge.

—— (1997) 'Theoretical orthodoxies': textualism, constructivism and the 'new ethnography', in M. Ferguson and P. Golding (eds) *Cultural Studies in Question*, London: Sage.

Murray, R. (1989) 'Fordism and post-Fordism' and 'Benetton Britain', both in S. Hall and M. Jacques, *New Times: The Changing Face of Politics in the 1990s*, London: Lawrence & Wishart, 38–54.

Nixon, S. (1993) 'Looking for the Holy Grail: publishing and advertising strategies and contemporary men's magazines', *Cultural Studies* 7(3), 466–92.

Norris, C. (1992) 'Old themes for New Times', *New Formations* 18, 1–25.

Pollert, A. (1988) 'Dismantling flexibility', *Capital and Class* 34 (Spring), 42–72.

Rustin, M. (1989) 'The trouble with New Times', in S. Hall and M. Jacques (eds), *New Times: The Changing Face of Politics in the 1990s*, London: Lawrence & Wishart, 303–21.

Urry, J. (1989) 'The end of organised capitalism', in S. Hall and M. Jacques (eds), *New Times: The Changing Face of Politics in the 1990s*, London: Lawrence & Wishart, 76–94.

6

THE Es AND THE ANTI-Es

New questions for feminism and cultural studies

The spectre of humanism

I want to address two questions in this chapter. First, what consequences does recent poststructuralist and postcolonialist writing (notably that of Butler (1990, 1993) and Spivak (1987, 1993)) have for what I might loosely call feminist cultural studies? And second, is it possible to use this work to inject some renewed intellectual energy into those areas which cultural studies has, over the last few years, neglected? I have argued elsewhere that a return to more sociological questions, particularly where these have a relevance for policy, should not be shunned by cultural studies' scholars for whom the politics of meaning have recently taken precedence over the need to intervene in political debates armed with data, facts and figures and empirical results (McRobbie 1996). Of course there is an important place for the deconstruction of the meaning and significance of what is taken to constitute hard facts and the role these play as a pre-requisite for engagement in certain kinds of political discussion. However, little attempt has been made so far to explore how post-structuralism can be made use of more productively in the context of these fields of intervention.

The second question this chapter asks looks, then, not only towards the emergence of a more applied feminist cultural studies, and to a reconciliation of sorts between the post-structuralists and those who consider themselves on the side of studying concrete material reality. It also envisages a return to the 'three Es'; the empirical, the ethnographic, the experiential, not so much against as with the insight of the 'anti-Es', that is anti-essentialism, post-structuralism, psychoanalysis. While there has been an enormous output of feminist post-structuralist writing of late, there has been some resistance to looking outside theory and asking some practical questions about the world we live in. At every point the spectre of humanism haunts the practice of those who align themselves with the 'anti-Es'. Ethnography? That truth-seeking activity reliant upon the (often literary) narratives of exoticism and difference? Can't do it, except as a deconstructive exercise. Empiricism? The 'representation' of results, the narrative of numbers? Can't do it either, except as part of a critical

75

genealogy of sociology and its role in the project of modernity and science. Experience? That cornerstone of human authenticity, that essential core of individuality, the spoken voice as evidence of being and of the coincidence of consciousness with identity? Can't do it, other than as a psychoanalytic venture.

This leaves us feminists who are concerned with the politics of culture high and dry when it comes to contributing to political debates outside the academy. It also allows the more practically oriented, down-to-earth feminist essentialists (Dworkin 1981; Itzin 1992; MacKinnon 1979 and others) to dominate the terms and the means by which academic feminism filters into the broader political arena, particularly the media. These new questions that I put here to feminist cultural studies also have relevance, therefore, to how we conceive of ourselves as intellectuals. Feminist cultural studies is not, of course, a unitary discipline. It intersects with film and media studies and it also connects with sociology, literature, history and with debates in Marxist, feminist and post-modern theory. Its interests frequently overlap with those found in women's studies and there are also shared areas of interest with feminist psychology and feminist anthropology. The boundaries and limits drawn in this chapter are admittedly my own. They represent the shaping and development of my own intellectual formation. This means omitting important but, to me, less familiar work. Within this limited orbit (which I have chosen to call feminist cultural studies but which could be as easily labelled feminist media studies or feminist cultural sociology) there has been a substantial difference between those who are concerned with textual meaning, and whose interest is therefore on issues of representation, and those who are indeed more focused towards cultural and media policy and whose emphasis is therefore on more materialist matters.

Feminist materialism, in the late 1970s, meant drawing on the vocabulary of neo-Marxism to explore how class relations and class struggle co-existed with patriarchal relations without dissolving the latter into the former. The second feature of this materialism involved a more specific turn to class and culture. By looking at the history and culture of working-class women and girls at home, in the community, in school, in leisure and at work, a series of ethnographic studies and accounts of lived experience gave testimony to the resilience and to the historical continuity of oppositional class relations created in this context by women. This work fell under the culturalist framework outline by Stuart Hall in his seminal 'Cultural Studies – Two Paradigms' (Hall 1980). Within this perspective women and girls were understood as active class and gendered subjects, doubly subordinated by class and sex but able to tackle the forces of domination through supportive networks and through the creation of distinctive but informal cultural forms and networks which were manifest in the institutions of school, workplace and community. Ethnographic studies demonstrated both the economic underpinning of these forms and what they achieved in terms of winning space or autonomy for the girls or women involved.

However, it is now so long since this kind of work has had any significant place in feminist cultural studies that its existence has almost been forgotten.

This is because work of this type was shown to operate along highly voluntarist lines, as though the girls and women constructed these oppositional cultures unconstrained by other social forces. Little attention was paid to the already existing 'scripts of resistance' which, structuralists argued, were then simply activated by the women in particular pre-defined ways. The transparency of language, as reflective of both consciousness and identity, was most problematic for those who aligned themselves with post-structuralism and psychoanalysis. The spoken testimony of girls and women was here taken as expressive of a full human being, rather than understood as partial, fragmented, articulations of available language codes. Finally, the very category of woman or girl used in this kind of work remained unacceptably problematic for most anti-essentialists. It was assumed that there was a direct and unmediated relation between their voices, their identities and their existence as women or girls. Post-structuralists turned this upside down and argued that these were in fact Marxist–feminist representations of the category of working-class women or girls. Feminist research in these contexts actively produced such subjects. 'She' might have no other recognizable identity outside this particular academic context. Likewise, 'consciousness' could be seen as a particular type of extrapolation, a means by which a specific and partial set of verbal themes are brought together and understood as representing a whole social being, as in 'the consciousness' of working-class women. In fact this was, in itself, a highly edited representation of a certain set of themes from which other discordant themes (such as racism) were carefully removed or ignored.

For all the above reasons the term 'representation' then came to occupy a much more significant place in feminist writing. It was understood mostly in the context of Althusser's usage of the term representation in his theory of ideology (Althusser 1971). Drawing both on Freud and Lacan, Althusser argued that representations were not expressive of some prior reality, but were instead actively constitutive of reality. Feminists used this work from the late 1970s onwards to move away from early critiques of the mass media which were concerned with either negative or positive images of women. The issue was no longer that images of women were unreal, untruthful or distorted, and that what was required instead were better or more positive images of women which would somehow fit with feminist requirements. The emphasis now shifted to sexual representations as concrete and material accounts of what it was to be a woman. Femininity was nothing more that a set of highly orche-strated representational practices which together produced this coherence of female gender as easy and naturalized. By showing how these signs were grouped together and endlessly repeated across a whole range of female genres (women's magazines, popular romances, melodrama, etc.), feminist media and cultural studies found a stronger theoretical direction for itself. This entailed use being made of Barthesian semiology, Lacanian psychoanalysis, and Foucault's concept of discourse. Representation as a term provides a key link through this work. It informs Laura Mulvey's seminal analysis of women as object of the gaze in classic Hollywood cinema (Mulvey 1975/1989), as it does Judith

Williamson's *Decoding Advertisements* (Williamson 1978), as well as informing Rosalind Coward's contributions to early issues of the feminist journal *m/f* (Coward 1978). It is thus through the currency of textuality and representation that the field of feminist media, literary and cultural studies acquires for itself a more international dimension. This is partly because of the dominance of the Anglo–American media industries, but it is also because structuralist and post-structuralist methods of analysis could easily be applied to texts independent of context. What was important after all was the genre. So even if magazines, soap operas or popular fictions did not have global distribution, they had frequently spawned local equivalents, allowing feminist media scholars across the world to participate in these discussions. Structuralism and post-structuralism travelled further and faster than their culturalist counterparts.

The effect this theoretical concentration has in feminist media and cultural studies is to push more materialist or indeed culturalist concerns back towards sociology. Socialist–feminist work accommodates empirical and institutional studies, policy-oriented work, studies of employment, discrimination and so on, while post-structuralist feminism concerns itself with subjectivity, difference and meaning. By the mid-1980s, however, this dividing line also begins to crumble as feminists increasingly look to the work of Foucault. Here the emphasis is on how discourses comprising words and statements and other representational forms brought together into a field of coherent textual regularity actively produce social realities as we know them. Thus, institutions are considered not from a viewpoint which asserts their existence as external things, but rather as they are envisaged in discourse – how they are talked about. The emphasis is also on how institutions instigate regularities of conduct and experience, and constitute their subjects accordingly. Even staunchly materialist concerns like rape in fact comprise various competing accounts as to how the scenario and the victim of rape are 'envisaged'. As we know in this respect, some count more than others, and for this reason a good deal is at stake in how the woman victim is represented in court.

From this point on, a different dividing line comes into being in this now very broad field of feminist scholarship. There are those for whom the category of 'women' represents an unproblematic and fixed set of meanings which are understood as shared by all who count themselves as female (the essentialists), while there are those others who see the category of 'women' as continually contested. Under the influence of Foucault and the post-structuralist critique of humanism, and thus of the coincidence of consciousness with identity, feminists begin to dispute the existence of 'women' *per se*. Denise Riley and others argue that woman is not an unchanging uniqueness, but instead she is herself the product of particular historical and discursive practices which name and classify her and which give her meaning as a coherent entity which otherwise she would lack (Riley 1988). Gender discourses rush to fill over all the cracks of fragile unstable sexual identities. They pronounce coherence, as Butler puts it, through 'announcing'; 'It's a girl!' (Butler 1990). The woman is a subject rather than an agent, and human action is no more than the human enactment of pre-existing scripts and scenarios. As Michèle Barrett puts it, there is a shift from 'things to words' (Barrett 1992). The material existence of women is borne through different, often competing, discursive strategies which in naming, classifying or speaking the truth of 'woman' also bring her into being. Barrett describes the shift of emphasis in feminist scholarship away from 'things' like 'low pay, rape, or female foeticide' to a concern with words, texts and representations. This has come about through the influence of Foucault who 'challenged the familiar hierarchy of value of the materialist perspective, counterposing the "dumb existence of a reality" with the ability of groups of signs (discourses) to act as "practices that systematically form the objects of which they speak"' (Barrett 1992: 203, quoting Foucault).

Opposition to the increasing dominance of the 'anti-Es' in feminist scholarship takes a different political form in the US from that of the UK (bearing in mind the limits of these as symbolic geo-political axes). In America the fiercest feminist opposition to the work of Butler, Spivak and others comes from those who assert, against the emphasis on difference, the essential sameness of women's experience. This arises, they argue, from female 'bodily matters', from the essential experiences shared by and understood by women, that is childbirth, menstruation, menopause, and female illnesses. In addition, feminists like MacKinnon (1979) and Dworkin (1981) add to this the long catalogue of crimes and violations done to the female body by men, including rape, violence, pornography, sexual abuse and so on. It is around these issues that the modern women's movement comes into being. In America these women occupy a high profile in the media and in the academy, and in many ways have succeeded in defining the terrain of feminism in this context. Their opponents within feminism, including Butler, challenge their unwillingness to take on board differences of ethnicity, class and sexual identity. She and others have argued that difference can be understood in politically positive terms rather than signalling the end of feminism. The threat of fragmentation is too often used as a means of achieving an uneasy, unhappy unity, just for the sake of it. In addition, this writing locates women in a victim-like position from which there is very little opportunity to escape. There is a vicariousness, then, on the part of the successful well-qualified feminist representatives of the women's movement and their 'subjects', who appear to remain trapped in abusive and violent relationships and for whom feminism only seems to confirm the stark dualities of power between men and women without providing hope or opportunity for changing these relations.

This, then, is the materialist feminist essentialism against which writers like Butler position themselves. However, in the UK feminist intellectual work has grown out of a more socialist tradition. There has been much less concern to assert gender over and above class and race; instead the emphasis has been on thinking through these relations of difference. Historical materialism rather than bodily materialism has informed much of this work. The socialist feminist tradition has, from the start, recognized that economic inequalities, compounded through the double disadvantage of gender and class, offered a framework for more fully understanding how, in and across different historical moments, women have found themselves dependent, powerless or simply subordinate. The socialist feminist refutation of post-structuralism is more muted and confined by and large to occasional interventions and attacks, such as that by Anna Pollert whose real animosity is towards the other 'posts', that is feminist postmodernism and debates around post-Fordism (Pollert 1988). The 'anti-Es' group in the UK challenges the determining role allocated in Marxist feminist thought to the 'economic', and relocates materialism to the realm of discourse. It also explores the political consequences of difference and antagonism between women in relation to class, sex and race; it refutes, as described above, the existence of women's consciousness as a thing that can be equated with identity; and it also fully engages with the challenge the unconscious brings to political analysis. So, in a sense, the work of Butler and Spivak perhaps finds more fertile ground in the field of feminist scholarship in the UK where, in the light of the decline of Marxism, the 'anti-Es' in the arts, humanities and increasingly in the social sciences have assumed a position of theoretical dominance.

Feminism as anti-essentialism

Two of the most significant contributors to the debate on anti-essentialism are Judith Butler and Gayatri Chakravorty Spivak. Both of these authors force feminism to confront its own, often invisible, boundaries and limits as well as those strands in feminism which seek to attribute a 'fixed essence to women' (Grosz 1995: 47). It will be my contention that the deconstructive exercises of both these writers can be usefully applied to feminist cultural studies. How can this be done? First, by considering their shared concern with feminism as a representational politics, and second, by extending Spivak's specific comments on pedagogy and Butler's work on 'gender trouble' to cultural studies, and third, bearing in mind the comments made earlier about the need for applied and policy-focused work, by attempting to revise simultaneously feminist cultural studies to embrace again more fully the 'three Es'. Feminism from the viewpoint of Butler and Spivak, is required to consider its foundations, its hidden representational remit and its category of woman. Post-structuralist thinking suggests that a range of meanings are invoked around the notion of 'women', while feminism in the past has assumed a simple and single transparency of meaning. Only now is this historical assumption being interrogated. For example, Brunsdon, writing recently on film and TV scholarship, argues that in the 1970s there was a binary divide between feminism and femininity, and that this fuelled feminist analysis (Brunsdon 1991). The political aim was to pull women away from cultures of femininity (the nail polish) towards feminism. The intellectual aim was to win a legitimate place for gender studies in the academy. The feminist scholar of film and TV studies was inevitably counter-posed to the ordinary woman, the housewife watching the soaps.

When feminists talk about women, this too is a representation. It does not automatically and unproblematically refer to and reflect a pre-existing material reality. Instead, it constructs and gives an identity to a social group who might previously have been known as ladies, girls, housewives, or mothers. Feminism creates a category of women which does not reflect a pre-existing reality so much as constitute a new reality. This category now competes with the older categories through which 'women' are known, and in some cases supplants these old titles with this new, political term of representation. Anti-essentialism in feminism recognizes the fluidity of feminism's own categories. As Riley points out, feminism's women also change quite dramatically over time (Riley 1988).

> The modern 'woman' is arguably the result of long processes of closure which are hammered out by infinite numbers of mutual references from all sides of these studies and classifications which are then both underwritten and cross-examined by nineteenth- and early twentieth-century feminisms which adopt, respecify, or dismiss these 'women'.
>
> (Riley 1988: 41)

The focus of Riley, Butler and Spivak's work is to dislodge, or at least desta-bilize, the certainties expressed in much radical feminism about those qualities which define women. They recognize this definition as a perhaps necessary political fiction (Spivak talks of the 'strategic use of essentialism') which grants feminism the authority to speak on behalf of a 'global sisterhood', but they also reject it (Spivak with qualifications as we shall see later). No sooner, then, is this essentialism expressed, than it is challenged most specifically by 'other women' who see themselves being spoken of by European white representatives who are not necessarily of their own choosing. They then argue vociferously that this global category of 'women' is one which is based on a Eurocentric confidence which claims to know what all women need to achieve equality, while in fact the charter of universalist feminist aims which has emerged from this movement is informed much more by the specific demands of Western European women. Black feminists have argued that this essentialism has made it all the more difficult for them to engage productively with difference within the category of 'black women'. They, too, have been expected to display characteristics which mark them out through homogenized categories of race and gender.

Post-structuralism posits women as a non-self-evident category. It suggests that feminist essentialism is a strategy of power, an attempt to enclose and foreclose the field of feminism. This can also backfire in policy debates in that, as Nash points out, to attribute to women a set of essential characteristics or experiences (caring and compassionate, maternal etc.) can have the effect of reproducing existing inequalities. Feminists therefore can unwittingly 'contribute to the regulation and reification of gender identities, and along pretty traditional lines at that, a regulation and reification that it is surely one of the aims of feminism to disrupt' (Nash 1994: 69). But if, instead, the category of women is fluid, if it is a 'political signifier', then, argues Butler, the point is to resist the kinds of stabilization which seek to pin women down to something incontrovertible, and instead to 'expand the possibilities of what it means to be a woman' (Butler 1995: 50). This includes the possibility of redrafting or of redesignating the self, not in an unproblematically voluntarist capacity, but rather as a process which recognizes gender as more unstable and *potential* than is currently acknowledged in culture. If gender, as Butler argues, is a staging of the body, a performance enacted on a daily basis, if woman is therefore put on, or applied, then there can be no natural female body. Instead the body is only female and feminine to the extent that it is given these meanings right from the start. These acts of gender can, she argues, be rearticulated to broaden out the stagy narrowness of 'men' and 'women'. When post-structuralism uncouples the binary partners of male and female, a range of less rigid sexual possibilities becomes available. Change or agency is here conceived of as taking place within the politics of meaning, that is within the realm of signification. Butler uses the post-structuralist claim that meaning is never as secure and as tightly tied to its reference point as it seems. Other meanings haunt those which appear to naturally attach themselves to language. The politics of meaning come into play exactly where other more disruptive meanings which haunt, linger or simply hang around the edges of words get sharply eliminated, by the repetitive emphasis, 'Of course this is what a woman is!'. The fixing of men and women in this way is a means of guaranteeing the 'heterosexual matrix' in culture. But its own uncertainty can be exploited and gender can be rescripted.

However, even feminism has opposed this practice of resignification. It has had to know that its women are really women. Butler explores the theoretical underpinning of this requirement by undertaking a lengthy and convincing critique of Lacan, Lacanian feminism, and what has also been called 'New French feminism', that is the work of Cixous, Wittig and Irigaray. There is a tendency in this work to see women as relegated to some marginal or external zone, to some outside place which is also the only place in which they can speak as women outside the terms laid down by patriarchy (for example, through Kristeva's notion of semiotic or poetic language). Butler disputes this relegation to, and then reluctant occupation of, the outside, particularly since it is also a place to which, in Lacan's writing, the lesbian is expelled. She argues that it is only by virtue of this process of externalization, that those on the inside know who they are and can confirm their own normativity.

The force of the argument in *Bodies that Matter* (1993) is that men and women exist as such to guard the sanctity of reproductive heterosexuality. They need not be like this. Gender is a coercion, and it continues to harm and cause immense pain to those who find themselves excluded. There is, overall, a quadruple movement in Butler's writing. She initiates a challenge to normative understandings of sexual difference from an unstable (rather than absolutist and therefore separatist) lesbian position. She confronts the conservatism of Lacan and Lacanian feminism, she positively invokes the 'politics of the signifier' whereby things can be made to mean differently, thus also disputing the deep pessimism of psychoanalytic feminism which almost allows it to turn away from politics. She also then rebukes the more activist forms of feminism for their earlier fantasies of freedom, unity and universal sisterhood. This was a 'phantasmatic signifier', a utopian projection destined to disappoint. But disenchantment with these fantasies of emancipation need not lead to hopelessness or despair. Feminism can instead work through its many differences. It can make coalitions and alliances and, no longer moving resolutely towards some agreed goal, can also eliminate the older hierarchies which requested that some demands or some issues took precedence over others. Altogether this seems to me the most useful and hopeful critique and analysis to emerge through the dense difficulty of post-structuralist writing.

Back to reality?

Spivak has recently argued for the importance of empirical research informed by the critique of essentialism:

> One has to learn to honour empirical work. Bardhan talks about how stratified the idea of women is in a place like India. In Bardhan's work [she's a development economist] you begin to see how impossible it is to focus, even within endogamous or exogamous marriage lines, on something called a woman. She even diversifies the radicals who can join in the struggle. She diversifies the people who study them.
>
> (Spivak 1993: 17)

Spivak also points to where theory finds itself grounded. She asks that theory recognizes its own place in the classroom. The 'lived experience' of theory is that it is taught to human subjects. Here she does a triple move. She connects theory with the politics of its pedagogic practice, she argues in this context for the 'strategic use of essentialism' and she allows the 'three Es' to be recast in the light of her deconstructive techniques, as a strategic gesture. Thus when a student asserts her identity in Gayatri Spivak's seminar, as representative of black or Asian women, Spivak permits this essentialism in that it marks not a closed finality so much as an open opportunity for Spivak to de-essentialize the student's claim. 'Others are many' is how Spivak recalls her response (ibid. 1993). This takes from the student 'the authority of marginality' (ibid.: 18). By asking how the community, which the student claims to embody, benefits from this act of representation in the classroom, Spivak also asks the student to consider (and here I paraphrase) 'the coding that has produced you as this subject who can now speak on behalf of your own others?' (Spivak 1993: 19).

This grounded pedagogic interest on Spivak's part remains unusual in the great portals of theory. In the US context I have only otherwise come across Drucilla Cornell who addresses the connection between post-structuralism, psychoanalysis and empirical research, and she turns the argument around to expose the limits of what is traditionally designated as constituting the researchable. 'Ironically, the lack of emphasis on unconscious motivation and social fantasy in empirical research can itself be analysed as an aspect of a questionable Eurocentric assumption about the "nature" of social reality' (Cornell 1995: 146). However, this dimension is close to what Valerie Walkerdine has been doing in the UK for some years now. She stands almost alone as a feminist writer influenced by psychoanalysis and post-structuralism but anxious to consider how, in empirical terms, female subjectivities, particularly those of girls and young women, are constituted. Her concern is with the fantasy structures and the enactment of unconscious impulses that are demonstrated in the process of reading girls' comics and magazines, watching television or going to the cinema (Walkerdine 1990, 1993). Walkerdine's ethnographics are never truth-seeking activities, nor do they claim to be providing a full account. Instead, they are partial, elliptical, interrupted and attentive to the unconscious motivations of the researcher in relation to her subjects. Walkerdine shows how family structures position girls to make them be 'good'. In Foucault's terms, they are continually called upon to become 'docile bodies' even when, as Walkerdine argues, they are being subjected to pain, suffering and also abuse. Walkerdine's work reflects to this extent Butler's concern to 'expose and ameliorate those cruelties by which subjects are produced and differentiated' (Butler 1995: 141). This interest in the empirical reality of emergent female subjectivities is pursued in a different context by Brunsdon (1991). Instead of asking the students to inspect their own identities or subjectivities (as Spivak does), Brunsdon takes the combative presence of young women in her 'women's genres' seminar as the basis for an interrogation of what happens when feminist analyses become the authoritative texts, when feminism becomes part of the academic canon. The resistance she encounters is complex and worthy of further consideration she argues. These young women both draw from feminist discourse and repudiate it. Brunsdon queries the implicit assumption in much feminist writing that the aim is either to recruit 'them', or indeed to reproduce ourselves. The girls in question often seem to recoil in horror on being invited to identify with what a previous generation of feminist scholars have labelled 'women's genres', that is melodrama, romance, soap opera and, of course, 'weepies', but neither do they want to take up a recognizably feminist identity. What Brunsdon's article points to is the often overlooked importance of considering the powerful but also contested subjectivizing process of our own feminist discourse.

Let me now conclude this section by trying to think through how the 'anti-Es' might be brought to bear on a more applied or practical feminist cultural studies. Two short examples, taken from my own research interests, will hope-fully suffice. The first of these is the category of 'single mothers' and the second is that of the 'teenage girl'. In the context of recent inflamed political debates, usually initiated by publicity-seeking Tory MPs, it could be argued that the single mother is the fictive invention of a number of competing and opposing interest groups. These include not just the main political parties, but also self-help groups, feminist groups, local community groups, pressure groups and campaigning organizations. There is therefore no 'single' single mother. How-ever, the many pejorative accounts of this new social category should not lead us to ignore its performative character. The single mother is no longer simply 'divorced' (that is without a man). Nor is she 'unmarried' (and therefore help-less). She is single and a mother. This is indicative of competence, confidence and of a destigmatized identity. There is no longer the suggestion of failure, abandonment or dependency. Feminism has made this resignification possible but it cannot control the 'chain of equivalence' set in motion as this social category makes its way through the social and political body (Laclau and Mouffe 1985). Nor can feminism assume that the category does not have its own exclusionary force. If single is a counterpoint to married, how is the lesbian couple embarking on motherhood designated within the field of maternity and heterosexual parenting?

How is the single mother envisaged in the range of political discourses? Here, too, we see a range of competing representations, with the pressure group and feminist representations describing a female body struggling against poverty but marked by pride, respectability, determination and the desire to work. This is in sharp contrast to the degraded feminine status accorded by the right-wing tabloid press to the young single mother, who is presented as dependent upon the state, overweight, unkempt, unattractive, unhealthy, a heavy smoker and usually pictured pushing a buggy against a backdrop of a gloomy council estate. The repudiation of, or by, a husband or father of their children in the lives of these women can literally be read from their bodies – a failed or flawed sexuality. A feminist cultural analysis would consider these circulating defini-tions in all their complexity and would, in particular, show how women now stand in for and replace questions of poverty, the end of welfare (they are instead, as *The Sunday Times* puts it, 'wedded to the state'), male unemploy-ment, and the escape by women from violent or abusive relationships. The policy implications of an anti-essentialist approach to single motherhood would mean, in the first instance, recognizing that the term has become a 'floating signifier'; it can be and is articulated this way or that by all the competing political parties. It is no longer a category over which feminism has any control or authority. In this complex field of representation an empirical study of teenage mothers would not so much seek after the truth beneath the media stereotypes as inquire after the impact these many representations have on the self-representations of women who are subjectivized by what Nancy Fraser has called the Juridical–Adminstrative–Therapeutic apparatus (Fraser 1987). Indeed it is often anger at being so typecast which fuels the creation of a more political identity as a single mother. Feminism has played some role in constituting the possibility of new subject positions for these women. Butler emphasizes the limits and the exclusions of feminist representation, but in this case there was important early work done on de-stigmatizing single motherhood and on making it easier for women to leave violent husbands and survive economically as single parents. British feminism, with its close connections to the left and the Labour Party, has in this instance shaped the space of identification for women across the boundaries of social class.

Bearing in mind the emphasis in Butler's work on the compulsive repetitions of normative heterosexuality, which resonate through the field of culture, and the extent to which feminism has unwittingly confirmed this by leaving uninterrogated the binary divide between men and women, there is good reason to reinvestigate the landscape of the cultures of femininity, including girls' and women's magazines which have informed my own objects of inquiry in the past (McRobbie 1991). Clearly there was an exclusionary tension which ran across all these forms of media where active lesbian desire was unspeakable and unrepresentable, all the more so when the subject of interest in these magazines (that is the female body) actually required repetitive, sexualized looking by girls and women at other women's bodies. The precise discursive way in which some currents of desire were legitimated and others repudiated ought to have been the focus of attention, when in fact it was the meaning of heterosexual romance which formed the cornerstones of these and other studies. This is not to negate all such work on romance or, more broadly, on femininity. Not only was this work attentive to the way in which ideology successfully naturalized what was in fact socially constructed, but it also highlighted the bodily harm and injuries done to women and girls as a result. What was left unquestioned, however, was the extent to which, for all those whom these commercial cultures of femininity drew in, there were and are many whom it brutally excludes, for example black and Asian young women, disabled teenagers and of course gay or lesbian young people. Part of my aim at the very beginning of these studies (back in the late 1970s) was to gain legitimation for areas of research such as commercial cultures of femininity which in the past had been marginalized, ignored or trivialized. However, in the process of doing this what remained unexamined was the very category of 'girl' itself and the way in which this implied a regularity of subjectivities and experiences within which a norm of happy heterosexuality was an unspoken goal. Within this field of adolescent desire, lesbianism has only recently appeared as 'no longer a problem'. Indeed, the precise passage through the field of girls' culture of this new articulation of non-heterosexual desire ought now to be an object of feminist analysis.

Having expressed a kind of *mea culpa* position, let me now, very briefly, suggest that some elements within cultural analysis already provide an interesting grounding for Butler's much more theoretical work on rearticulation. Perhaps the attraction of Butler's *Gender Trouble* (1990) is that this is exactly what the sociologist of youth subcultures sees all around her – in the streets, in shops, in magazines and in nightclubs. Deviations from the deep binary divide of male and female have been a marked feature of post-war youth subcultures. Hebdige's (1988) use of the concept of bricolage to show how young people reorganize the existing and available codes of cultural meaning to produce new and oppositional relations is not so far removed from Butler's notion of sexual resignification. In the past I have argued that from within the heartland of commercial culture, new scripts of sex and gender have emerged precisely through this process of creating distinctive and sometimes spectacular sub-cultural styles. These in turn have then been seen as constitutive of youthful identities which are the subject of the historical tensions of racial, sexual and class differences which are then 'written on the body'. This indicates a line of connection between Butler's theoretical trajectory and that of a particular cultural studies' tradition. Butler's writing evokes, at some subliminal level, memories of the Gramscian Marxism of 'resistance through rituals' (Hall and Jefferson 1976) through to Hebdige's semiotic account of 'subculture, the meaning of style' from which her own notion of 'gender as performance' seems to unfold quite easily. At each point some note of political hope and some prospect of human agency is squeezed out of a sustained and rigorous post-structuralism.

The strategic use of the Es and the anti-Es?

Can feminist post-structuralism in cultural studies go beyond its function as a critique, as a warning device, a cautionary practice, which relentlessly and inexorably exposes the operations of power manifest in the positions from which we speak as feminists? Can it, as Jeffrey Weeks has put it, be more than a matter of 'tearing apart' (Weeks 1993) or, as Spivak says, 'looking rather than doing' (Spivak 1990)? I will argue in this final section that this body of thinking can actually enhance the focus and the clarity of how we might intervene in cultural and social policy issues. Laclau and Mouffe (1985) have begun to spell out how post-structuralist and psychoanalytic ideas can be applied to political practice, though there are also hints and suggestions in Butler's work about the impor-tance of being able to connect or culturally translate between theory and practice. Laclau and Mouffe acknowledge that culture remains underdeveloped as a political space in their work, despite it being the terrain upon which Gramsci developed the concepts of hegemony and articulation, both of which remain critical to the radical democratic politics now envisaged by Laclau and Mouffe.

What, then, can the anti-Es offer empirical, ethnographic or experiential research which facilitates or accelerates a more interventionist mode in the field of feminist cultural studies? I think it allows us to return to these forms of research without embracing them in a totalistic, exclusive or absolutist way. Doing empirical work need not mean becoming an out-and-out empiricist. And given the low profile that empirical research has had in cultural studies over the last 20 years, what this might mean now, in the late 1990s, is not just beginning to do empirical work informed by questions which emerge from a post-structuralist paradigm (for example, exploring the diverse and fluid subjectivities of 'young women'), it might also mean quite simply strategically speaking the language of empiricism as and when required. We can perform as empiricists in the public domain when that is appropriate. For example, the strategic (and often critical) deployment of the conventions of empiricism is a not unhelpful tactic for cultural studies' academics who are called upon to comment on political debates about violence on television, or on pornography. It is possible to perform in this capacity and to talk the language of results, data and statistics without necessarily endorsing this as the only way to explore the relations between texts and their readers. This is not a matter of bad faith, disingenuousness or falsification. The particular authority of the empirical mode can be occupied now with greater complexity. It can be both used where appropriate and deconstructed elsewhere for its narratives of truth, its representation of results. Research can therefore be rewritten and rescripted according to the politics of its location. Empirical work can still be carried out even if the feminist researcher no longer believes it to be a truth-seeking activity. Indeed, awareness of this and of the structures and conventions which provide a regulative framework for doing cultural studies' research brings not just greater reflexivity to the field, but also demonstrates cultural studies to be a field of inquiry that is aware of the power which its competing discourses wield. Cultural studies itself can thus be deconstructed to show how post-structuralist work has occupied a position of authority as theory which has relegated policy-oriented work to the margins of what is in fact an unstable and disputed field. The three Es can then be brought back in from the margins to expand the political potential of the field and to enter a dialogue with those other strands which appear to occupy the high ground.

Ethnographic work has attracted a good deal of deconstructionist attention over the last few years, notably by Clifford and Marcus (1986) and also by bell hooks (1990). The ethnographer is not the unique (and intrepid) self he or she presents him/herself as, but is rather a point deployed in an already existing discourse which produces a set of 'self-effects' in the text. The subjects of ethnography can no longer be exoticized others whose everyday lives are presented in a naturalistic way. But what does this leave? Certainly, it provokes a lively and interesting debate about existing ethnographies along the lines of what was left out. How does this particular kind of discourse in cultural studies create the category of 'working-class girls' for example? It also raises the question of doing ethnography differently to allow many voices to mingle so that the authoritative voice of the ethnographer is dislodged, though, as David Morley reminds us, as long as there is an author there is also an authoritative editorial and selective practice embedded in his or her mode of representation (Morley 1997).

In fact many of these questions were continually being raised, without the theoretical gloss of the anti-Es, by feminists doing ethnography in the 1970s.

Dorothy Hobson's work on working-class housewives was fully informed by anxieties about speaking on behalf of other women (Hobson 1978). Later, in the pages of *Feminist Review*, there were furious debates about, for example, whether heterosexual women could do ethnographies of lesbian young women. This debate continues today outside the direct influence of post-structuralism by feminists like Marie Gillespie, carrying out ethnographic research on Asian youth (Gillespie 1993). So, discussions of power and the rights of representation are not only tabled by the post-structuralists. What is specific to anti-essentialism in these debates is the insistence that there can be no true and authentic account, that the lives and identities being chronicled are necessarily partial, fluid, performed and constituted in the context of that particular ethnographic moment. But this does not negate the value of the endeavour. Recognition that my own category of 'working-class girls' produced the actual respondents in my research as more fully formed and coherent as individuals than they ever were, does not invalidate the usefulness of the category as a framework for academic feminism to work with as part of its own attempt to think both about the politics of representation and also to find a place for already devalued subjects in the academic curriculum. Thinking again about young women, or 'different, youthful subjectivities' (McRobbie 1994), feminist ethnography, now re-cast in the light of the anti-Es, might accelerate Butler's critique of feminism by illustrating and complexifying the relations between feminism and young women.

This leaves us with the category of experience. It too has been the subject of intense debate in feminist theory over the last few years. Its privileged site in humanist thinking has allowed it to be taken as a cornerstone of truth about the subject – testimony to the existence of a true self or a 'real me', and thus also a clear sign of the appearance of social reality in the context of academic research. However, Foucault's writings permit the category of experience to reappear in post-structuralist feminism by showing agency to be part of the practice of discursive incitement to do or to act (Foucault 1988). The subject is taught to experience and to expect certain normative experiences. She or he is also endlessly encouraged to 'feel it'. 'Can you feel it?' implores the DJ, 'How did it feel?' asks Oprah Winfrey. The subject is therefore produced as a 'feeling self' and experience is one of the means by which feeling is testified to. This pooling of experience is also, according to Foucault, a means of managing and regulating diverse populations.

But just because experience comes as a pre-packaged set of practices while disguising itself as what is unique and most true about ourselves, does not mean it cannot find a place in feminist cultural studies. We can stage experience as a way of speaking or writing, as a genre of populist language. Knowing, for example, how the codes of experience work in human-interest sections of national newspapers, or in daytime television programmes, experience can be adopted as a means of lobbying or campaigning so as to connect academic feminist research with a set of policy objectives. My own research experience on young women's magazines, for example, allows me to use this experience and to speak in a certain way in the media to counter the claims by right-wing moral guardians like Lady Olga Maitland that these publications encourage sexual irresponsibility and promiscuity on the part of their readers. That is to say we can temporarily 'humanize ourselves' as feminist academics to speak the more popular language of experience where political goals can be achieved as a result.

Conclusion

The perspectives I have labelled the anti-Es force us to review and reconsider what we as feminists are doing in our research practices and what relations of power underpin these activities. The anti-Es de-stabilize the old relation between feminists and what used to be called ordinary women by problematizing the politics of representation. They also disenchant and disappoint us by removing the possibility of there being a truth of womanhood towards which feminists can encourage women to strive on the basis that unity is a better guarantee of political action and change than the disunity which may follow from the disaggregation of the category of women. However, the more hopeful note in Butler's writing indicates that through the full recognition of difference, new and more sustainable alliances and coalitions can be built. On a more pragmatic level, we have to live with the fragility of such partnerships rather than waiting for a future where unity is somehow miraculously achieved.

If the vocabularies of post-structuralism help us to move feminist cultural studies on in this respect, then it is also important that they, too, are subjected to criticism. The open-endedness of meaning proposed by Derrida and others actually legitimates a forceful and even intimidating poetic ambiguity in writing which is underpinned by the strong disciplinary frames of literature and literary theory. Having deconstructed the special place of fiction or poetry in writing, it is possible for post-structuralist literary theorists to intersperse purposefully these models into their own readings of key literary texts. This gives to post-structuralist criticism the characteristics of a certain playful, meandering or poetic style, one which is much less acceptable as a practice in the social sciences. The commitment to meaning as an endless open chain of signification can be an excuse for producing texts which, to the social scientist, are highly impenetrable. To the sociologist or cultural studies' feminist concerned with making ideas accessible to a wider audience, this can seem like a real abrogation of political responsibility. The language of the anti-Es, in particular psychoanalysis, can appear far beyond an undergraduate readership never mind a wider audience. Thus it can easily be claimed that the anti-Es are as exclusive in their own practice as they are open-ended in the meanings they profess. Indeed, the latter becomes an excuse for the former. It is also the case that the process of actually translating these ideas so that they might have some broader political impact is often overlooked. More attention might therefore be paid to the practical mechanisms through which, for example, Homi Bhabha's or Dick Hebdige's writing is taken up and used in Isaac Julien's films or, for that matter, to how Butler's ideas find their way into discussions, debates and interviews in the gay and lesbian press. This at least would demonstrate that high theory can have relevance to cultural and political practice.

Similar questions can also be put to the impact of the anti-Es in feminist cultural studies. Having only recently achieved some degree of institutional recognition in the academy, the experience of being robbed of this authority and of being challenged as to whether it is possible to speak in this context, 'as a woman', is unlikely to be met with a wholly friendly welcome. And to stop thinking universally on behalf of all women runs the risk of retreating into an equally fictive sphere of thinking about 'some women only'. To pursue anti-essentialism uncritically can run the risk of making it a new point of faith, a new kind of thing. And for all the connections and alliances which the anti-Es appear to make possible, there is also the possibility of narrowing down the political field so that it becomes the site of endless dispute and antagonism in a negative rather than in a productive way.

In addition, there is also the danger of re-reification where theoretical journeys, whose own essence or truth can only be grasped by exhaustive reading of a great legacy of philosophers and thinkers, makes it more difficult for 'theory' to consider its own place in contemporary political culture. For these reasons, perhaps the critical task now is to return in feminist cultural studies to the empirical, the ethnographic and the experiential, and to use what has been happening in the theoretical world of anti-essentialism, psychoanalysis and post-structuralism to explore the social and cultural practices and new subjectivities which have come into being.

References

Althusser, L. (1971) 'Ideology and Ideological State Apparatuses', in L. Althusser, *Lenin and Philosophy and Other Essays*, London: New Left Books, pp. 121–80.

Barrett, M. (1992) 'Words and Things: Materialism and Method in Contemporary Feminist Analysis', M. Barrett and A. Phillips (eds) *Destablising Theory: Contemporary Feminist Debates*, Cambridge: Polity Press, pp. 201–20.

Brunsdon, C. (1991) 'Pedagogies of the Feminine: Feminist Teaching and Women's Genres', *Screen*, 32 (4), pp. 364–81.

Butler, J. (1990) *Gender Trouble: Gender and the Subversion of Identity*, New York: Routledge.

—— (1993) *Bodies That Matter: On the Discursive Limits of 'Sex'*, New York: Routledge.

—— (1995) 'For a careful reading', S. Benhabib, J. Butler, D. Cornell, and N. Fraser (eds) *Feminist Contentions*, New York: Routledge, pp. 127–45.

Clifford, J. and G. Marcus (eds) (1986) *Writing Culture: The Poetics and Politics of Ethnography*, California: University of California Press.

Cornell, D. (1995) 'Re-thinking the time of feminism', S. Benhabib *et al.* (eds) *Feminist Contentions*, New York: Routledge, pp. 145–57

Coward, R. (1978) 'Sexual Liberation and the Family', in *m/f* 1: 7–25.

Dworkin, A. (1981) *Pornography: Men Possessing Women*, London: The Women's Press.

Fraser, N. (1987) 'Women, welfare and the politics of need interpretation', *Thesis* 11(17) Australia.

Gillespie, M. (1993) 'The Mahabharata – from Sanskrit to Sacred Soap: A Case Study of the Reception of Two Televisual Versions', D. Buckingham (ed.) *Reading Audiences: Young People and the Media*, Manchester: Manchester University Press, pp. 48–74.

Grosz, E. (1995) *Space, Time and Perversion*, New York: Routledge.

Hall, S. (1980) 'Cultural Studies: Two Paradigms', *Media Culture and Society*, 2(2): 57–72.

Hall, S. and Jefferson T. (eds) (1976) *Resistance Through Rituals: Youth Subcultures in Post-War Britain*, London: Hutchinson.

Hebdige, D. (1978/1988) *Subculture: The Meaning of Style*, London: Routledge.

Hobson, D. (1982) *'Crossroads': Drama of a Soap Opera*, London: Methuen.

Hoggart, R. (1957/1970) *The Uses of Literacy*, London: Penguin.

hooks, b. (1990) 'Representing Whiteness in the Black Imagination', L. Grossberg, P. Treichler, C. Nelson (eds), *Cultural Studies*, New York: Routledge, pp. 338–47.

Itzin, C. (ed) (1992) *Pornography: Women, Violence and Civil Liberties*, Oxford: Oxford University Press.

Laclau, E. and Mouffe, C. (1985) *Hegemony and Socialist Strategy: Towards a Radical Democratic Politics*, London: Verso.

MacKinnon, K. (1979) *The Sexual Harassment of Working Women: A Case of Sex Discrimination*, New Haven, CT: Yale University Press.

McRobbie, A. (1991/2000) *Feminism and Youth Culture*, Basingstoke: Macmillan.

—— (1994) *Postmodernism and Popular Culture*, London: Routledge.

—— (1996) 'All the World's a Stage, Screen or Magazine: When Culture is the Logic of Late Capitalism' *Media, Culture and Society* 18(2), pp. 335–42, and also reprinted in this volume, see chapter 2.

Morley, D. (1997) 'Theoretical Orthodoxies: Textualism, constructivism and the "New Ethnography", in Cultural Studies', in M. Ferguson and P. Golding (eds) *Cultural Studies in Question*, London: Sage, pp. 121–38.

Mulvey, L. (1975/1989) 'Visual Pleasure and Narrative Cinema', *Screen* 3(16): 6–18.

Nash, K. (1994) 'The Feminist Production of Knowledge: Is Deconstruction a Practice for Women?', *Feminist Review* 47, pp. 65–78.

Pollert, A. (1988) 'Dismantling Flexibility', *Capital and Class* 34 (Spring), pp. 42–75.

Riley, D. (1988) *Am I That Name? Feminism and the Category of 'Women' in History*, Basingstoke: Macmillan.

Spivak, G.C. (1987) *In Other Worlds: Essays in Cultural Politics*, London: Routledge.

—— (1990) 'An Interview', *Radical Philosophy* (Spring), pp. 32–40.

—— (1993) *Outside in the Teaching Machine*, New York: Routledge.

Walkerdine, V. (1990) *Schoolgirl Fictions*, London: Verso.

—— (1993) '"Daddy's Gonna Buy You a Dream to Cling To (and Momma's Gonna Love You Just As Much As She Can)": Young Girls and Popular Television', D. Buckingham (ed.) *Reading Audiences: Young People and the Media*, Manchester: Manchester University Press, pp. 74–89.

Weeks, J. (1993) 'Re-Discovering Values', in J. Squires (ed.) *Principled Positions: Postmodernism and the Rediscovery of Value*, London: Lawrence and Wishart, pp. 189–211.

Williamson, J. (1978) *Decoding Advertisements*, London: Marion Boyars.

7

AFTERWORD: IN DEFENCE OF CULTURAL STUDIES

So vitriolic has the debate about the value and place of cultural studies become, it would seem that a lot more is at stake than a mere disagreement among academics. Indeed so much has been said or written on this issue during the last few years that it is tempting to turn one's back. The question of what cultural studies is, or should be, has occupied too much time and taken up too much space. Much more refreshing is the work which gets on with the job, combining clear-headed political analysis with an understanding of the importance of cultural forms. A recent article by Tricia Rose strikes me as exemplary. In 'Rewriting the Pleasure/Danger Dialectic', Rose explores the way in which, through a range of news media, the American new right has attributed to young black women ideas of 'moral pathology and negligent motherhood' (Rose 1997). At the same time an accusatory and blaming vocabulary shifts public opinion away from compassion towards punishment, to lay the groundwork for further cuts in welfare programmes.

Rose argues for the importance of cultural forms like cinema to describe the complexity, the pleasure and danger of growing up black and female, by doing away with sexual absolutes such as the virgin or the whore. Rose examines Leslie Harris' 1993 film *Just Another Girl on the IRT*, a low budget realist narrative which explores the question of teenage motherhood without demonizing it. The film, Rose argues, is an attempt to reconfigure the 'black urban teen mother – to normalize her sexual desires and fears'. This short and clearly written piece by Rose provides a commentary upon the contemporary politics of race, sex and youth in America. It is a fine media or cultural studies teaching text. Few students, black or white, could fail to be engaged by a viewing of the film followed by a discussion of the article. And in many ways this is the bottom line. Who is the audience for our academic endeavours? To whom are we speaking? Or rather, whom do we prioritize? Is it worth expending time and energy on what are called in the US the culture wars (culminating in the 'Sokal affair') or can we afford to ignore these altercations?[1]

Media studies under attack from the media

Media studies is, the journalists claim, a 'non subject', wrongly elevated to the status of a discipline. Throughout 1995–96 the tabloids attempted to set up a media moral panic against media studies. On one occasion it even made front page news. The *Daily Express* on 21 August 1996 ran the headline 'Farce of Useless Degrees'. The taxpayers' money was being wasted in students signing on to do 'Mickey Mouse' courses in soap opera, and even the then Prime Minister, John Major, joined in the chorus of disapproval. Standards were being lowered and the classics of English literature were being overlooked in favour of courses about Hollywood cinema. It is an easy and familiar scenario to envisage, with origins from the Thatcher years against a backdrop of fears about multi-culturalism in the curriculum and the abandonment of the canon. Given the centrality of the tabloids in leading the political agenda, it wasn't long before the quality media was conducting a more esoteric critique by drawing in key figures from the arts world, from the *Guardian*, from BBC2's flagship late night news programme *Newsnight*, to left wing playwrights such as David Hare. This argument winds its way through an endless number of venues, eventually coming to lay most of the blame at the doorstep of the postmodernists and those who favour cultural relativism in favour of truth and greatness and pre-serving a distinctive national culture. The condemnation of media and cultural studies almost becomes a point of faith among quality broadsheet editors. It is impossible to recall any principled defence of the area by a practising journalist.

Often it is the most nationally respected journalists like Polly Toynbee (now of the *Guardian*) and Jeremy Paxman (the presenter of *Newsnight*) who are the most vociferous. Toynbee wrote in the *Radio Times* that media studies was a 'useless degree if ever there was one' (17–23 August 1996). Editors of national newspapers joined in, saying they would never employ graduates in any of these fields, preferring applicants from the more familiar disciplines like English, History or PPE (Politics, Philosophy and Economics). By this point it begins to look as though a campaign is afoot to limit places or even run down media studies degrees. Not surprisingly alarm bells start ringing inside the university departments. Confident not only about the overall quality of their provision and in the otherwise cold climate of academic rationalization and accountability enjoying being a first choice for students and in some cases being able to ask for higher A level points than even medicine or law, such accusations from the media and possibly also from the government prompt an immediate response.

Since there is neither the media space made available (with the exception of the odd page in the *New Statesman* or in *The Times Higher Educational Supplement*) nor any other opportunity to publicly counter the notion that media studies is a low-level interdisciplinary mishmash dreamt up in the low status polytechnics (now new universities), the standard academic response has been to rally as professionals and lobby under the umbrella of the Standing Conference on Media, Communications and Cultural Studies. So far this has been fairly effective. By 1997 academics were able to give a sigh of relief, some of the pressure was off, and with the election of the new government it wasn't long before there was discussion about jobs and employment in the cultural and creative fields. This is not enough to guarantee the secure future of media and cultural studies but the setting up of the Creative Task Force in July 1997 to some extent legitimated teaching in these areas. If there were jobs then the courses must, at some level, be relevant. In fact it has since transpired that membership of the CTF includes no representative from higher education. Available documents show there to be a consensus that media studies creates the highest pool of unemployed graduates, that its teachers are below par in comparison to practitioners, that courses are out of date and that employers do not want to recruit media studies graduates. According to the minutes of a CTF meeting held on 17 December 1997, employers in the creative industries look for high flyers from top universities with degrees in traditional disciplines.[2] The CTF wonders, ominously, whether the existing courses are worthy of the government funding they receive.

Some of the antagonism between the media and media studies can be traced to the training of journalists and broadcasters which in the past consisted of a class-divided model. The metropolitan media, and in particular the BBC, looked to young Oxbridge graduates while the rest of the media relied on in-house training schemes and the tradition of working your way up through the local or provincial press. The huge expansion of the media, along with the changing gender composition of this labour market, as well as the media emerging as the most desired place to work for thousands of young media studies graduates, has all but overturned these traditional pathways. The reaction against media studies appears at times to overlap with a general concern on the part of the broadcasting and journalism élite about what is happening in their own profession. A number of different strands get conflated. Commercial pressures and competition for ratings have resulted in 'dumbing down'. There has been a fall in standards in the quality of writing and ideas in journalism (often in favour of lifestyle pieces). These shortcomings are blamed on the perceived low level of education among those entering the profession, which can in turn be explained by the growth of media studies. As though this was not enough, media studies then has the cheek to set itself up as a discipline and profess to know about and do research on these same professionals. The dislike on the part of the media in having the spotlight turned on their own professional activities actually dates right back to the early days of media studies when the Glasgow Media Group and others introduced the idea of bias. At that point the antagonism was against research on the media, now it is directed against teaching the media and the influx of graduates whose training has been in these areas. It remains completely open to question how in fact aspects of this training are translated into practice in the professional field, since little research has been carried out to date. To blame the changes in the professional field on the rise of media studies is actually to foreclose a more important debate about the changing world of work and employment in this field.

But while many leading figures in the media studies field abhor the uninformed but confident downgrading of media studies on the part of largely Oxbridge graduates who never came across any aspect of this field in their own education, there seems to be private agreement, particularly amongst the 'old guard' of media studies, that all is not well. Indeed many of those who were once themselves on the receiving end of media attacks by prominent journalists (the Glasgow Media Group, for example) are now most vociferous in condemning cultural studies. Some of the criticisms from the press, especially the ridiculing of the language of post-structuralism and the application of psychoanalytical concepts to popular forms, touch a raw nerve. This gives further grist to the mill of critics like Frith and Savage (1992) and McGuigan (1992) who a few years earlier had already begun to query what they saw as an unhealthy drift away from the empirical social science tradition which has underpinned much of mainstram media studies. These various critiques by Frith and Savage, McGuigan and others have been widely circulated and discussed and it is sufficient here to merely flag Frith and Savage's argument that cultural studies has slid into an apparent evasion of politics in favour of an endorsement of consumer culture. McGuigan follows this up at much greater length by exploring the origins and growth of 'cultural populism' in the field and Garnham (1995, reprinted 1997) makes a substantial plea for the importance of political economy in the study of culture. All four writers bewail the marginalization of questions of economy in the field in favour of what they consider the superficiality of debates about pleasure. Likewise they query the vehemence with which cultural studies refutes an analysis of culture which reduces the movements of culture to the movements of the economy.

To preserve the coherence and the respectability of the whole field, especially in the light of the new prominence it has acquired in the public stage, cultural studies must either be disciplined and pulled into line or sacrificed as worthless. At the same time a campaign can be mounted to overturn the flimsy and insubstantial public image of the inter-disciplinary field. This entails a concerted effort to gain prominence and respect by becoming players in the field of higher education politics. In these sets of manouevres, key government agencies which deal with ensuring the quality of both teaching and research and which allocate funds accordingly, as well as the research councils, are all being addressed. In the highly competitive, as well as under-funded world of higher education, the battle to gain status has in this case required a jostling for position. While the manouevring may be necessary, the willingness to trash cultural studies as though it was an undifferenciated field of muddy thinking and third rate scholarship cannot go unanswered.

'Cultural studies in question'

Much more savage than the acrimony between media and media studies is the introduction to the recent collection 'Cultural Studies in Question'. This introduction by Marjorie Ferguson and Peter Golding (1997) represents the culmination of what was set in motion by Frith and Savage in 1992. While Frith's disparaging tone actually belongs more to the style of music journalism which both he and Savage also practice, and while McGuigan at least does the work of reading and commenting at length on the cultural studies work with which he disagrees, which means that his book *Cultural Populism* contributes directly to a lively debate, the tone of Ferguson and Golding is unfortunately close to the sneering sarcasm and feigned incomprehension of the *Daily Telegraph*. The introductory essay in CSIQ is scornful from the start. This is in some ways unusual in academic circles. It recalls a kind of exchange which predates feminism. Not that feminism somehow softens the terms of disagreement or forces male academics to restrain from their preferred mode of intellectual combat. It is simply that, typically, differences of opinion are aimed more generously, or there is an assumption of goodwill. To resort to the tactics of sneering is to avoid the challenge of sustained and dynamic discussion.[3] Ferguson and Golding disparage the way in which the areas of study within the cultural studies rubric proliferate like a 'whole earth intellectual catalogue' (Ferguson and Golding 1997, p. xiii). This is a subject with a 'penchant for a pedagogy of infinite plasticity' (ibid., p. xiii). To this it might be said that the extension of an interdisciplinary field to embrace 'colonialism and post-colonialism, race and ethnicity, popular culture and audiences' (ibid., p. xiii) might only be seen as a cause for concern among those who think such things are not really worthy of study, or who see such a range as weakening the basis of an already weak or questionable foundation. To add insult to injury, it is not enough that the wide embrace is intellectually shaky. So, too, are the practitioners who become, when they describe themselves as such, according to Ferguson and Golding, something of a 'sub species' (ibid., p. xiv). There is a suggestion that it is inherently suspicious to subscribe to a mode of study which over a period of thirty years or so finds itself moving through a body of work and ideas. Cultural studies finds itself easily reduced to a list of fads through which its impressionable acolytes wander. They can therefore have no real conviction if they find themselves so easily attracted by a stream of fashionable theories. The authors also suggest that the kind of attention shown to gender and race means that cultural studies work has 'lost sight of fundamental questions of structured inequality' (ibid., p. xix) as though the cultural analysis of race and gender is not informed by issues of structural inequality. Judith Butler has recently described how the 'neo conservative left' in the US make this same charge that questions of sexuality and identity are 'merely cultural', i.e. distractions, and not an intrinsic and fundamental part of the whole complex structuring of social inequalities (Butler 1998). Reneging on the earlier commitment to exploring how the media and cultural forms operate within a capitalist economy to secure existing power relations, cultural studies scholars are lured instead by the 'superficially glamorous' (Ferguson and Golding 1997, p. xx). This echoes the critique by McQuail that this is a field for the 'flighty and opinionated', a comment which carries heavily gendered connotations as Ann Gray has pointed out (Gray 1998, McQuail 1997). These are the terms by which the male teacher will undermine the conviction and confidence of the assertive female pupil who dares to challenge his authority.

Although the work of John Fiske bears the brunt of attack from these and many other critics (most recently Miller and Philo (1998), and Mulhern (1995)) it is the British cultural studies tradition represented by the work of Stuart Hall which seems to fuel this introduction or, rather, since Ferguson and Golding fail to name names, it can only be assumed that they are actually talking about Hall, or perhaps those who they consider follow, more weakly, in his footsteps. The 'cunning use of inverted commas' (Ferguson and Golding 1997, p. xxi) in much cultural studies work as a means of suggesting a kind of double take on the immediate or superficial meaning is for these authors nothing more than the 'coded cant of imprecise analysis' (ibid., p. xxi), and this is compounded by an over-reliance on a series of concepts, each of which, it has to be said, is associated with Hall's writing over the years. But what to Hall and others are useful concepts, the 'tools of the trade', are to Ferguson and Golding 'the calling cards of the cognoscenti' (ibid., p. xxii). Hall's writing finally comes under the microscope when the authors comment on *Policing The Crisis* (Hall *et al.* 1978) which they recognize as seminal, and yet complain of its over reliance on 'analysis by metaphor'. To reduce in this way such an important book which is still in print twenty years later and on every reading list, is bad enough. To fail to fully acknowledge how this work and, following it, the BBC *Open Door* programme, *It Ain't Half Racist Mum*, written and presented by Stuart Hall, provided a pathbreaking analysis of race and its representation in 1970s Britain, is extraordinary. It is not surprising that the authors give themselves away when, without offering any evidence, they proclaim that 'the era of cultural studies expansionism is ending' (Ferguson and Golding 1997, p. xviii). In light of the above, how is it possible to read this as anything other than a wish fulfilment, or indeed as a decision already taken?

Cultural studies seems to be guilty of a number of things. It has not played the academic game by appearing to invent methodologies as they are required and having a certain confidence about doing this, which can be perceived as a disregard for tradition. In so far as much of the Ferguson and Golding critique is directed against gender and ethnicity elements in cultural studies, one obvious answer to this charge is that part of the establishment of feminism in media and cultural studies necessarily entailed a critique of existing methodologies. If the editors had cared to take more than a cursory look at the field they would have come across a series of lengthy debates on the role of biographical and auto-biographical writing in feminist scholarship, on the validity of 'intuition' in the research process and the application of these in a range of fields including social history, sociology and media studies (Brunsdon 1997, 1999). The question Ferguson and Golding's attack on cultural studies raises is about who casts judgement. Who decides when a discussion among feminist academics is worthy of attention? These editors have taken it upon themselves to cast judgement. Surely under the rules of academic discourse this ought to involve serious discussion rather than cheap polemic? They also suggest that cultural studies has been too excited by new theories and new areas of study. This provides the critics with grounds for arguing that the 'merely cultural' (Butler 1998) is 'merely fashionable' (Ferguson and Golding 1997). Instead of sticking with the same paradigms, which is a noticeable characteristic of the political economy approach, cultural studies has moved through a changing set of paradigms. But there is nothing inherently wrong with this. Who ever said that in dealing with questions of culture, politics and power, it is necessary to remain faithful to the methods and the principles which informed investigation over twenty years ago?

Ferguson and Golding are not alone in collapsing a wide and diverse body of work into what they perceive as its weakest elements which are then taken to characterize the whole field. Neither they, Miller and Philo or Mulhern demonstrate in their various essays any willingness to engage with the new arguments around race and ethnicity and the enormous impact they have had in shaping the cultural studies field. They completely fail to mention the profound impact of books like Said's *Orientalism* (Said 1978), the recent rediscovery of Fanon's work on the internalization of racism on the black psyche (Fanon 1992), Gilroy's relentlessly argued rejection of 'ethnic absolutism' (Gilroy 1987, 1993a), Hall's work on 'new ethnicities' (Hall 1992), Lola Young's work on race, sexuality and representation (Young 1995) or bell hooks' analysis of whiteness in the black imagination (hooks 1992). Instead there is a suggestion that by focusing on notions of difference, by introducing aspects of psychoanalysis, and by being over-concerned with texts, representations and meaning, writers like these have given up all interest in where the roots of racial oppression really lie, which according to Garnham is in the international labour market (Garnham 1997).

In direct response to these critiques Lola Young has recently repeated how texts, images and representations are indeed of key importance to black people, as the means by which they are seen to exist (Young 1997). There is no point in pitting one level of inequality against the other. Discrimination in the labour market is intricately connected to how black people are understood, how employers see them. Where does discrimination come from, if not from these knowledges of 'the other'? The critique of post-colonial cultural studies on the part of the old left in media studies is also undermined if we take seriously Stuart Hall's suggestion that in a sense 'the other' is no longer so 'other'. Things have changed in the twenty or so years since the sociology of race attempted to chart the existence of racial inequality. Not only have black scholars like Gilroy, Hall, Bhabha and Mercer debated at length the value of concepts like multi-culturalism and anti-racism, but the position and identity of black people has also changed (Hall 1998).

None of the critics deal head on with what might well be the underlying issue throughout these debates, which is the pivotal position occupied by Marxism (and to a lesser extent feminism). The critics of cultural studies can only interpret recent work on cultural identity and difference and also feminist work on pleasure as a kind of decisive shift away from the Marxism. However, their own Marxism (or not) remains completely undiscussed. We can only assume that the Marxism of the political economists remains primarily concerned with how capitalist corporations work to reproduce and accentuate unequal relations of power and powerlessness. Ferguson and Golding accuse cultural studies of vacating the terrain of structural inequalities but they offer no engagement with what is at stake in retaining a commitment to Marxism in the late 1990s. Golding neither locates himself within or outside Marxism. While Golding's work has been indisputably within the political economy tradition, Marjorie Ferguson has never defined herself within either Marxism or feminism. Her book on women's magazines disregarded feminist scholarship entirely and opted instead for a Durkheimian approach which understood femininity as a 'cult' (Ferguson 1982). So it is galling to find this author accusing feminists of moving away from what should be their concerns in favour of some kind of indulgent interest in pleasure and the body.

Feminism and social change

It is interesting that the wrath of the critics falls disproportionately on broadly feminist work. They either ignore the significance of black scholarship or they voice their disapproval of post-colonialist criticism. But they appear to feel themselves on stronger ground when it comes to the commodities and cultural forms associated with women. So when feminist writers find value and meaning for their audiences and readers in otherwise devalued forms such as magazines, popular romances, fashion or shopping, perplexity gives way to anger. There is a sense that feminist 'revisionism' amounts to an outright betrayal of the efforts of the political economists of the mass media to show how dangerous, pernicious and oppressive are its forms.

There are real political issues at stake here, notably where we as feminists stand in what has become known as the 'post-socialist era'. Do we maintain the same level of opposition to and critique of commercial capitalism and the free market? Do we believe in the same values which fuelled the left in the post-war years, or do we have to reassess in light of the seeming inevitability of capitalism? Do we simply observe and criticize from the sidelines, dispassionately but with the sort of disappointment which comes with the decline of socialism, as a living political force? Or are we ourselves, within the media and cultural studies field, in disarray? Is this tremendous quarrel which has broken out on the question of cultural studies a symptom of the despair about how the Marxist left can respond to a whole range of issues, including the endorsement of the free market (and the Murdock empire) by New Labour and simultaneously the diminishing of the language of social democracy from the New Labour agenda? Meanwhile there remains enormous energy in the debates and discussions engaged in by black intellectuals and those working on questions of race and ethnicity, and likewise among feminists in cultural studies, and those who have created the field of 'queer theory'. This vitality alone suggests that political goals can still be aimed for, despite the claim by the political economists of the mass media that there has been an abandonment of politics.

Feminists like myself have argued (as I do on two occasions in this volume) that it is true, for example, that commercial girls' magazines like *Just 17* or even *Sugar* or *More!* – can indeed take on a feminist agenda and promote feminist issues quite aggressively. They can and do encourage readers to confront sexual inequality, to take action against harassment and to aim for goals which in the past would have been unavailable or virtually unachievable. This must inevitably create a political dilemma for those who see the media primarily in terms of the loss of a public sphere, the narrowing of interests to conform with the processes of deregulation, privatization, de-democratization and the centralization of media power in the hands of half a dozen multi-nationals. Is it possible that such a media can incorporate the political aims of feminism, or at least some of them, while pursuing an aggressively capitalist pathway?

I am not implying that there is no longer any problem for feminists with the world of consumer capitalism. Far from it. Indeed in one of the articles in this volume I part company quite sharply with some strands of contemporary feminist writing which appear to endorse such a position. I have indicated my own surprise where either there has been a tendency to overlook exclusions from consumer culture through low income and poverty or indeed where aspects of commercial capitalism are somehow seen as beneficial to women in their struggle for equality (see Chapter 10). It is not the case that capitalism has softened or changed, or become less ruthless, more ethical, or more feminized (whatever that might mean). Nor is it the case that there has simply been progress, which explains why I can be more positive about young women's magazines today and yet critical of those feminists who describe the emancipating role of the department store at the turn of the century in similar terms.

So what does it mean when capitalism, in this case the world of magazines, absorbs feminism? Is this just another ploy to look up-to-date? And what kind of feminism is being absorbed? In Chapter 4 I examine changes visible in girls' magazines by arguing for renewed interest in production values. I suggest more attention should be paid to who is pushing through such changes, and to the professional ideologies at work in the studios where the magazines' editorial features, images and lay out are put together. Editors and journalists are continually engaging in power battles over content and, alongside the traditional emphasis on the body, beauty and the products which falsely promise the achievement of these goals, other issues are also being addressed as part of those power struggles.

Many of the young women working on magazines (and interviewed in the course of a research project on the fashion industry) said how they had 'done media studies', or had written their final year dissertation on some aspect of gender inequality (McRobbie 1998). This is by no means a simple transmission of radical values from one generation to another, as Charlotte Brunsdon has testified (Brunsdon 1997), nor am I unaware of the small scale of changes we are talking about. But this reflexivity is virtually unexplored territory in the map of media and cultural studies. Researching the fashion media it was clear that some of what was learned at university was being put into practice within the heartland of the multi-media empires. My own encouragement to students to find these kinds of jobs could be seen as a compromise on the part of a feminist scholar like myself. But students have to get jobs and earn a living and if they can change media institutions from within then why not? If this is bad faith or recantation to the old left of media studies then it is true that there is a chasm opening up between feminists like myself who do not discourage students from getting jobs inside big advertising agencies, and those who see this either as a betrayal or as a hopelessly unrealistic and optimistic assumption about how much can be changed by these means. I see it as extending the net of politics, working inside the institutions for change and improvement without losing track of the need for struggle, organization and association within the workplace.[4]

Ferguson and Golding are probably happier dealing with radical feminists. Intellectual separatism is more manageable despite the anti-male rhetoric. The same goes for liberal feminism. Where empirical studies can show existing inequalities in media labour markets, and where questions of representation still ponder over good and bad images of women, there can still be a consensus about what constitutes the field. Post-structuralist feminists, in contrast, dispute the terms upon which such judgement about good or bad images are based. Homi Bhabha, in his pathbreaking article on the racial stereotype and the power of visual representation, argues for the instability of the stereotype and the anxious repetition to tie down the meanings attached to 'the other' to which this instability gives rise (Bhabha 1994). All this intellectual disorderliness, even the use of terms like fascination, ambivalence and instability, gives to the field of media and cultural studies an image which is too shaky and unstable for its official custodians to be able to deal with. They see this as weakness and loss of nerve or as an abandonment of rigour.

And yet, just as it is inaccurate to perceive the cultural turn as a shift away from politics, so also is it increasingly untrue to say there is no economy in cultural studies. Recent work by Nixon (1996), Du Gay (1996) and also by myself (McRobbie 1998) explore the economies underpinning the new culture industries. In Nixon's case this is the magazine market for young men and, in my own case, the 'micro-economies' of fashion design, while Du Gay has recently (in collaboration with Stuart Hall) argued that 'the economy' or 'an economy' is also something which is imagined and represented. The specific social processes which are normatively invoked in the discourses of 'the economy' are themselves the outcome of political struggle. The economy is as much about the struggle for meaning as it is about inflation, interest rates or the global market. What is excluded and included in the circulating flow of economic meanings which now dominate the front pages and not just the city pages, with all the talk of soft landings, silver linings and protective mechanisms, is also a way of defining the kind of society in which we live. 'The economy' dominates and this is made to look inevitable. It is along these lines of inquiry which Du Gay, writing within a Foucauldian framework and drawing explicitly on Donzelot, envisages a new kind of cultural economics.

Poetry or sociology?

Of course it can go badly wrong in the hands of the merely pretentious or those who, for whatever reason, perversely prefer their writing to remain opaque, but the political economy critics of cultural studies have absolutely no understanding of the attempts made by writers like Dick Hebdige or the feminist philosopher Denise Riley to experiment with the form of their academic writing, or simply to foreground the 'writerly'. As social scientists they lack empathy for the arts and the humanities and have no sense of the visual or the poetic. This puts them at some disadvantage when it comes to understanding the 'aetheticisation of everyday life' and the increasingly prominent role of culture (Jameson 1984, Lash and Urry 1994). The formalist strategies of writers like Hebdige and Riley are designed to enhance and emphasize the argument but they do not adhere to the rules of a social science methodology (Hebdige 1978, Riley 1988). Riley is also a published poet and Dick Hebdige's most recent work takes the form of performance or installation art (Riley 1996, Hebdige 1998). Riley's seminal essay on feminist post-structuralism integrates and absorbs the argument into the actual form of her chosen voice and mode of address, the shape and the tone of the writing (ibid.). *Am I That Name?* is a poetic rumination. The shape and movement of the writing describes the author's lucid exploration of the power and politics of classification on the question of 'what is woman?' and Riley's own attempts to slip that net. Likewise, Hebdige's equally seminal *Subculture: The Meaning of Style* displays all the signs of the 'cut up' method which, he argues, punk borrowed from Dada, Surrealism and from William Burroughs to give it the distinctive, jarring, torn, broken, angry and splintered aesthetic (Hebdige 1978). We could take this further and suggest that many of the best known works of cultural studies adopted an experimental, open-ended form. Hoggart's peculiarly entitled *Uses of Literacy* is possibly the best and earliest example (Hoggart 1956). At the same time some of the collectively written work produced at the Birmingham Centre for Contemporary Cultural Studies (CCCS) in the late 1970s was indeed put together with little thought being given to a consistent style, never mind a poetic tone. At the time of writing the ethos was more that of political pamphleteering than it was academic career making. There were always close links between the Birmingham Centre and the wider field of cultural and artistic practice. Some people left to manage bands hoping to find ways of integrating aspects of cultural theory and sexual politics in music making. Others moved into film production enamoured both by Laura Mulvey's *Visual Pleasure and Narrative Cinema* and by Gramsci's arguments about working within popular culture (Mulvey 1989). Nor was this intersection between art, cultural practice and theory the sole concern of the Birmingham CCCS. These issues were debated in what was the Polytechnic of Central London (now the University of Westminster) under the influence of Victor Burgin and Mitra Tabrizian, and also at Leeds art history department under the guidance of Terry Atkinson and Griselda Pollock. Most fruitful perhaps have been the collaborations between Stuart Hall and film-maker Isaac Julien (Morley and Chen 1996). What is important here is the emphasis upon cultural politics and on the exchanges between academics and practitioners. But what has been the norm in cultural studies, to the point that it feels like stating the obvious, is actually a relation between theory and practice.

Not everybody can be a poet, artist or writer. Often in the midst of Deleuzian ramblings the reader almost cries out for some facts and figures. But in much cultural studies writing what the critics take for celebration is actually more an enthusiasm for dialogue with artists, writers or film-makers. Three of the articles in this volume have attempted to convey how some forms of contemporary dance music bring into being new kinds of association and community between black and white young people. Through tracing these movements it is possible to see a politics in art which does spread some rays of light against a backdrop where hardship and injustice remain rife. Paul Gilroy sees black music as having played this transcendent role in making life worth living by offering some sense of change and hope for those for whom vocabularies of political analysis and theory have been unavailable or, rather, who have not been allowed access to the educational, cultural and social codes of power. Inter-disciplinarity as well as the intersection of art work with cultural theory in this context is no mere academic preference. Given the sparsity of sustained scholarship by black writers since the turn of this century who, like their working-class and female counterparts, were and still are kept waiting at the the gates of academia hoping to be let in, it is not surprising that black students of the social sciences have turned to fiction or autobiography and used this as a kind of interdisciplinarity by necessity. This in turn becomes a principled position, the mixing of poetry and sociology, history and art.

Identity politics and the 'neo-conservative left'

The repudiation of identity politics by the academic left in America, who see it as a retreat from real, materialist politics in favour of something more individualist and lifestyle-related, is a way of resisting the current uncertainty about political priorities. The assumption is that if you are in this identity camp you no longer care about or campaign around issues like poverty, low wages, the return of the sweat shop or the disappearance of the welfare state. This is exactly the sort of suggestion found in attacks on cultural studies, which is taken as synonomous with identity politics. But culture doesn't stop where what are designated real issues like single parenthood begin, as Tricia Rose so well describes.

The underlying concern must be the disunity among the academic left and the need to urgently re-establish shared political and intellectual priorities. But if it is the case that no such clear set of priorities can be arrived at, how can left politics proceed? Nancy Fraser argues that the left needs to recognise a dual system of needs and recognition, with the first emerging from the unequal distribution of material resources and the second from the unequal politics of recognition (Fraser 1998). This Habermasian model acknowledges the integration of these systems but also allows for their conceptual difference. Butler argues against this bifurcation of sexuality into a separate sphere by returning to the issues which concerned socialist feminists in the 1970s. These demonstrated how central women's role in social reproduction was to the maintenance of the whole society (Butler 1998). Likewise Butler reminds us of the legal and material obstacles faced by gays and lesbians as they attempt to create their own families, partnerships and livelihoods. The danger with Fraser's model is that inevitably, for the left (and also for the liberals), the materialist, redistributional ethos takes precedence over that of recognition.

For Butler (and Laclau and Mouffe 1985) the proliferation in recent years of social movements for whom material and symbolic injustices are interwoven do not add up to some hierarchy of the oppressed. The challenge in the post-Marxist era is to recognize the diffusion of different political movements (which means alliances rather than faith in eventual unity) and to conceptualize these movements so as to broaden the span of radical democracy. However, as Butler reminds us, the job of alliance building and the task of reconceptualizing socialist politics is far from easy, especially when there is as much opposition from what she calls the 'neo conservative left': 'How quickly – and sometimes unwittingly – the distinction between the material and the cultural is re-manufactured when it assists in the drawing of the lines that jettison sexuality from the sphere of fundamental political structure!' (Butler 1998: 42). She also suggests that the marginalization of the cultural, and the location of the sexual within that sphere, along with the insistence that the cultural is separate and autonomous, is also a strategy, a means of containing the current energy, dynamism and theoretical challenge of queer politics and scholarship. Translated into the context of this current discussion it seems that the political economists want to redefine cultural studies to fit with their conceptual schema which entails what Butler also describes (and here I paraphrase) as a 'caricaturing, demeaning and domesticating of difference' (Butler 1998: 44).

The interventions of Ferguson and Golding, as well as Miller and Philo, are clearly a bid for power. They want to be listened to by the new Labour government, to be consulted and brought into the daily life of government as experts and spokespersons for media studies. They also want to be in a strong position inside the academy to define the territory and police the boundaries of both media and cultural studies – and with cultural studies tamed and cowering in the corner it, in turn, must defer to these masters. As far as strategies go, this does have its limits. The attempt to create a consensus is bound to be challenged by feminist academics like myself as well as black scholars who cannot fail to perceive the underlying agenda. Will the more traditional social science focus for media studies really win over the media establishment? Will it be listened to by government any more than it ever has been? Its disengagement with cultural practice and its dismissal of alliance building with the creative arts makes it unlikely that it will occupy a strong lobbying or campaigning role in debates around the future of the culture industries and the role of the Creative Task Force.

Indeed, there is such an accumulating richness in the arts and culture in Britain today, much of which comes from these 'queer' and 'other' places, that the inability of the critics to see or listen to these voices shows them, as social scientists, to be inattentive to those aspects of everyday life which are all around us and which, as Stuart Hall has pointed out, tell us at street level about changes in the lives and identities of black people in Britain today (Hall 1998). There is a distinct lack of sociological imagination here which stops critics like Ferguson and Golding from noticing how ordinary people actually make a small record of their lives through forms of cultural and symbolic embodiment including music, dance and fashion. Perhaps it is the scale and intensity of social change in these areas, particularly among women and black people, which destabilize and literally turn upside down the world as seen by the political economists and media academics like Ferguson and Golding. But there are, thankfully, enough examples to demonstrate that the flickering lights of culture can still illuminate our pathways and provide commentary and critique. Poetic documentaries like Patrick Keillor's *London* (Keillor 1994), Talvin Singh's album *Anokha: Sounds of the Asian Underground* (Singh 1996), Chila Burman's images of her father's ice cream van on the beaches of the Wirral and James Kelman's Glasgow, are all low budget, independent productions. They are also signs that, despite the world being carved up according to the logic and the seeming inevitability of the free market, new forms emerge which demonstrate the inter-connectedness of identity and materiality, and which urgently argue for extending the net of radical democracy through the communicative possibilities afforded by culture.

Notes

1 US Physicist Alan Sokal submitted a hoax article to the literary theory journal *Social Text* in 1996. His attempt to expose post-structuralist thinking as relativist and nonsensical gained him front page coverage on newspapers across the world.
2 This information is taken from the minutes of the December 1997 meeting of the Creative Task Force, chaired by Chris Smith (Secretary of State), Department of Culture, Media and Sport.
3 I regret sliding into something near to a sneer in Chapter 4.
4 The *Independent* newspaper recently ran a feature on the personal assistant to the editor of the new women's magazine *Red*. The young women lists as one of her activities in her spare time, working for the 'Domestic Violence Intervention Project': 'Sometimes I find it very hard to move from what seems like one extreme to the other. The magazine world can seem a bit frivolous at times, yet *Red* remains refreshingly down to earth.' ('Job With A Red Hot Future', interview with Caitlyn McCarthy by Katie Sampson, The *Independent* 8 July 1998, p. 20).

References

Bhabha, H. (1994). 'The Other Question: Stereotype, Discrimination and the Discourse of Colonialism', *The Location of Culture*, London: Routledge.

Brunsdon, C. (1997) 'Pedagogies of the Feminine', *Screen Tastes: From Soap Opera to Satellite Dishes*, London: Routledge.

—— (1999) *The Feminist, the Housewife and the Soap Opera*, Oxford: Oxford University Press.

Butler, J. (1998) 'Marxism and the Merely Cultural', *New Left Review*, No. 227, January, London: Verso.

Du Gay, P. (forthcoming) *The Economics of Globalisation*, London: Sage.

Fanon, F. (1992) 'The Fact of Blackness', J. Donald and A. Rattansi (eds), *'Race', Culture, And Difference*, London: Sage.

Ferguson, M. (1983) *Forever Feminine. Women's Magazines and the Cult of Femininity*, London: Heinemann.

Ferguson, M. and Golding, P. (1997) *Cultural Studies In Question*, London: Sage,

Fraser, N. (1998) 'Heterosexist Capitalism?', *New Left Review*, No. 228, March, London: Verso.

Frith, S. and Savage, J. (1992) 'Pearls and Swine: The Intellectuals and Mass Media', *New Left Review*, No. 198, London: Verso.

Gilroy, P. (1987) *There Aint No Black In the Union Jack*, London: Hutchinson.

—— (1993a) *The Black Atlantic*, London: Verso.

—— (1993b) *Small Acts*, London: Serpents Tail.

Garnham, N. (1995, reprinted and revised 1997) 'Political Economy and Cultural Studies: Reconciliation or Divorce?', University of Westminster, reprinted as 'Political Economy and the Practice of Cultural Studies', M. Ferguson and P. Golding (eds), *Cultural Studies in Question*, London: Sage.

Gray, A. (1999) 'Audience and Reception Research in Retrospect: The Trouble with Audiences', P. Alasuutari (ed.) *The Inscribed Audience*, London: Sage (forthcoming).

Hall, S. (1992) 'New Ethnicities', J. Donald and A. Rattansi (eds), *'Race', Culture and Difference*, London: Sage.

—— (1998) 'Aspiration and Attitude: Reflections on Black Britain in the Nineties', in *New Formations*, no. 33, Spring, Frontlines, Backyards issue, 38–47.

Hall, S., Critcher, C., Jefferson, T., Clarke, J. and Roberts, B. (1978) *Policing the Crisis: Mugging, The State and Law and Order*, London: Macmillan.

Hebdige, D. (1978) *Subculture: The Meaning of Style*, London: Methuen.

—— (1998) Lecture delivered at Goldsmiths College, Department of Media and Communication, London.

Hoggart, R. (1956) *The Uses of Literacy*, Harmondsworth: Penguin.

hooks, b. (1992) 'Representing Whiteness in the Black Imagination', L. Grossberg, C. Nelson and P. Treichler (eds), *Cultural Studies*, New York: Routledge.

Jameson, F. (1984) 'Postmodernism: Or Culture, The Logic of Late Capitalism', *New Left Review*, No. 146, London: Verso.

Keillor, P. (1994) *London*, Channel 4 film production, London.

Laclau, E. and Mouffe, C. (1985) *Hegemony and Socialist Strategy: Towards a Radical Democratic Politics*, London: Verso.

Lash, S. and Urry, J. (1994) *The Economy of Signs and Spaces*, London: Sage.

McGuigan, J. (1992) *Cultural Populism*, London: Routledge.

McQuail, D. (1997) 'Policy Help Wanted: Willing and Able Media Culturalists Please Apply', M. Ferguson and P. Golding (eds) *Cultural Studies in Question*, London, Sage.

McRobbie, A. (1998) *British Fashion Design: Rag Trade or Image Industry?*, London: Routledge.

Miller, D. and Philo G. (1998) *Cultural Compliance: Dead Ends of Media/Cultural Studies and Social Science*, Glasgow Media Group, Glasgow University, London: Longmans.

Morley, D. and Chen, H.-S. (1996) *Stuart Hall: Critical Dialogues in Cultural Studies*, London: Routledge.

Mulhern, F. (1995) 'The Politics of Cultural Studies', *Monthly Review*, July–August.

Mulvey, L. (1989) *Visual and Other Pleasures*, London: Macmillan.

Nixon, S. (1996) *Hard Looks: Masculinities, The Visual and the Practices of Consumption*, London: University of London Press.

Riley, D. (1988) *'Am I That Name'? Feminism and the Category of Women in History*, London: Macmillan.

Riley, D. (1996) *Douglas Oliver, Denise Riley, Iain Sinclair*, Penguin Modern Poets 10, London: Penguin.

Rose, T. (1997) 'Rewriting the Pleasure/Danger Dialectic: Black Female Sexuality in the Popular Imagination', E. Long (ed.), *From Sociology to Cultural Studies*, Mass., and Oxford: Blackwell.

Said, E. (1978) *Orientalism*, London: Penguin.

Singh, T. (1996) *Anokha: Sounds of the Asian Underground*,

Young, L. (1995) *Fear of the Dark*, London: Routledge.

—— (1997) Inaugural lecture, delivered at Middlesex University, London.

Part II

8

RECENT RHYTHMS OF SEX AND RACE IN POPULAR MUSIC

Popular music has occupied an unstable and uncertain place within the mainstream of cultural and media studies. More significant, however, the fact is that what were the accepted critical categories and grids of classification in this field of study are now urgently in need of revision. The world of popular music has moved rapidly and changed dramatically through the availability of new musical technologies and techniques. It has so forcefully been deployed in both these respects by subaltern social groups that now, particularly in dance music, in rap and in hip hop, popular music culture defines and redefines its own landscape of mutating types and tastes and styles at breathtaking speed. Music critics, never mind the academics, have to run to keep up. In short, it destabilizes both theory and politics. This is most visibly played out in rap where many performers are deliberately provoking a hostile response as much from the black 'parent culture' as from the world of white consumers. Of course the relationship between black intellectuals like Paul Gilroy in the UK and Tricia Rose and George Lipsitz in the US, all of whom have written about rap, and the rap artists who actually produce the music, is particularly intense. To pose Dr Dre and Snoop Doggy Dogg, on the one hand, with their evocation, not to say celebration, of bullets, whores and bitches, and Paul Gilroy on the other, is already to ask a question about the politics of representation, about who speaks on whose behalf, about generation, education and about, as Gilroy has eloquently put it, the need for there to be difference (and difficulty) within 'black'; and for this not only to be recognized but also reaffirmed as it is so clearly in rap. It is not my intention here to provide a summary version of the more extensive debate on rap (and more recently on ragga) which has drawn into the arena a whole number of black intellectuals and politicians in the US, including Henry L. Gates Jr, Cornel West, Michael Dyson, Jon Michael Spencer, Houston A. Baker Jr and Jesse Jackson. It is sufficient here to note the existence of this debate and to signal its presence in the UK through the work of Paul Gilroy and also in the recent *Arena* documentary by the black and gay film-maker Isaac Julien (1994).

But what of the place of popular music in media and cultural studies? This has followed an idiosyncratic route, one result of which has been the undertheorization of popular music in comparison perhaps to the overtheorization which, from the mid-1970s to the late 1980s, was a dominant feature of film and television studies, a tendency which, it will be argued here, has recently produced an anti-theoretical thrust in new rock studies, particularly in the work of Simon Frith. Another way of describing this route is to suggest that 'theory' or, as Stuart Hall has put it, 'the politics of theory', has for some reason never formed the same close attachment with music as the object of study as it did with almost all other areas of study within the field of media, cultural studies and communication (Hall 1989). Thus, for example, work on reception theory, on theories of reading, on the question of subjectivity, on audiences, on the psychoanalytically-influenced questions of the look or the gaze and, more recently, on the post-colonialist concern with 'fascination' and 'the other' has, at the most, only noted the world of popular music, pop stars or pop 'fandom'.

In the British context at least this can be accounted for partly in terms of the dynamics involved in the institutionalization of media and cultural studies. Here the centres of gravity can be located in four schools of thought. The 'political economists of the mass media' have been associated with Leicester, Loughborough and the University of Westminster. This is perhaps the most consolidated and concentrated area of study with a strongly Marxist and neo-Marxist identity. While its departure from the orthodoxy of economistic Marxism is perhaps more marked than some of its 'culturalist' critics suggest, this school is more concerned with, say, over-arching theories of capital accumulation in relation to the mass communications industries than it is with 'theories of the gaze', or with the psychoanalysis of desire. Its orbit has been that of the global communications networks with their shifting patterns of regulation and control. With this there has been a strong interest in broadcasting policies and legislation. Television, the press, film and video have figured most visibly here, with music recognized as representing at most a vital strand in the whole provision of mass entertainment. The distinctiveness of musical styles and tastes and the nature of the music audience have been overshadowed by music's place within the huge entertainment multinationals. The exception to this is the recent work of Andrew Goodwin who in *Dancing in the Distraction Factory* considers the role of the pop video as both an autonomous cultural form and as a key part of the marketing strategies of a handful of major record companies (Goodwin 1993).

The second school has offered a more 'natural' home to popular music studies, although it too, for quite different reasons, has inadvertently perhaps marginalized the area. Cultural studies, with its early home in Birmingham, was most open to popular music initially through the central role it played in the formation and identity of youth subcultures. However, as various critics pointed out, it was 'style' which provided the theoretical ignition point in the sub-cultures work; later in, for example, the seminal *Policing the Crisis: Mugging, the State and Law and Order*, the music of young black people is signalled as part of a distinctive cultural identity. However, the theoretical vocabulary of the study, in particular the ideology and hegemony 'couplet', is more concerned with the practices of social control than with the cultural rhythms of discontent (Hall *et al.* 1979). Nonetheless there is a line of interest here which is the unmistakably important place of a whole range of musics within the black British community. This serves as a point of connection between the different 'ports of call' which have been part of the history of what Gilroy later hailed as the black diaspora (Gilroy 1993). Indeed black music provides the soundtrack to the work on race and identity associated with Birmingham and then more broadly with cultural studies. The chapter titles of *The Empire Strikes Back* (Gilroy *et al.* 1982) evoke the political resonance of reggae, and in *There Ain't No Black In The Union Jack* (Gilroy 1987) Gilroy foregrounds the place of black music as a necessary resource, a tool for survival, a space for the transcendent yearning for freedom and equality, for the pain of subordination and for the fleeting pleasures of 'sexual healing'. From this point onwards music comes to occupy a critical place in debates about race and ethnicity. But in Britain this is still largely dependent upon Gilroy whose recent *Black Atlantic* develops further the theoretical analysis of black musics in terms of the nexus of production–performance–participation (ibid., 1993). To look at music in the more conventional language of individual performers, distinct musical texts or tracks, or music audiences, argues Gilroy, is to miss the existence of black music as a more fluid, more open set of meta-communicative strategies, which quite literally 'ask' or 'provoke' others into response. Thus the boasting claims of rappers and MCs repeat the 'call and response' structures of gospel. Thus, also, girl rappers like Salt 'n' Pepa reply to and issue further challenges, on the grounds of gender and sexuality, to the inflated claims of potency and performance of their male counterparts. The centrality which Gilroy grants to these forms is incorporated into one of the central arguments of *Ain't No Black*, which is that historically excluded from the channels of access to mainstream politics, black politics by necessity has been rehearsed and pursued in culture. However, where music is the focus of attention in contemporary black cultural studies, Gilroy still finds himself occupying a lonely space. Virtually all the other post-colonialist intellectuals have looked instead to film, literature, photography, art and to forms of popular culture other than music.

There is also a gender question here. Alongside the emergence of black intellectuals like Gilroy and Hazel Carby there was also a distinctively feminist cultural studies which came into being from the late 1970s onwards. This refined itself theoretically either in the field of film where psychoanalysis came to dominate or in television studies where there was a substantial revision of the critical language of media studies through the contributions of Charlotte Brunsdon (1981), Dorothy Hobson (1982) and, more recently, Ann Gray (1987). However, while the broader field of popular culture – including girls' and women's magazines and popular romantic fiction – also developed a subtle vocabulary of ideologies of femininity and, later, of desire, fascination, consumption and pleasure, popular music still found itself relegated to the margins.

While the position of women in music begged an urgent question, writing on this subject, apart from an overview article authored by myself with Simon Frith in 1978 (Frith and McRobbie 1978) has actually remained within a firmly journalistic format (Steward and Garratt 1984) or has been extremely sporadic, buried in academic music journals or, as in the case of rap, connected more directly with black American debate.

In the third school we find the work of Simon Frith and those whose work is either associated with him or deeply influenced by his 'rock' pardigms (as Larry Grossberg puts it, in his contribution to *Microphone Fiends*, the 'rock formation'). It is not insignificant that two of the volumes in this review are co-edited by Simon Frith. Virtually all academic efforts in the sociological or cultural analysis of popular music have, in some way or another, gestured towards Frith. Two points need to be made here. First that Frith has also for almost twenty years worked as a music journalist, for the *Melody Maker, New Statesman* and *Observer* in the UK, and more recently for the *Village Voice* in New York. The second point is that Frith writes most confidently on popular music when the work is firmly estab-lished within a historical or a sociological framework. The real strength of Frith's writing is when he has defined as his object of study the rise, for example, of music as home entertainment, or when he is casting a broad sociological view over the role and meaning of rock lyrics (Frith 1988). While Frith's natural academic allies are now in departments or institutes for the study of popular music, and while he retains close connections with fellow journalist Jon Savage in Britain and Greil Marcus in the USA, the expansion of both mainstream media studies and of cultural studies has precipitated on his behalf a necessary engagement with the politics of theory. This has taken the form of a series of interventions, either an advocacy of empirical work on popular music within a cultural studies framework (see Frith 1992), with Sara Cohen (Cohen 1987, 1991) and Ruth Finnegan (Finnegan 1989) being cited as exemplary in this respect, or as a rather sweeping condemnation of cultural studies for what Frith and Savage (Frith and Savage 1993) jointly characterize as a new complicity between aca-demics and marketing directors (i.e. 'cultural populism') on the basis of their assessment of recent cultural studies work on consumption. Alternatively it has comprised even more sweeping attacks on postmodernism, once again on the rather shaky assumption that this is now a theoretical point of faith with cultural studies writers. What has not been addressed in this diversion into cultural studies is perhaps what could be described as the crisis in rock, the kind of conceptual realignment which has taken place over the last few years in response to the emergence of race and ethnicity as critical themes in cultural analysis, which means that the old reliable categories now become questionable, if they still exist at all.

The final school is perhaps the most familiar to media studies academics, that is, the school of textuality. It is sufficient here to note the institutional connec-tion with the British Film Institute and the spread of textual approaches to media forms, particularly film and television, across a wide range of prestigious university departments. Rarely does the study of pop music texts, or even of pop videos, play a key role in the research interests or publishing outputs of such departments. This means precisely that theoretical developments leading away from the specificity of the text towards the world of readers, viewers and consumers remain fixed on the idea of audience ethnographies in relation to television or film. The consumption of popular music at home or in the concert arena has failed to attract the interest of those 'new ethnographers'. In this way an important strand of shared social experience which is constantly played out in the presence of frequently very loud music, in cars, in personal stereos, in the bath, and also during working hours, is not registered, let alone theorized.

Sex and race revolts

The two themes which can be traced right through the volumes under review are unmistakably those of sex and race. What marks them out as particularly noticeable is the different theoretical vocabulary which has come into being around them in quite a short space of time. One way of understanding this might be to suggest that it is in musical forms, particularly those associated with youth cultures, that an avant-garde of ideas emerges. Or at least since music (with music video) is the most pervasive and noticeable of the youth cultural forms then perhaps it is not surprising that it is here that statements are made, positions and identities staked out. It is the one cultural space which unequivocally belongs to young people despite the interests and interventions of the music industry. Just think how many rap songs make direct reference to place, city or neighbourhood. Just think how 'rock' in the past has so urgently and anthemically proclaimed the entitlement of youth to a place in the nation state (e.g. Springsteen's *Born in the USA*).

Rap and hip hop music are the main focus of attention in *Microphone Fiends*. Although Ross recognizes that against a backdrop of post-industrial decline the structural positions of black and white youth are not as different as might be imagined, there is still in this American writing a sense that rap and hip hop are by and for black youth and that it is only when rap artists are signed by the major record labels that they cross over. The mass audience is therefore assumed to be white. While this might be empirically the case, and while it is understandable that black critics situate rap within the broad framework of a black aesthetic primarily for a black audience, this leads too easily into an argument about black as marginal and white as mainstream. And the idea of authenticity also creeps in to give support to the debate about the dangers of contaminating 'real' rap by 'selling out' to the majors and in the process editing out the anger.

What such a position does is to reinforce the boundary which puts rap in one corner and 'rock' in the middle. Perhaps the case for hybridity in music (Puerto Rican rappers like A Lighter Shade of Brown, and in the UK of course Apache Indian, Fun^Da^Mental, as well as the mixed-race line-ups of so many UK soul bands like Galliano and the sound systems of On U Sound and Tackhead) is easier made from this side of the Atlantic, but this does not mean that Gilroy's argument against 'ethnic absolutism' has no place here (Gilroy 1993). The absence of an anti-essentialist perspective in *Microphone Fiends* does not devalue the new critical vocabulary which is developed in these pieces. Lipsitz, for example, sees rap as the voice of aggrieved communities pushed down so mercilessly that it is a testimony to the power of black youth that it rises up with such magnificent fantasies, with graffiti tags, with names which place, displace and 'mock the world'.

Lipsitz describes the jagged movement through the city of the hip hop crews as they repossess it. Hip hop takes on board symbolically not just the laws of private property but also capital's other prized possession, the commodity form itself. The apparent celebration of consumption, the songs about cars, jeeps and trainers, jewellery, clothes and chunks of gold confound sociological analysis by their inflated, ironic and also prosaic tones. The puzzle to the conventional radical imagination is why those for whom so often 'money's too tight to mention' should profess such love for and faith in the commodity. Gilroy (1994) has recently unpacked this deep irony, but Lipsitz here sees in it a kind of aesthetic of mimicry and, otherwise, a hyperbolic version of the desperate narcissism of adolescence and the sheer need for pleasure; while Rose points out that rap is never either fully on the side of the commodity or in opposition to it. This reflects a point I shall make later in relation to girls and music – it is that we should be less surprised than we sometimes are that the space of political articulation in culture from groups who have grown up under different historical conditions from those on the left, or even those within the anti-racist orbit of the late 1960s, is entirely different. It cannot be neatly anchored into a more familiar and therefore more comfortable language of socialist analysis.

What we see in the deliberately provocative 'shocking' language of rap is a response which is not just addressed to the hostile white environment into which these young people found themselves flung, but which is also a generational gesture of defiance to other sections of the black community, including the intellectuals to whom they will not be accountable. Thus the black politics of rap refuses to be tied down to any consensual notion of inequality, discrimination or even injustice. But this does not mean it must devolve into representing a subcultural separatism. Rap does not stand for the inevitable stratification of the black community; instead it provokes a dialogue, a fluid set of exchanges, a kind of dance of differences, where strong identity does not mean unchanging identity and where rap insists on being listened to. In this sense it parallels theory; it says in musical form what Laclau argues for theoretically, a pluralism which continually interrogates its boundaries, which is always crossing over (Laclau 1990). For Tricia Rose rap is quite literally 'black urban renewal'. Set against the no-longer-needed populations and wasted labour powers of the post-industrial society, rap 're-imagines urban life' with its open air communities circled round the ghetto blaster, with its street corner microphones-cum-soap-boxes plugged into the city electricity supplies (i.e. the lamp-posts) for the necessary amplification. It is hard not to participate in the pleasure of this 'aggressive insubordination'.

With these kinds of political gymnastics going on, and with the smooth, beautiful soundtrack of the cinematic parody of ghetto nihilism, *Menace 2 Society*, demonstrating more than even Snoopy Doggy Dogg that music actually stops nihilism in its tracks, that it holds it back, that it articulates a space of work and creativity and *tension* which is also one of hope, a hair's breadth in these cases away from the enveloping despair of poverty and drugs, then it is not surprising that 'rock' is dislodged, not to say negated. Once rock also stood for these things, but with less good reason, and it also spoke for 'youth' but, as we know, for only one section of it.

Grossberg recognizes this and proclaims the death of rock not just from the viewpoint of 'new ethnicities' but also as a whole new media economy comes into being where images connect more directly with sound through the growth of the promotional video as well as MTV. With the fragmentation and undermining of the older rock identities, what springs up in its place is a musical and visual language of 'authentic inauthenticity' most clearly expressed in the Pet Shop Boys. This is the crisis of rock, that it can no longer claim to be authentic. While Frith refuses the challenge posed by a fullblown crisis of rock, he too points to the new musical economies of global markets, of record companies through their TV companies making 'independent documentaries' about their own stable of stars for sale and broadcast across the world. The issues raised by both Frith and Grossberg are fleshed out into debates about nation, state and policy in the various contributions to *Rock and Popular Music*. But by this time rock is a more questionable category than many of the contributors seem willing to admit. The anti-theoretical stance in the book is also evident in its conventional approach to questions of policy, state and power. This is despite the suggestion of a Foucauldian approach hinted at in the title of the first section, 'Government and Rock'. The avoidance of such a perspective is a pity because the application of Foucault would surely unveil the power of 'rock' as residing precisely in its pleasurable incitements to be aroused in body and, particularly in the case of black musics, also in 'soul'.

Meanwhile, once again the musicians do what theory here ought to be doing. In articles written before Kurt Cobain of Nirvana killed himself, Joanne Gottlieb and Gayle Wald in *Microphone Fiends*, and Simon Reynolds and Joy Press in *Sex Revolts*, point out that Cobain consciously addresses the femininity embedded in the male psyche; he grapples with it and, as we now know, submitted to it in a kind of death drive taking him literally back to where his music also goes, which is to the 'blissed out' oblivion of the pre-oedipal (Reynolds 1988). Michael Stipe of REM also explores the death of rock through the terminal sadness of his lyrics. Like Cobain he occasionally appears on stage in a dress and in this respect he too is acknowledging what all the previous 'rebel rockers' with their eyeliner and pouting could not bring themselves to admit, that they were not 'men'. So in both these musicians' sense of displacement, in their moving over to let both the feminine in and also to let women speak on their behalf as Courtney Love so volably did, they do the work of theory and analysis in their requiems to rock.

Unfortunately there is not much room left now for sex, although the drift of the argument can already be seen in the inflated sexual rhetoric of the rappers and the deflated sexual sadness of the white boys. But where does this leave the girls? The piece on Riot Grrrls in *Microphone Fiends* is particularly interesting for its rcognition that the kind of 'independent' music produced by the American Riot Grrrls no longer exists out on the margins of musical culture in the way their punk feminist predecessors did back in the late 1970s. The boundaries between what constitutes 'alternative' culture and what constitutes the 'main-stream' are decidely blurry in this discussion' (p. 252).

Thus Courtney Love and her band Hole, with the angry 'pornographic' baby doll sexuality they parodied, moved rapidly from the outer reaches of subculture right into the heartland of American popular culture. The point being that, as Sarah Thornton rightly points out in her contribution to *Microphone Fiends*, the youth mass media, particularly the music press and the style magazines, do not just represent subcultures but actively construct them. They are part of the noise of the music. So developed are they this time that with the help of cheap new print technology the 'micromedia' of youth cultures become mass media almost instantly. For our purposes here this means that deviant femininities and sexualities are no longer confined to the margins; they too are now part of the mainstream. Like the rappers, in their response to the black radicals and intel-lectuals, the Riot Grrrls are addressing much vitriol to the older generation of feminists who were much too polite and 'ladylike' in their sexual politics. 'How far did it get you?', they seem to be asking. And this time there are more young women listening to, or at least watching, MTV.

Looking more at the mainstream of the record industry, Lisa Lewis in *Sound and Vision* disputes the idea that, here, women performers are still fodder for male consumption. By examining in depth Cyndi Lauper's role in producing as well as performing in her videos, Lewis shows how much more active women are in every stage of musical production than is commonly imagined. Moreover, she suggests that new female audiences are created in response to these more active sexualities being presented on screen. She takes the argument even further, suggesting that authors and audiences 'align' themselves in the text and in front of the text and that the transparent popularity of this new femi-ninity provides spaces for further changes in the field of popular music. How-ever, it is left to Reynolds and Press to produce what is by far the most systematic and also ferocious critique of the complicated misogyny of 'rock'.

In *Sex Revolts* these writers draw imaginatively on theorists like Theweleit, Kristeva, Deleuze and Guattari and apply this critical psychoanalytic vocabulary to the posturing of the rebel rockers. It is virtually impossible to do justice to this huge 'book of accounts' except to say that by subjecting the history of postwar rock (i.e. almost entirely white males) to detailed analysis of lyrics, looks and performancers, the authors equate the rebel with masculine irresponsibility, with grievances that 'they' are somehow constrained through 'momism', family and everything else that ties young men down. The Rolling Stones with their 'effete dandyism and cruel machismo' come in for particular attack on the grounds that they take up the 'privileges' of femininity (Jagger in skirt at Hyde Park, Brian Jones adopting a conscious androgyny) while simultaneously belittling women for their frivolousness and stupidity.

This is a theme which is then amplified and extended as rock progresses through to punk in the 1970s. The authors cast a much more scathing eye over Malcolm McLaren's attempt to bring the figure of the 'Cambridge Rapist' into the iconography of punk than other writers on punk have done so far. They then take the reader through an exhaustive trip of male fantasies as expressed in rock, from the odyssey of the road and the flight from domesticity, through the elevation of the machine to the search for symbolic world domination found in Jim Morrison's drug-induced, self-aggrandisement ('I am king', he proclaimed and believed). This flight of the male super-ego in rock is also an attempt to stave off 'abjection' and the fear of being engulfed by the disgusting and the feminine. In an extraordinary analysis of the Sex Pistols' song 'Submission', the authors see the male terror of being suffocated by female appetite, and in John Lennon's 'Mother' they see him howling out for more nurturing, for more of everything. In *Sex Revolts* the history of rock (occasionally opened up to include recent black music) becomes indeed much more than that. It becomes a history of post-war culture. The authors even look at what happens to these heroes when they tire of rampant individualism and want to come home. From Van Morrison to Bono to Sting they all then imbue that too with either a heavy dose of mysticism or with the comfort and relief of 'true love' at long last.

I want to end with a few points which relate first to *Sex Revolts*, possibly the best book ever on 'rock' and also one which, through a rigorous feminist critique, also contributes decisively to the death of rock. The music can never quite sound the same again. However, the positions taken up by these rock heroes are also already in place in culture, waiting for them, even if they are reworked to sound new or more extreme than what has come before (which is exactly the task rap sets itself). Second, how on earth do we reconcile the force of this analysis with the way in which the music itself is still good enough to make us want to listen to it? Why, if Nick Cave is so enmeshed in the ethics of violence and is one who sees women as death, do I make the trip to Shepherd's Bush last month to see him play live and find it an indescribably pleasurable performance? Do I forfeit both my femininity and my feminism in the process, or is the consumption of music a more complex, more layered experience than the lyrics and the attitudes described on the printed page imply? Is it that men still have, in art and in culture, a kind of patriarchal entitlement to exploring the extremities of emotion? It is vitally important that Reynolds and Press impress upon us the magnitude of this power. But it is also important and intellectually necessary that extremities do get to be expressed. So, in a sense, both the expressions themselves and the Reynolds and Press critique help us try and work out where we stand as women. For some young black women music writers like dream hampton, for example, the question is simple (hampton 1994). She is with Snoop Doggy Dogg on the basis of his racial anger and she can easily throw off the derogatory sexual stereotypes. Indeed the real issue is that there is often as much identification with these extremities on the part of women as there is with the men. The 'difference' is, in psychoanalytic terms, that girls and women never quite manage to separate from the 'parent culture' with such tidal waves of energy and force. As Jacqueline Rose and Juliet Mitchell have both pointed out, psychic history and patriarchal power still weigh heavily enough on daughters to position them in endless vacillatin and ambivalence. They are both at home *and* on the road (Mitchell 1974; Rose 1987).

This article first appeared in (1995) *Media Culture & Society*, Vol. 17 and was published as a review article in response to the following publications:

Reynolds S. and Press J. (1994) *Sex Revolts*, London: Serpent's Tail.
Ross A. and Rose I. (eds) (1994) *Microphone Fiends: Youth Music and Youth Culture*, New York and London: Routledge.
Frith S., Goodwin A. and Grossberg L. (eds) (1993) *Sound and Vision: The Music Video Reader*, London: Routledge.
Bennett T., Frith S., Grossberg L., Shepherd J., Turner G. (eds) 1994, *Rock and Popular Music: Politics, Policies, Institutions*. London: Routledge.

References

Baker Jr, H.A. (1993) *Black Studies, Rap and the Academy*, Chicago: University of Chicago Press.
Brunsdon, C. (1981) '*Crossroads*: Notes on a Soap Opera', *Screen* 22(4): 32–44.
Cohen, S. (1987) 'Society and Culture in the Making of Rock Music in Liverpool', PhD Thesis, Oxford University (published as Cohen, 1991).
—— (1991) *Rock Culture in Liverpool: Popular Music in the Making*, Oxford: Clarendon Press.
Finnegan, R. (1989) *Hidden Musicians*, Cambridge: Cambridge University Press.
Frith, S. (1988) *Music For Pleasure*, Cambridge: Polity Press.
—— (1992) 'The Cultural Study of Popular Music', L. Grossberg, C. Nelson and P. Treichler (eds) *Cultural Studies*, New York and London: Routledge, pp. 174–86.
Frith, S. and McRobbie, A. (1978) 'Rock and Sexuality', *Screen Education*, 29.
Frith, S. and Savage, J. (1993) 'Pearls and Swine: The Intellectuals and the Mass Media', *New Left Review*, No. 198: 107–16.
Gilroy, P. (1987) *There Ain't No Black In The Union Jack: The Cultural Politics of Race and Nation*, London: Hutchinson.
—— (1993) *The Black Atlantic: Modernity and Double Consciousness*, London: Verso.
—— (1994) 'Downtown and Doggystyle: Bio-Politics and Etho-Poetics in the Black Public Sphere' in *Public Culture*, Fall.
Gilroy, P. *et al.* (eds) (1982) *The Empire Strikes Back*, London: Hutchinson.

Goodwin, A. (1993) *Dancing in The Distraction Factory: Music, Television and Popular Culture*, London: Routledge.

Gray, A. (1987) 'Reading The Audience', *Screen*, 28(3): 48–62.

Hall, S. (1989) 'The Meaning of New Times', S. Hall and M. Jacques (eds) *New Times: The Changing Face of Politics in the 1990s*, London: Lawrence & Wishart, pp. 15–33.

Hall, S., Critcher, C., Jefferson, T., Clarke, J. and Roberts, B. (eds) (1979) *Policing the Crisis: Mugging, the State and Law and Order*, London: Macmillan.

hampton, d. (1994) 'Women and Rap' unpublished paper delivered at New Directions in Popular Music Conference, New York University.

Hobson, D. (1982) *'Crossroads': Drama of a Soap Opera*, London: Methuen.

Julien, I. (1994) 'A Darker Shade of Black', *Arena* – BBC Television (March).

Laclau, E. (1990) *New Reflections on the Revolutions of Our Time*, London: Verso.

Mitchell, J. (1974) *Psychoanalysis and Feminism*, Harmondsworth: Penguin.

Reynolds, S. (1988) *Blissed Out*, London: Serpent's Tail.

Rose, J. (1987) 'Femininity and Its Discontents', *Sexuality: A Reader* (*Feminist Review* special issue), London: Virago, pp. 177–98.

Spencer, J.M. (ed.) (1993) *The Emergency of Black and the Emergence of Rap Black Sacred Music: A Journal of Theomusicology*, 5(1) Special issue, Spring, Carolina: Duke University Press.

Steward, S. and Garratt, S. (1984) *Signed, Sealed and Delivered: True Life Stories of Women and Pop*, London: Pluto Press.

9

PECS AND PENISES

The meaning of girlie culture

In February 1996 Tory MP Peter Luff presented a Private Member's Bill which sought to require that 'teen' magazines carry a sticker giving the appropriate age-range of readers. Luff had purchased a copy of the innocently-titled *Sugar* for his daughter and had been horrified by the contents. Instead of harmless boarding-school stories there was graphically illustrated information about sex, and about how girls can give and receive sexual pleasure. At about the same time the family entertainment magazine *TV Hits* (purchased and read mostly by young adolescents) carried in its advice column a question, and fairly detailed answer, about oral sex. In the few weeks following, and running up to the presentation of the Bill, a moral panic of some scale reverberated across the media. This took the by-now predictable course of outrage and condemnation about the corruption of childhood innocence, followed by calls for 'something to be done'. In the event the Bill failed, as expected, but strong pressure was put on the publishers to set up a regulatory body to monitor their own practice and to ensure the appropriateness of the information given in the magazines. In itself this is not a bad thing since it will force the magazine industry to account for itself. In the past, girls' and women's magazines have been considered so trivial that nobody ever thought to ask them to take responsibility for what they publish.

What was most noticeable, however, was how opinion was divided along the lines of gender. It was men like Darcus Howe, presenting Channel 4's *The Devil's Advocate*, who were most outraged and it was they who did not like the idea of their daughters finding out about sex in a way they did not think appropriate. It seemed as though men still thought that sex for girls and women should be presented in the guise of Barbara Cartland-style romance, in soft focus and without too many questions being asked. Anything more than this appeared to make them feel uncomfortable, as men or as fathers, even though they would in all probability expect their teenage sons to be reading *Penthouse* under the bedclothes. And of course in another guise it is men who provide the primary consumer market for explicit sexual material in films, magazines and newspapers like *Sunday Sport*. At any rate these men did not seem to like the new frankness and the rude jokes found on the pages of the new magazines.

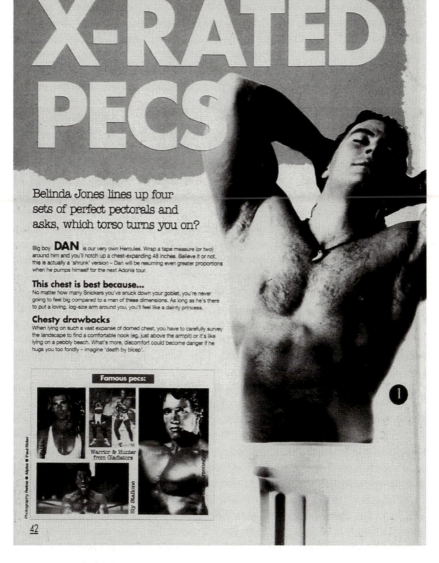

Figure 9.1 X-rated pecs

There were, in contrast, very few women on the television panels or in the studio audiences who took the same view. Most thought it better to know the facts at an early age to avoid unwanted pregnancy and to be confident enough to have sex without feeling forced into it. The information provided in the magazines, they argued, gave girls a bit of bargaining power – they would know what to expect, and they would be in a stronger position to negotiate new emotional and physical experiences. Counsellors from family planning agencies argued that magazines like these served a useful function and were more effective at getting the safe sex message across than most other means. They also reminded us of how many young women still remain uninformed about sex and their own bodies. There even emerged a current approval for the joky way in which sex was talked about in the magazines. The double standard for too long had meant that only men and boys could treat sex lightheartedly. Pleasure and enjoyment, fun and jokes on the subject of sex were hardly going to threaten the moral fabric of the nation, especially when 'dirty jokes' told to and by men had for so long been a part of male culture. This point was made by several groups of young women themselves, who held their ground against the formidable presence of Darcus Howe by insisting that reading about different ways of having sex did not necessarily mean that fourteen year olds across the country were going to go out and do the things about which they had just read. It was also noticeable that all the editors of the magazines from *Just Seventeen* and *Mizz* to *Sugar* and *More!* were also female. They too spoke in the language of what is now called 'popular feminism'. Female assertiveness, being in control and enjoying sex, are now recognised as entitlements, and the struggle for equality with men and boys starts young. Forced to defend the kind of features they regularly run about masturbation, fantasy and orgasm, what was significant was the surprise, indeed shock, on the part of the men that women – and young women especially – actually wanted to read this stuff. It was as though they were suddenly forced to recognise that 'girls' were no longer sweet and innocent and that women were no longer 'ladylike'.

Commercial culture, in the form of the magazines, has devised a better way of 'doing' sex education than any of the official agencies. By developing a humorous language of 'pecs and penises', the magazines have broken the grip of clinical terminology. If, as Darcus Howe sharply pointed out, the magazines were doing more than educating young readers into the use of condoms, what kind of sexuality are the readers being presented with? Is it better or worse than the diet of romance and beaches-at-sunset which used to fill the pages of *Jackie*?

Although when set against the landscape of major political debate, issues like this are of minor importance, they nonetheless touch upon a bigger set of changes which have indeed exercised politicians. This has been most manifest in anxieties about young single mothers and the decline in family values. It has also surfaced in debates about young women becoming more aggressive. But what I am referring to here is the deeper change in consciousness which has affected the outlook, values and expectations of women and young women, from different social backgrounds, from different parts of the country, from different cultures. It is difficult to generalize across such a large sector of the population. It is not as though women share anything like a single set of values or beliefs. Nor has change affected women homogeneously. By exploring the

Figure 9.2 Sugar! Sex special: Courtesy of EMAP–ELAN

climate of change in the culture of young women today one is tapping into something which exists in a state of disaggregated latency, a 'semi-structure of feeling' to rephrase Raymond Williams, which surfaces at unexpected moments in unexpected ways. But its presence is a sure sign that there has been some deep and apparently irreversible shift across the whole social domain. These transformations find symbolic form in the consumer-culture of young people, and in particular young women's culture. If they strike a note of discord or discomfort among some feminists, as much as among the male moral guardians of left and right, then this does not mean that feminists of my generation should discount them as politically insignificant.

Indeed it is disappointing that feminists have tended only to see the negative dimensions in girls 'behaving badly' on the pages of magazines and on television programmes like *The Girlie Show*. It is not enough to write this off as girls simply becoming like boys. Yet even if they are playing at what it is like to be a lad, this in itself is an interesting phenomenon. Our own surprise at the apparent pleasure young women seem to get from subjecting men and boys to the kind of treatment they have come to expect, by virtue of being a girl, is a mark of just how unexpected this kind of response is. One young woman recently described to *Women's Realm* how 'we sit in a cafe on the quayside eyeing up male runners as they pass by. For years men have talked about women as though they're pieces of meat. Now we say "look at the state of that bum, two out of ten", or "Get a load of this crumpet"'. This kind of reverse sexism can also be seen as a riposte to an older generation of feminists whom younger women now see as weary, white and middle class, academic and professional, and certainly not spunky, vulgar or aggressive. Coming across as loutish and laddish is a provocation to a generation of feminists now established as figures of authority. This dynamic of generational antagonism has been overlooked by professional feminists, particularly those in the academy, with the result that the political effectivity of young women is more or less ignored. And yet various studies show, for example, that the politicization of older Asian women around issues of domestic violence comes from the agitation and encouragement of their daughters and from younger women in the community. To these young women official feminism is something that belongs to their mothers' generation. They have to develop their own language for dealing with sexual inequality, and if they do this through a raunchy language of 'shagging, snogging and having a good time', then perhaps the role this plays is not unlike the sexually explicit manifestoes found in the early writing of figures like Germaine Greer and Sheila Rowbotham. The key diference is that this language is now found in the mainstream of commercial culture – not out there in the margins of the 'political underground'.

Charlotte Brunsdon has recently argued that in commercial culture, particularly in Hollywood cinema, feminism increasingly plays a role as reference point; it informs a good deal of narrative action, but at the same time it is also disavowed, even repudiated (Brunsdon 1997). In the end the heroine opts for marriage to some Richard Gere-type male. But this does not wholly invalidate the presence of feminism as a tension, a productive force for moving things on. Here feminism can be seen as having entered the public psyche. In a similar way teen magazines often seem to set out deliberately to provoke a feminist response as a way of setting themselves apart from an older generation concerned with more serious issues. They do this by 'doing gender' in an exaggerated and ironic way. If 1970s feminists argued that make-up and fashion turned girls and women into commodities, then these magazines overdo the make-up and the fashion, without resorting to the old sexist repertoire of female competition, anxiety and neurosis. As Brunsdon notes in relation to *Clueless*, the Hollywood film devoted to teenage female consumerism, cultural forms like these turn femininity into a performance. Gender is dramatized and girls can even play the old-fashioned game of romance as long as they know it is all a bit of a joke. Ironic distance works to give girls room to breathe; it gives them space to explore new emotional ground on their own terms, it designates a place of playful thinking and exploration, away from the watchful eye of their elders. The editors of the magazines understand this, partly because many of them are still in their twenties and close enough to their readers to recognize the need for separation and autonomy. This is the trick of the successful magazine: it intervenes in a space which attempts to defend itself from the critical voice of mothers, teachers and feminist academics. It is one thing to do 'women's magazines' at university, by which time many young women are thinking about looking for jobs in this kind of field: it is quite different to be thirteen and have your culture ridiculed for not being serious enough, or for not covering the right kind of feminist issues.

Women's studies academic Stevi Jackson, for example, seems bewildered by the contents of the new magazines (Jackson 1996). Her argument is strongest when she suggests that magazines still take heterosexuality as the norm. She deplores the ways in which female sexuality continues to be organized around fashion, beauty and personal appearance as if for male consumption. But she has to admit that many feminist lessons have been portrayed. Yet even if heterosexuality is taken for granted in the magazines, does this mean that we consign them to the dustbin of patriarchy? Or can we see them as disruptive, more open-ended, more disputatious forms? Jackson is right to say that heterosexuality is the norm. It would be difficult to imagine *More!* (designed for eighteen year olds but read gleefully by fourteen year olds) carrying a 'Position of the Fortnight' feature for lesbians. This in itself shows how magazines see their own limits and, in so doing, it also reveals how sexuality remains something continually inscribed within boundaries – but boundaries which are fluid and permeable. Lesbianism on these pages remains a social issue rather than a sexual desire. Even when *Just Seventeen* ran a piece recently about 'Girls Who Fancy Girls', the feature itself seemed strangely enclosed. It did not tip over onto the fashion pages; it was as though the feature was describing a separate world. Lesbianism remains perhaps the touchstone, its existence marking the line between 'popular commercial feminism' and 'real feminism'. But there is no inherent reason why this too might not change. Consumer culture shows itself elsewhere open to those who can afford to participate, as the growth of the pink pound demonstrates. In the more sophisticated world of women's magazines, including *Elle* and *Marie Claire*, 'lesbian chic' now has an uncontroversial existence.

Nowadays there are many competing feminisms; who is to say which version is better than any other? Or at least let us put that question on the agenda. The tone in Jackson's article is that of the feminist expert, surveying the state of women's and girls' magazines from afar. Almost inevitably they fail to meet the mark. However, the question that feminism rarely asks itself these days is what exactly it is looking for in young women. What does it expect of them, what should they be like? What should magazines be saying to them? What kind of relationship does 1970s feminism envisage itself having with young women growing up in the 1990s? More generally, how does feminism today connect with 'ordinary women'? What does it mean if, as I suggest here, 'ordinary women' are themselves set upon improving, often against the odds, their own lives and those of their daughters? How does feminism connect with this new emergent consciousness of women and girls? How does it relate to the kind of feminist issues daily debated on television programmes, and even in the tabloid press? Are they just watered down, sanitized and de-politicized versions of feminism? Are they cynical attempts to up the ratings or the circulations by exploiting women's anxieties about sex, or are they actually capable of bringing about some change? How does one group of feminists, represented let us say by Stevi Jackson in one corner, respond to another group of young women, editors and journalists of magazines like *Just Seventeen*, *Mizz* and *Sugar*, many of them graduates of media studies and even women's studies, who also define themselves as 'feminist'?

It is my contention that there has been over the last few years a terrific determination among women to somehow transform and improve the conditions of their own existence and to find equality with men at home, at work and also at leisure. This has often been a long and painful process, but the gains of it are being passed on to daughters and to young women. There is an exchange going on between and across generations of women in living rooms and behind closed doors, inside the family, where the idea that women can achieve a good life for themselves – and that they need not rely on men or marriage to achieve – is increasingly prevalent. This accounts for the tremendous degree of change in family life. Nowadays if a young girl gets pregnant and wants to keep the baby her mother will encourage her to delay marriage rather than rush into it. In the old days it was a question of 'Will he do the decent thing and marry you?'. Now it is more likely to be 'Stay at home and continue with your studies, marriage can wait'. This kind of shift in attitude shows just how far sexual politics has penetrated the private sphere of the family. Paradoxically it would also be seen as a sign that solid family values actually prevail, since research shows that it is in this kind of context that young single mothers and their babies do best.

There is an enormous energy in the way in which sexual politics now bursts across our television screens. From *Newsnight* to *Oprah Winfrey* social issues of the day almost inevitably touch on changes for women in work, in the family and also even in the field of leisure. The private and public tensions around what it is to be a woman or young woman today also account for the energy and exuberance found in the popular cultural forms like magazines. Female independence has entered into contemporary common-sense, it is the very stuff of women's genres today; from women's and girls' magazines and television sitcoms to radio programmes like *Woman's Hour*. It has a particular resonance in British society where high divorce rates and the rising number of single-parent families have encouraged women to concentrate on careers and on organizing their own lives, with or without men. Sex, having fun and enjoying a sense of freedom, is one dimension of this new independence. If women are marrying later and if they are working hard for qualifications and good careers, then the idea of enjoying their leisure time becomes part of their social expectations. And if pleasure and leisure have left older women and mothers behind, they are not going to grudge their daughters the right to have some fun. I think in many ways it is this kind of sensibility which accounts for the hedonism and rowdy behaviour on the part of young women which has recently been brought to public attention. Beatrix Campbell recently explored the fashion for young women going out on the town and actively seeking pleasure (Campbell 1996). If this includes drinking or drugs, they make sure one of the group remains sober or clear-headed so that she can look after the others. Other writers have described how young women are as keen participants as their male counterparts in the dance culture based on taking ecstasy. As Sheila Henderson reports in *Druglink*, they quite openly talk about wanting to 'get out of their heads' (Henderson 1993). Indeed in the days following the death of Leah Betts an articulate eighteen year-old young woman joined a panel discussion on *Newsnight* refusing to condemn the drug, arguing that overall it was safer than alcohol, and that in terms of enjoyment it was 'a lovely drug'.

None of this is very appealing to politicians. The Labour Party has gone out of its way to support the family values platform and Jack Straw was predictably critical of the girls' magazines for encouraging the wrong kind of attitude. Women MPs from the Labour Party have had little to say of late on any of these issues and it was up to the Tory Teresa Gorman to challenge her party leader last year for unfairly scapegoating single mothers. Pressure groups and self-help groups have been much more vocal and articulate. And yet for the Labour Party this truly is a lost opportunity. To recognize the role of choice and diversity in family life and in sexual identity, to address women on their own as well as in the context of the family unit, to commit themselves to improving further the career opportunities for women and girls, and to develop a set of social policies which take into account the transformed landscape of family life today, would hardly be more radical for women than we find expressed in contemporary commercial cultures. Indeed, if anything, Labour is more anxious to break any conceivable connection with these kinds of ideas. The image of social respectability combined with respect for traditional family values leaves New Labour with nothing to say about current changes in family life. Questioned on these matters on the *Today* programme (following his speech on family values as necessary for the creation of a 'decent society' during a recent visit to South Africa), Tony Blair could not or would not say the word 'gay' in relation to family life – indeed he could hardly bring himself to say the words 'single parent'. All he could do was repeat the fact that children were best looked after by both parents living in the traditional family unit.

It is the care of children which really is an important issue, one which seems to have completely slipped the political net. If parents are going to divorce and possibly re-marry how can ways be found of avoiding the children absorbing the anger and disappointment that typically comes with the end of a relationship? Are there ways in which this kind of pain can be minimized, and can parents learn to act with the requisite responsibility? Should we be looking for guidelines on these kinds of family values? Feminism has played a role in making it possible for women not to feel that they have to remain miserable in marriage. Men, too, will often prefer to risk the emotional turmoil of divorce rather than put up with a partnership which is based only on antagonism and resentment. Is it not better that we recognize these as the new facts of life and try to think how children can survive and flourish when marriages dissolve, rather than try and return to a situation where marriage is for life?

Underpinning this is an even more awkward issue. Do new family values really mean remaining sexually faithful to one partner for life? Is this what is now expected of us? In the highly sexualized consumer culture in which we now live this seems extraordinarily limiting in human and social terms. But if we have to abide by these new rules in adult, if not in adolescent life, do we simply retreat into the world of sexual fantasy? Where sexual pleasure is now regarded as a social entitlement, and where sexuality is so prominently a part of consumer society, can we now be expected to relinquish this expectation and rely instead on finding ways of spicing up a marriage which has gone stale? Or must we confront something which really is a challenge to how we live as human beings today? How do we reconcile the diversity of sexual desires with our social responsibilities as parents? This poses a bold political challenge and New Labour might gain more respect by confronting such issues. Maybe Tony Blair is actually saying, without stating it, that sexual culture has gone too far and that we need to constrain desires and forego their dangerous currents in favour of the pleasures and rewards of everyday family life. The problem about developing policies based on values and ideals like these is that those who cannot fulfil such ideals, who through no fault of their own cannot get the 'true happiness' package together, are condemned as failures.

Ask most men or women how they would like to live and the chances are they might describe a scenario not unlike that envisaged by Tony Blair. But material and other circumstances simply do not allow that to be a reality for many people nowadays. Of course most women would want a partner who loved them, had a brilliant job, was a wonderful parent and a responsible, upright citizen. But we have at least learnt that this is a Barbara Cartland fantasy. Breaking down the myth of romantic love which most women have been exposed to in popular culture – and in teen magazines as they used to be – has been necessary for survival and for participating in a much crueller and more disappointing world. It has been a hard lesson for women to learn. To now have these fantasies foisted back upon us by the likes of Jack Straw is little less than insulting. In short, social and cultural change have moved further and faster than either the Labour Party or many feminists are willing to admit. We now have to run to catch up. The danger for feminism is that it remains unwilling to recognize that there are now many ways of being a woman or girl in contemporary society. The danger for Labour is that it fails to find a way of talking to women and to families at the same time. It also has to face up to the fact that the myth of the 2.4 family unit is as unrealistic as the belief that girls are still sugar and spice.

References

Brunsdon, C. (1997) *Screen Tastes*, London: Routledge.

Campbell, B. (1996) 'Girls on Safari', *Guardian*, 15 June.

Henderson, S. (1993) 'Time for a Make-Over' and 'Keep your Bra and Burn your Brain?', *Druglink*, Sept/Dec.

Jackson, S. (1996) 'Ignorance is Bliss: When you are Just Seventeen', *Trouble and Strife* 33.

10

THINKING WITH MUSIC

Who is that by?

Nowhere is the marriage between art and science more happily secured than in the extraordinary profusion of cheap-to-produce popular musics which over the last fifteen years or so have created a music-society to rival and even outstrip the image-society in which we now live. This forces a reassessment of what music means in everyday life but so prolific is the output of so many different genres, which converse with and against each other, that few critics seem capable of creating a credible map or writing a story of contemporary pop. Music-making defiantly slips the net of language, setting itself, as Susan Sontag memorably put it back in the 1960s, 'against interpretation'. Current music styles leapfrog backwards and forwards in time, snatching phrases, chords and strains of sound from unlikely sources, placing one on top the other, and making issues of authorship and ownership irrelevant. 'Who is that by?' becomes an absurdly naïve question. These musics play teasing, competitive games with the audience for whom, listening on the car radio or even half submerged in the local swimming pool, there is always the chance that they will never hear the same track again. (For a moment, last summer, I thought of getting out of the water at Archway pool in North London to ask the DJ/swimming attendant the name of the hip hop track that was playing. Its fluid interplay of spoken word and backing track so evoked the bare-bone aesthetics of rap that it was good enought to drown in.)

Hip hop and dance musics propose newness, not just from the application of bedroom size computer technology to old, discarded fragments of sounds, but also by forging a different relationship with their audiences. So energetically bound up are they with their own musical inventiveness, with what can, at the present moment, be done with music, that the DJs, musicians and producers can virtually ignore the audience in the same arrogant way that early punk did. So dispersed and fragmented, so volatile and widely spread, are the various audiences for contemporary music, that it seems almost pointless to think who it will please or who would want to buy this record. This allows music to turn in on itself and enjoy a moment of almost sublime self-confidence. This challenge to the audience is reflected in the challenge to the critic – or to the sociologist – we too seem suddenly redundant. What role is there now for criticism or analysis?

Indeed our critical vocabulary seems sadly lacking. None of the old words, like collage, montage, or postmodernism, seem capable of capturing the velocity and scale of this output. Likewise, the older ways of making sense of music by placing different styles into different categories, or by posing the commercial against the creative or experimental, or by talking about white or black music as though they were quite distinct, are equally inappropriate. Now, in the late 1990s, we have to start with an assumption of musical hybridity, with global cultural cross-over and profound inter-penetrations of style, coupled with a reliance on often quite basic machines to engineer a quality of DIY eclecticism with which even the huge and wealthy record companies have trouble knowing what to do. Music, in short, has become 'artificially intelligent'.

Faced with the sheer challenge which music production poses, music writing and commentary in the more academic journals has actually pursued a fairly predictable course. The claim that current dance music styles appear to embrace a refusal of meaning, in the same way that they suggest a refusal of authorship and authenticity, is patently banal and unsatisfactory; and the conclusion which follows, which sees only political nihilism in sharp contrast to the political verve of punk, is equally fallacious and ahistorical.

Jeremy Gilbert has recently argued that 'However nihilistic they may have seemed at the time, not even Joy Division . . . can really be located outside this discourse of protest' (Gilbert 1997). But the problem with this kind of account is that it posits a style of music, i.e. punk, even in its most nihilistic form, as being inherently close to politics, as though politics was this quantifiable, identifiable thing at the centre of social life. Current dance music in comparison pursues a logic of pure pleasure rather than politics, and thus confirms the essentially apolitical identity of young people in Britain in the late 1990s. Gilbert explains this in terms of the rave generation's frustration with 'mainstream political culture'. Rave too is nihilistic but it just, and no more, manages to rescue itself from the slur of having no politics whatsoever by refusing at least to share the nostalgic stage of national pride with Blur, Oasis and the other white boys of Britpop. In a similar vein, the search for politics continues in Hemment's suggestion that 'The ecstatic dance is not in itself political, but it is a micropolitical event – an intervention in the formation of desire' (Hemment 1997). Finally, Hesmondhalgh warns against too easy a confirmation of the democratic potential of dance music on the grounds of these same features of authorless music, imagined and produced largely outside the corporate cultures of the big music companies (Hesmondhalgh 1997). This is misleading, he argues, because it overlooks how dance music producers also get sucked into the star mythology of name DJs and the attraction of a record deal with a major company. Yet, despite this, Hesmondhalgh still wants to hold the torch for dance. Even though drum 'n' bass has become 'yuppie cocktail music', he acknowledges in this music the 'often thrilling mixture of the dark and the uplifting'. In all three cases, and indeed across the field of writing academically about music, where it is recognised that in some complicated way something political is at stake, there is this same tension.

It is certainly not satisfactory to discount the political dynamic from the viewpoint that 'it's just music, after all'; nor are most left critics willing to adhere to the argument that the writing and the discussion somehow spoil the whole experience, that it robs the music of its whole reason to exist (as one of my own students recently put it). Perhaps the approach should be not to search for a political and theoretical vehicle of such sophistication that it does justice to the significance of the phenonemon (which is how the presence of Deleuze and Guattari in the footnotes inevitably appears), but rather to be more realistic about the politics of music and the people who make the music, and adopt a more pragmatic, sociological approach, based on the question of what academics can say or do which might be useful. This would not mean the courting of political approval from a government attuned to the significance of the culture industries (indeed with a culture industries strategy high on the agenda) by producing a string of policies, or 'good ideas' out of a hat. Quite the opposite. It might well mean asking very awkward questions of a government determined to use pop to look modern. But neither would such an approach simply succumb to the temptation to replace politics with theory, as though 'making sense' is achieved exclusively at that point where some convincing analogies can be drawn between a musical form and the frequently opaque writing of a number of French philosophers (enjoyable though such an attempt might be).

Livelihoods in music

The more politically relevant point is surely that music today is also a place of employment, livelihoods and labour markets. This fact is obscured because being creative remains in our collective imaginations as a sort of dream-world or utopia, far apart from the real world of earning a living; and the irony is that the philosophers are as spellbound by the idea of art and creativity as the rest of us. Baudrillard, for example, is reported to have said that the real attraction of retirement is that it means he can become a real writer, an artist no less. The popular music industry has drawn upon the conventional language of genius, talent and charismatic personality, which is how modern society has understood the role of the artist. The artist is the romantic outsider whose exceptional gifts are manifest in how different he (occasionally she) is from the rest of us. But this is now a hopelessly anachronistic way of understanding music (and art) production in Britain in the 1990s. For a start there are a lot more people making music and hoping to earn a living from doing so – this is no longer a completely futile dream. The old jobs, which for many people meant a lifetime of unrewarding labour, have gone for ever and there has been instilled into a younger generation, at some deep level, a determination for work to mean something more than a hard slog, for work to become a labour of love, a source of creative reward, a sort of poetics of living. For working-class boys (less so for girls) without qualifications, to turn youth culture into a job creation scheme has become one possible thing to do. Too easily do we forget, in the demonic media-typecasting of young, often black, males on the fringes of criminality, the small humiliations and indignities of low paid, low status labour.

What an escape then, to move into music. It has been through this process of 'choosing culture' that the discovery of talent, imagination and even musical genius has occurred, in some cases transporting the individual from a career in crime (e.g. the rap artist Coolio) in the space of one record. In Britain the startlingly diverse and imaginative urban soundscapes of Manchester and Glasgow, Bristol and London, are an index of the scale of wastage which was (and still is) the mark of a class-divided society, where middle-class children had (and have) every ounce of talent nurtured like a precious thing as a matter of course while the rest could quite easily have never known they had it in them. But even this does not exhaust the issues posed by the changes brought about by the culture society. How much music and how many musicians can the new culture-society accommodate? What kind of livings are being made? How can we gauge the span of talent and creativity? Who judges what constitutes musical genius? Indeed, this line of enquiry can even be taken to the opposite extreme by suggesting that, at some level, to those now doing the producing, the questions, how good is it? or, is it great art? are somehow less relevant. These are replaced instead by a sense of exploring further some very particular musical direction in a way which is uninterrupted by other, commercial constraints. We can see this particularly in the new musics being produced by figures like Roni Size and his colleagues, and also Björk.

With creative work now accounting for a much greater number of livelihoods, it may well be the case that in the process some of the old romantic notions have already slipped by the wayside. Artistic work has become more ordinary, it has been edged off its pedestal and turned into more common currency. It is not just that the art schools are churning out more graduates; further down the hierarchy there are any number of BTEC courses in sound production, studio engineering and computer programming, and the students who enrol on these have been mixing tracks in their bedrooms since they were twelve and see quite clearly that electronics and engineering no longer mean working for the Electricity Board or for British Steel. The emphasis on the skill rather than on stardom does not mean that the utopian dynamics of these new apprenticeships for the night-time economies of dance and club culture are denied. Quite the reverse. Here we have, with the growth of cultural capitalism, something similar to the scenario Marx himself looked forward to: cooking, looking after the children and doing the ironing in the morning, writing lyrics and composing tracks on the home computer in the afternoon, and playing them for money in the evening! Caspar Melville describes how this happens in the world of drum 'n' bass: 'It is not unusual for producers like Grooverider and 4Hero to make a piece of music in the daytime and play it "out" at a club in the evening' (Melville 1997).

How this kind of activity will work out in the post-welfare society remains to be seen. How much of the labour market can culture mop up? What kind of livings are there to be made in this cultural society? Are we witnessing the emergence in Britain of a new kind of low pay, labour intensive, cultural economy comprising of a vast network of freelance and self-employed 'creative people'? What sort of issues for government will be thrown up by the emergence of this kind of workforce as a long-term phenomenon? Are they all dutifully paying their national insurance stamps? Have they already attended to their private pension plans? How does self-employment tally with the high cost of parenting? It is doubly difficult to get a real grip on these economics when they encompass such vast differences of income, from the now incredible wealth of The Prodigy to the modest living of Grandmaster Flash, for example. At the same time, what all these performers (including the twelve year olds in their bedrooms) have in common is the possibility of producing cheap music by having access to sophisticated, home-based computer equipment.

The opportunities made available by these machines were spotted early by figures like Grandmaster Flash who learnt how to refine the art of mixing from the electronics course he was doing at technical school and then proceeded to combine this knowledge with his curiosity for old records, which stemmed from his fascination with his father's record collection, locked away and out of reach of children's hands. As he said to David Toop, 'I would tiptoe up to the closet, turn the knob, go inside the closet and take a record' (Toop 1984). Being able to make music within the budget of pocket money and a Saturday job has also been a key factor in the prodigious expansion of tracks, twenty years after the birth of hip hop. It is how the first Prodigy album was cut, with Liam Howlett literally walking in to the record company off the street with a sequence of rave songs recorded in his bedroom. This is now common history, but the celebrity culture which almost immediately gears itself up for marketing musical success obscures what the local economies look like in the longer term. As far as I know, no attempt has been made, for example, to chart how current DJ careers are pursued in Britain, how many of them there are plying their trade, and how sustainable these careers are.

An avant-garde of the self taught?

But obviously all this activity does count more than just economically. Contemporary music culture embraces the banal and the sublime but because most popular music still registers in the cultural hierarchies as 'untutored' or 'untrained', associated with talent, emotion and sensuality, its cerebral and socio-economic significance is often overlooked. (In a recent *Desert Island Discs* Sue Lawley rather snootily asked Jools Holland if he was 'self-taught'.) Critics

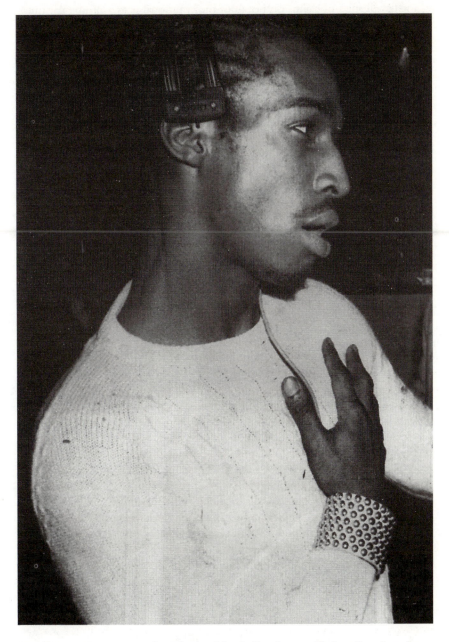

Figure 10.1 Adventures on the Wheels of Steel: Grandmaster Flash at Broadway International: Courtesy of Pat Bates

can make all sorts of claims on behalf of the emotional power of popular music but rarely, if ever, do they dare propose a thinking role. As French sociologist, Pierre Bourdieu, would explain, if it is sensual and immediately gratifying then it must belong to the lower social classes and thus be perceived as incapable of the depth and complexity found in the high arts and enjoyed by the educated social classes. It has been up to black writers in Britain like Paul Gilroy to demonstrate just how much thinking there is in black music. Such music can hardly contain the investment of artistry and politics and history and literary voice so that, as an aesthetic, it is, by definition, spilling out and over-flowing, excessive, a first destination for social commentary, dialogue and rap which leaves those of us still caught in the 'prison house of language' far behind. But no establishment person on the quality press or elsewhere ever gives it the accolade of calling it a spectacular avant-garde, which is what it is. (Although it is also perhaps true that the popular, black idiom of this kind of musical activity also exposes the underpinnings, limits and exclusions of the term 'avant-garde'.)

It is not just music which is directly connected with black culture which provides a language of analysis and critique for its practitioners. Popular music in Britain provides an accessible, relatively open aesthetics for those who want to play. It can be something to think with and with which to explore class and history, city and space, sexuality, identity and tradition. And it is because this capacity has been grabbed as a kind of philosophical lifeline by some of the most interesting figures in this particular urban, post-war landscape that much music means more than just pop. The way in which British pop has become particularly aware of its capacity for reflecting on all sorts of sexual anxieties, as well as other national obsessions, has been commented on since the early 1980s. The Pet Shop Boys and Morrissey are usually held up as prime exemplars of this, masters of surface poise, gentle irony, and explorers of white, polite masculinity. There is a problem, however, when debate gets narrowly focused on the work of performers like these 'big names'. It becomes even more difficult to shift from a mode which considers their work and its meanings, and how these develop and where they come from, to one which is concerned with livelihoods and politics. So enormous is their personal wealth that they have hardly to worry about paying their mortgages or about what will happen if they get sick. The challenge then is to find ways of making connections between these, and other, success stories and the question of employment in music and, by extension, in the culture industries. We can begin to do this, I would argue, by returning to questions of social class (as well as gender and ethnicity), history and biography.

Histories of music, politics of class

Three useful examples of how music can function as a way of thinking as well as a place of working came to my attention almost by chance last summer. I felt like reading about music again, and I was suddenly overtaken by a desire to go to hear music in the way I used to, when in the early 1980s in Birmingham there was such a rich musical crossover of reggae (Steel Pulse), disco (Sheila B Devotion), punk and two-tone, as well as various well-intended efforts at neo-Marxist pop. I re-read Simon Reynolds' influential *Blissed Out* and found myself absorbed in his interview with Morrissey (Reynolds 1990). It showed Morrissey to be remarkably aware as a child that pop culture provided him with a kind of personalized map, a way of making sense of place, identity and

Figure 10.2 Morrissey: Courtesy of Rankin

existence. He told Reynolds how at the age of six he had his own magazine, 'listening to the Top 30 every Tuesday only to run off instantly to the type-writer in order to compile my own personal Top 30 which totally conflicted with how the world really was . . . It was a Top 30 of contemporary records, but the new entries were very unlikely, and obviously I favoured certain musicians, like T Rex'. This does not simply repeat to us what we already know about how popular culture has replaced nursery rhymes and fairy tales as a source of image, narrative and information, it also reveals an incredibly intelligent child looking to the charts as a way of working things out. In a more middle-class environment this would no doubt be gently discouraged. But in a single-parent and class-dislocated household, Morrissey was free to consume as much pop as he wanted. You get the impression of him being a rather pompous, old-fashioned child, giving pop his full unbridled attention.

A week later the *Guardian* ran a lengthy interview with Terry Hall, who had started off with The Specials and then set up the Fun Boy Three, and has recently released an excellent new album, *Laugh* (*Guardian* 10 July 1997). This was a distressing story of a working-class boy making it into the local grammar school only to be perceived as socially vulnerable by a teacher, who then subjected him, along with another thirteen year old, to kidnapping and sexual abuse. Unable to describe to his parents at home on the council estate what had happened to him, his school work went out the window and his days at grammar school were numbered. His talent was only able to surface inside the 'safer' confines of Coventry's grim and hard-edged two-tone youth cultures of

Figure 10.3 Terry Hall: Courtesy of Elaine Constantine

the early 1980s; here he wrote *Ghost Town*, a classic single which conjured up the history of black ska music by allowing it to gently haunt the outskirts of the song, envisaging and documenting the new intersections of black and white youth in Britain's inner cities.

The same week that this interview was published I slipped into a sweatbox in Islington to hear Jah Wobble's *Invaders of the Heart* play on one of the hottest nights of the year. It was a great performance in the King's Head, with a line up of reggae musicians and the drummer Jaki Liebezeit from Can. Wobble's bass playing (and his looming, expressionless, physical presence) led and connected the whole set, from a pared down jazz introduction, through a reggae section which combined Celtic instruments and Blakeian lyrics, through to a solid dance dub ending. The thudding bass line also told a story of class and history, of manual labour and then later of urban multi-culturalism. In his earlier incarnation with John Lydon this was put to spectacular effect in the first Public Image single (I forgot I had it, but recently rediscovered it in my box of records). The dark rumble (much more ominous than anything The Prodigy have come up with), combined with Lydon's psychotic screechings, make it one of the most memorable (and influential) records ever made.

Wobble had done a number of extended interviews following the release of his most recent work (Fox 1998; Feay 1997). He recalled walking out of a shabby, run-down East London school ('this was no Dead Poets' Society') and stumbling into Lydon with whom he then went on to share a squat. Eventually he picked up a bass guitar left lying around by Sid Vicious. Interwoven with this narrative was another one, of Dickensian cityscapes, of fifteen mile hikes round Lea Valley, to Greenwich and back to Cambridge Heath Road, of reading Yeats in Shadwell public library, of parents and grandparents who made their living from the river and its trade, of falling into music after falling out of hopeless jobs. He also told of abandoning music for a time after Public Image and taking a job with the London Underground, and then finding his way back into music, and rediscovering his ability and talent and a sense that it couldn't be wasted.

Apart from the fact that this particular story vividly illustrates the cultural studies work of at least three of my colleagues, produced over the last twenty years – including Phil Cohen's seminal essay on youth cultures and the break up of the working-class community in East London (1996), Hebdige's still magnificent structuralist reading of punk (1979) and also Willis's *Learning to Labour* (1979) – all three interviews prompted more general questions about how academics engage with the sort of people who have been living and breathing what we scholars then write about or analyse. For example, it seems scandalous, after thirty years of comprehensive education and the so-called decline of class society and its replacement by the consumer culture, that there remains a need to draw attention to the forces which continue to conspire against young people having access to forms of encouragement, and to finding ways of making good use of their talent. To be still in the business of showing the obstacles overcome, and the sheer

Figure 10.4 Jah Wobble: Courtesy of John Sleeman

contingency of achieving against a backdrop of active discouragement, is as politically demoralizing as it is potentially patronizing.

Better however to run that risk than to disappear entirely into the more intellectually tantalizing but politically less useful project of searching for a theoretical language to measure up to the dizzying brilliance of contemporary music making. Of course the one should not conteract the other. But the stakes are high when (mostly male) academics set themselves the task of making sense of modern music. They are, it seems, haunted by the image, style and reputation of the (usually white) music journalist (again, you only have to check the references for the mentions of the halcyon days of the *NME*). In this context the writing has to somehow be a parallel text to the music. This is a boy's language which avoids at all costs soft subjects like those raised above, in favour of a breakneck breakdown of mutating styles, names, gadgets and equipment.

Alternately, the aim is to elevate the music to the realm of the philosophical by introducing poetic fragments from Foucault, Deleuze or Guattari. This would be more welcome if the authors were willing to take their arguments further and ask what exactly it means that the ecstatic, dancing, raving bodies of working-class boys (girls have always danced) in a field off the M74 correspond at some level to the 'bodies without organs' which are so central to Deleuze's concept of the social? Or indeed to challenge the new hegemony of the 'super-human' black body and the power attributed to it in contemporary hip hop music, as Gilroy has recently and provocatively suggested (Gilroy 1997). But even the inclusion of these questions should not overshadow other issues, such as those involved in earning a living, or learning a skill in the new culture industries. The Creative Task Force, for instance, might well find itself confronted with more challenges than it has so far anticipated in all the rounds of hand-shaking. Alan McGee, a member of the Task Force and manager of Oasis, has suggested that young musicians might be spared the pressure to find a proper job while receiving the Jobseeker's Allowance. Others are talking about the revival of the Enterprise Allowance Scheme, while my own recent research on creative workers in the fashion industry has shown clearly how hard it is to survive in the longer term in the freelance economy, never mind put money into a pension fund. So the current flowering of talent and energy across the creative industries will need more than just symbolic support, it will require a post-industrial strategy which, in its most hopeful mode, might mean that among those less supported by their own cultural capital, less is left to chance.

References

Cohen, P. (1996) *Rethinking the Youth Question*, London: Macmillan.

Feay, S. (1997) 'Here Comes the Stubble', *Independent On Sunday*, 1 June.

Fox, E. (1998) 'Songs of Innocence and Experience', *Guardian*, Weekend Supplement, 7 September.

Gilbert, J. (1997) 'Soundtrack for an Uncivil Society: Rave Culture, The Criminal Justice Act and the Politics of Modernity', *New Formations*, No. 31.

Gilroy, P. (1997) '"After the Love has Gone": Bio-politics and Etho-poetics in the Black Public Sphere', A. McRobbie (ed.), *Back to Reality? Social Experience and Cultural Studies*, Manchester: Manchester University Press.

Hebdige, D. (1979) *Subculture: The Meaning of Style*, London: Methuen.

Hemment, D. (1997) 'e is for Ekstasis', *New Formations*, No. 31.

Hesmondhalgh, D. (1997) 'The Cultural Politics of Dance Music', *Soundings*, Spring, No. 5.

Melville, C. (1997) 'New Forms and Metal Headz: Jungle, Black Music and Breakbeat Culture', unpublished MA Dissertation, Goldsmiths College, London.

Reynolds, S. (1990) *Blissed Out*, London: Serpents Tail.

Toop, D. (1984) *The Rap Attack*, London: Serpents Tail.

Willis, P. (1979) *Learning to Labour*, London: Saxon House.

11

'COME ALIVE LONDON!'

A dialogue with dance music

Interviewing the Moschino crew is an odd experience. 'Where is the going Jackiz?' 'The *Guardian* Guide'. 'Rich'. 'Have Mercy! Come Alive!' 'I am a *Guardian*', confesses Alfa Romeo. 'The Guardian of the ladies'. 'Indeed', I say. 'Indeed!' they all repeat, adding this new word to the mantra. ('Rich!' 'Have mercy!' 'Come alive!' 'Indeed!'). 'Can we do shouts out?' Drew asks. 'Shouts out *Guardian* Guide listenders! (I realise he thinks the *Guide* is a radio show.) 'Daryl, er, Geena, Shequera, my big ego self, boy, the rollin bass renegade master, Drew!

(Jacques Peretti, *Guardian* Guide, April 11–17 1998, p. 32)

Boyzone

Three recent books, *Dis-Orienting Rhythms: The Politics of New Asian Dance Music*, edited by Sharma, Hutnyk and Sharma (1996), *More Brilliant Than the Sun: Adventures in Sonic Fiction* by Kowdo Eshun (1998) and *Energy Flash: A Journey Through Rave Music and Dance Culture* by Simon Reynolds (1998) have each, directly or indirectly, taken issue with Paul Gilroy's writing on music and have therefore sustained and developed the specific debate on popular music, race and anti-essentialism (Gilroy 1987, 1993). While the significance of these exchanges on race informs much of this review, there are other issues at stake, namely gender. But instead of conforming to that pattern established back in the late 1970s of indicating the scale of the absences of 'women in popular music' and then following this up as did Simon Frith and myself, with an analysis of 'how women are represented in rock', it makes more sense now to explore the dynamics of masculine investment in popular music as a special form, a cultural phenomena to which men have uniquely privileged access (Frith and McRobbie 1978). This access is based upon the enduring nature of cultural tradition, on a canonical history comprising mostly of great male figures, on the gendered character of leisure and commercial popular culture, on the differential pathways now taken by young men and women of both working-class and black origin through schooling and education and into work and, more recently, on the gender-segregated division of labour which has sprung into being around new musical technology.

144

These features should not however blind us to a few small ironies. First, that dance music should find itself written about in a way which removes girls and young women from its broad frame of reference. The actual act of dancing virtually disappears from these accounts. Granted, the distinguishing feature of so much dance music (in particular the dub-inflected trip hop of Tricky and Massive Attack) is that you do not or cannot dance to it but still the active participation of girls on the dance floor would warrant more than the passing references by Simon Reynolds to the E-induced distinctive jerky moves associated with male ravers stripped to the waist and girls dressed in skimpy lycra tops. In Reynolds' case the less than comfortable descriptions of the dancefloor are there it seems to back up his claim made in the opening pages of the book that the real stars of club culture are the crowd, the mass of bodies 'iridescent with sweat'.

A seond irony in relation to sexual politics is that it is young, black (and white), urban disadvantaged males who have almost single handedly carved out a distinctive musical aesthetic which is as innovative and as important as reggae. Berated for being failures at school and shunted into the remaining low paid, low skill jobs or into the emergent New Deal schemes, it is from this social group that most of the music being discussed in these books has emerged. An extraordinarily high form of aesthetic engagement is coming from a very low status sector of the population. Of course those who make it in the field of dance music quickly move up the social scale. The rewards are potentially as high as they are for any successful pop musician but, by and large, those who enter this field have low qualifications or no qualifications. It is not surprising then that girls, whose levels of achievement in school have soared in recent years, are under-represented. The field in which, in my mind, the greatest amount of creative energy is currently manifest is virtually a female-free zone. Behind the decks, in the studios, across the pirate airwaves and in the newspapers and magazines, the voices, bodies and images are male. So, to a certain extent, we can read this explosion of experimentation as being born out of the intensification of racialized economic marginalization and the simultaneous appropriation of studio-produced dance music as a haven for black and white males. As a result, the music is a vehicle for distinctively gendered psychic material. Black science fiction, the iconography of horror movies and the world of *Robocop*, *Terminator* and *Bladerunner* all feed into (as soundtrack samples) the undertow of fear, panic, paranoia and urban dystopia which runs through drum 'n' bass music. The reliance on samples, the infatuation with science and engineering, the layered flowing and seemingly authorless quality of the music as well as its supreme self-confidence, the sense that in the great tradition of Miles Davis, Herbie Hancock and others, it is actually making some important breakthrough, creates a field of such intense self reflection that there is, it seems, no opening at all for prosaic questions about the politics of music in general and more specifically the sexual politics of dance music.

It is as though everone now knows that girls and women are more equal but equally everyone knows that this is more or less an exclusively male terrain. This is not to say that sex and gender simply melt away. Popular music will always be a vehicle for analysing sexual anxiety and Simon Reynolds describes accurately the fine line between sexual intoxication and constraint in the intimate dialogue between Tricky and Martina on Tricky's album *Maxinquaye*. It is private but also exposed, close but claustrophobic. The lyrics say strange things like 'we never kiss' and Tricky talks about getting undressed *before* he goes out. The listener wonders whether it is the cannabis-induced heaviness of body and its ego dissolving 'trickery', which Tricky is more in love with. At any rate the musical duet pursues a traditional course of male evasiveness and female need. 'Will you spend your life with me?' asks Martina. Reynolds attributes an exceptionally significant role to drugs in dance culture. Both he and Pini refer to the communality and the dissolution of boundaries and inhibitions brought about by taking Ecstasy (Pini 1997). For Pini rave culture and E provides young women with a more relaxed, less aggressive environment in which they can explore body pleasures through dancing, while Reynolds boldly emphasizes the role of drugs in enhancing musical creativity. The music is the drug, he acknowledges, but the drugs also provide the narrative of euphoria, rush and exhilaration followed, at a later stage, by the darker, gloomier downside, each of which find expression in the music. If punk music dramatized sexual antagonism and provided a platform for sexual anger on the part of young women, dance music celebrates sex without the burden of gender. The freedom or escape is also an escape from the whole bother of gender, but as gender dissolves in the dance floor the men behind the turntables are left unchallenged in their control over the whole field of music production.

Sex is an issue in *Dis-Orienting Rhythms*, mainly during the interview with DJ Radical Sista who angrily repudiates the still prevalent stereotype of energetic young Asian women being seen as inevitably locked in family battles. Her mother objected in the first instance to her being a DJ and playing her records in public, she 'chased me round the house with a roller pin!', but she soon came round and 'even started taking bookings for me' (Housee and Dar 1996: 87). In Kowdo Eshun's *More Brilliant than the Sun*, sex and gender disappear altogether as irrelevancies in the cyborg world where the body is merely an appendix to the machine, where the interface between the human and non-human breaks down and where musical imagination, thanks to computer technologies, allows for a kind of lift off and escape into some inter-planetary zone. All that is conceded here to sex and the body is the autoeroticism of machine-made music as a counter to the more normative and regulatory injunctions to have sex or feel sexy which is one of the means by which black music has been integrated into commercial culture. This refusal of soul is also Simon Reynolds' starting point in *Energy Flash*. I will return to it shortly, but perhaps the additional point is that in this world where the subcultural capital (Thornton 1996) evolves so forcefully around the acquisiton of a very distinctive kind of knowledge, one which can trace lines, tracks, influences and sounds from the intergalactic imagination of Sun Ra to A Guy Called Gerald at the drop of a hat, and where this knowledge, in Bourdieu's terms, appears to be acquired effortlessly as some natural gift, where, to put it bluntly, men simply know about these things, it seems either too sociological or too political to inquire into the gendered dynamics of knowledge production and distribution in this field (Bourdieu 1984). So it is the scale and the depth of the knowledge about music demonstrated in both Eshun's and Reynolds' books, and the manner in which this knowledge is narrated, how their stories are told, which also confirms the almost hermetically sealed world of male expertise. There is no greater risk than being exposed as possessing poor taste on these matters. Sarah Thornton in her account of club culture deftly avoids being seen as hostile or antagonistic to this whole scene on the basis of gender by discounting women's participation as not her immediate concern (Thornton 1996). Instead she examines the hide and seek games played by underground cultural producers, including DJs, promoters and musicians, with the mainstream. Drawing on Bourdieu she argues that the subcultures are as intricately tiered and rigidly hierarchical as any of the more approved forms, in particular the fine arts and classical music. But by avoiding engaging with the perceived poor taste of girls and women in the field of subcultural capital, while also noting it, Thornton is abiding by the rules of the game. This is also a historical and generational position to take. Whereas in the late 1970s it was as normal in writing to challenge male hegemony in music and youth cultures as it was in music itself, by the 1990s feminism is perceived as such an 'unhip' or even 'sad' label to be associated with that it is more usual to make some signal to the sociological existence and relevance of persistent gender differences, and to move quickly on. The alternative is to locate oneself more fully, indeed unambiguously, as a writer within the academic terrain of women's studies and the sociology of gender. Maria Pini's study of women and rave culture makes no attempt to secure subcultural capital for herself on these terms and instead provides a detailed ethnographic account of young women's experience of raving (Pini 1999). She argues that raves offered women an unprecedented space to autonomously explore the physical pleasures of dance as well as the excitement of Ecstasy-induced euphoria and communality. These experiences are also 'subject producing', that is to say they interpellate and create new ways of being female in the leisure field. Some of Pini's interviewees were single mothers in their mid-twenties. For them getting the time to disappear to a rave for up to twenty four hours (leaving the child with its father or grandparent), was a way of overcoming the isolation and hard work of being poor and looking after a young child. But these kinds of concerns immediately put Pini into a very different intellectual and political space from that occupied by all the authors here. I am probably closer to Pini's position than Thornton's. The absence of attention to the domestic, the mundane or even the material in subcultural and music writing, in favour of the abandonment found in these dark spaces, was a focus of attention in one of the first pieces I ever wrote on youth culture

(McRobbie 1999). But the problem with avoiding an engagement with the boys, or in coasting along with them in the hope of acquiring the same kind of facility with the history of sounds, means acquiescing in the rules which govern access to and engagement with these significant cultural forms. It is also to absolve oneself of a commitment to the politics of music, something which is directly confronted in the *Dis-Orienting Rhythms* collection.

The sounds of the Asian underground

The authors here agree that recent writing on hybridity and on the forging of new ethnic identities in urban Britain, which finds expression in popular music, ignores or overlooks how these categories are easily packaged and commodified by the international record industry which is well placed to market these sounds as a new take on the exotic otherness of marginal cultures. The contributors also fear that such emphasis upon difference minimizes or overlooks the human suffering of being deemed different or other. The idea of cultural fluidity and migration is, they argue, conceptualized from the viewpoint of the western metropolis, producing a version of hybridity tilted towards the familiar land-scape of consumer culture. This leaves behind the material and geographical existence of the Third World. There is, they remind us, racial violence and terror every step of the way in the journey from 'there' to 'here'. Not only is there an absence of materialism, there is also a process of cultural filtering where traditional cultures remain invisible in contrast to the contemporary urban cultural mix which is more amenable to theorizing in an anti-essentialist way. Post-structuralism can also mean the 'erasure of the subaltern subject' and in much of this kind of writing, the authors argue, there is little sign of how living human beings survive on a day-to-day basis in racial subordination. Hutnyk suggests that cultural studies is 'aesthetically obsessed' and this leads to a lack of concern with concrete political realities. The banning of a pop video by Fun^Da^Mental, on the basis that it depicted a racial attack, never raised a comment in cultural studies, nor did the introduction of the Criminal Justice Act with the various infringments of liberty which it permitted.

Sharma *et al.* rightly point to the important relation music has played in the lives of young people and also in forging political identities. They remind us of the role of the Anti-Nazi League in the late 1970s and early 1980s and, despite the decline of this kind of activity in the 1990s, they demonstrate the connections between, for example, the student activism in the anti-racist politics of Tejinder Singh and the music of his band Cornershop (who recently had a number one UK hit with 'Brimful of Asha'). In any discussion of the new Asian dance music there is an insistence upon the relevance of a political vocabulary which highlights the scale of racial violence in Britain today. Hutnyk decries the unwillingness of fellow radicals to follow through their denunciation of racial violence with support for community self-defence.

This is an important volume for the history it describes of young Asian people's immersion in popular music, and from this the emergence of a distinctive new Bhangra sound. Any suggestion that certain types of music are primarily or indeed exclusively associated with any single ethnic group is immediately opposed as the authors recount their involvement in soul and rare groove, or in the London jungle scene of the early 1990s. *Dis-Orienting Rhythms* is part record, part testimony, part challenge. In its attempt to combine analysis of music and lyrics as sources of meaning and opposition with a description of the forces which deny the reality of day-to-day racial violence and harassment, the collection looks to Gilroy's seminal *There Ain't No Black In The Union Jack* (Gilroy 1987) as a model. What remains less fully developed is the critique of post-structuralism and of those strands of post-colonialist theory which privilege textuality over what the authors would see as social reality. But to use the latter as a means of relegating the former to a less political space in some notional hierarchy of commitment runs the danger of replicating a long-standing antagonism between what is seen negatively as intellectualism, or theoreticism, in favour of activism. There is also a tendency in the collection to concentrate on those musicians and those parts of the Asian dance music scene which very clearly give voice to anger and frustration (e.g. Fun^Da^Mental, Asian Dub Foundation etc.). The problem lies in the longer term in continuing to expect more of the music politically than musicians are often prepared to commit themselves to. Almost inevitably, given the nature of the music industry, these lines of connection between music and politics are going to be put to the test. As the big record companies offer lucrative deals, the musicians, if signed, will be forced to abide by company code of practice. At the very least this means saying good things in public about the company itself, evidence of which can already be seen in the interview with producer Bally Sagoo. Sagoo acknowledges that there are very few Asian people employed in the music industry. Most have to hold onto their day jobs with British Gas he says, 'while they are doing gigs in the evening or they're singing songs in the charts' (Housee and Dar 1996: 99). On the other hand, he diplomatically continues, 'I've got a great A and R guy and a great relationship with Columbia' (ibid: 99).

'Black Atlantic futurism'

Kowdo Eshun's book is neither traditionally academic in style nor is it popular journalism. Eshun declares his intention to break with the idioms of writing about black music. He is not interested in biographies of great musicians or in charting musical histories. *More Brilliant than the Sun* is theoretically ambitious and deliberately un-disciplined in its structure and organization. But it also perceives itself to be an intervention in black politics. Explicitly taking issue with Gilroy he argues that the narratives of both suffering and redemption carried in black music and promised by it demonstrate how hard black people have struggled to gain for themselves the status of being human. They have sought against the odds to be included. Eshun, in contrast, prefers to construct a musical history based on the desire to escape from the bondage of humanism and the required subjectivities of 'being black'. Drawing loosely on strands of post-structuralist thinking Eshun appears to be arguing that there is no essential black subject and that the experience of slavery created only 'negro subjects' fit for work in the US who were not designated human. Consequently the notion of being human is a 'pointless and treacherous category' and, in addition, 'most African Americans owe nothing to the status of the human'. Eshun looks then to those dynamics in black music which have cut their losses with the aspiration to acquiring human status and have instead embraced a kind of 'Afrodiasporic futurism'. Instead of 'yearning for human rights', *More Brilliant than the Sun* seeks to tell another story. This is one of a post-soul 'Black Atlantic futurism'. Eshun traces a line which begins between 1968 and 1975 and which he labels the Afrodelic Space Program. Eshun applauds all attempts in black music to evade the temptation to be 'real', to have 'soul', and for this reason he looks to the work of a range of musicians who combine an extraordinary degree of inventiveness on the basis of machine technology with a science fiction imagination. He celebrates every point at which music is furthest removed from those roles and sounds normatively expected of black musicians and black music. He includes in this the moments at which Miles Davis and Herbie Hancock 'turned effects into instruments'. The more frequently advanced technology and its futuristic metaphors are applied to music the better.

Despite Eshun's extraordinary flights into narrative experimentation himself (which makes the book at points almost impossible to follow), it is a convincing story. Sun Ra wanted to be 'alien', and often said he came from Saturn. The Afrodelic Era of the early 1970s saw Hancock cast himself as an Afronaut, and Eshun describes his music as a 'psychosonic geography of gangstadelia', while Afrika Bambaataa a few years later looked to the industrial, programmed music of Kraftwerk for inspiration. He too wanted to 'artificialize himself'. This accelerates in the early 1980s with 'turntablization' and the percussive techniques of scratch, introduced into music partly through the efforts of Grandmaster Flash (see figure 10.1, p. 138) who also took on the image of himself as a scientist whose studio was a 'research centre'. From this point onwards the story unfolds with increasing velocity. The discovery of the breakbeat is as big a breakthrough as dub was to reggae, and drum 'n' bass music takes off into the outer space of pure experimentalism with figures like A Guy Called Gerald (whose best-known CD is titled *Black Secret Technology*), Goldie, 4Hero and Grooverider now cast as 'sonic engineers'. These explorations of sound also rely on a set of accompanying cultural artefacts, often incorporated as samples from the world of science fiction, including J.G. Ballard, Phillip K. Dick, The X Files, Ridley Scott's films, and the tradition of dystopia in film. These tastes (like the music of Kraftwerk and Depeche Mode) also indicate a fascination with 'whiteness in the black imagination' (hooks 1992).

Eshun argues that these sources were exciting to black teenagers from the mid-1970s onwards and contributed directly to a cultural break with the past. The intergalactic imagination embraced and embodied by Bambaataa and also by George Clinton coincided with what Ian Penman called the 'smoky logic of dub' (Penman 1998). Dub plate technology along with the birth of the break-beat take black music into a new time and space. Pursuing a vaguely Derridean pathway he describes how dub and breakbeat, through the productive use of space, break and echo in the sequence of the music, act as forces of disorganization, haunting the edges of musical narrative and throwing the listener into sonic disarray. The extraordinary experimentation with sound forged on crude technology by dub producer and pioneer Lee Scratch Perry in the 1970s finds contemporary examples in Tricky's reworking of the idea of voice in music. As Eshun points out this is voice put through the computer and thus made alien, non-human. It is also an 'asthmatic croak', a voice 'in smoke' and in dialogue with the narcotic power of cannabis.

Throughout the book drugs belong both to the world of science and technology, a kind of legitimate part of sonic experimentation, and they also help to envisage these other outer and imagined worlds, in Benjamin's sense of the phantasmagoria. This sensibility of bridging two worlds, that of the scientific and the imagined, also pervades the writing. In the paragraphs above I have mercilessly reduced the flights in language in Eshun's book for the purposes of clarity, summary and critique. Eshun clearly wants to emulate in his writing the brilliant experimentations in sound he attributes to figures like Lee Perry, he wants to simultaneously invent new concepts (he calls himself a concept engineer rather than a writer) and he also wants to imaginatively explore the world of 'sonic fiction'. But does he carry it off? Is his text a counterpart of Lee Perry or Sun Ra, and is this not an excessively inflated ambition? I would have thought that very few critics would be so kind as to suggest that Eshun does carry it off. For my own part I found only nuggets of brilliance hidden away in the many pages of indulgence. He says he wants the book to be an irritation, a kind of 'scratch version' of music history. But this is too laboured to the point of transparency. The reader requires that he takes the needle off the record. A book is a different thing.

Eshun argues that music does not need explication or a separate theoretical language to justify its existence. Music generates its own theory. The terms and phrases invented by figures like George Clinton or, more recently, by Roni Size, Goldie or LTJ Bukem are, he suggests, theoretical terms, the means by which music explains itself to itself. In so doing, music is also explaining the world. Eshun refutes the laboured attempts by sociologists and others to reduce music to its socio-political context. The banality of cultural studies or the social sciences fails miserably to grasp how these musics (embodied in the image of Lee Perry's Black Ark 'space craft' sudio) actually produce themselves as systems of meaning. These are meanings which blur the boundaries of subject and object and which transcend the normative discourses about who and what we are. Hence the interest in refusing the dull logic of real time and space and attempts to carve out another time and space, an 'outer space' in a future time.

But saying music is philosophy does not mean we cannot ask socio-economic or cultural questions about it. How useful is a theory whose logic ends up in space? Is it not the case that the concepts invented by these musicians are not so much elements of theory as technical terms, a way of explaining what is being done, in quite practical and down to earth terms? Eshun's case veers towards defending music and its internal philosophizing systems as sufficient in themselves. This completely defies the need for politics and also contradicts his engagement with Gilroy. In many ways Eshun's account is actually a further extension of Gilroy's argument that black music is, for good historical reasons, an excessive, transcendent, abundant and multi-functional aesthetic. The logic of racialized exclusion created a confinement inside the space of music which in turn made it the spectacular site of innovation, experimentation, argumentation.

There is also an unstated subtext throughout these ruminations by Eshun which can only be described as hallucinatory. There seems to be a point in the book at which a narcotic effect intersects with a philosophical ambition, both of which are intensified by the further seductions of computer and the internet. But to mistake hallucination with some kind of freedom from constraint is surely an illusion, as though drugs do not also have their own regulatory and normative dynamics. Drugs seem here to enable the escape from humanity, collectivity and community which Eshun so desires. But this is a wearied post-hippy cliché. While in this context Eshun offers an alternative narrative of drug use to that which envisages only all too human misery and even nihilism, it would be more interesting and more convincing if he spelt this out. Presumably the debate about how pharmaceuticals can be understood as creative devices needs to be updated in relation to the E and post-E generation. To what extent do drugs, set within the musical milieu described by Eshun, 'mix' the line between what Gilroy would term the tradition of 'black musical genius' and the 'purple haze' of psychic despair and dispossession? Eshun's flight into musical euphoria is so confident, so energetic, exuberant and extraterrestial that it cannot counter the 'return to earth'. Is this escapism not another, more dramatically imagined, form of redemption, one which might make sense aesthetically, but which veers dangerously close to being a new version of the nineteenth century romanticism of art for art's sake? In abandoning the politics of race Eshun comes close to embracing a familar vision of the artist; drunk, drugged, or simply blissed out. He eshews the outdated conceptual world of a black politics forged in community and 'universal love'. One might legitimately ask, who is the subject of this music if not part of some (albeit 'post-human') community or collectivity? Is it not the case that dance music has created a 'new community'? And if 'the love has gone' we have to ask what has replaced it? Is the auto-eroticism of Kraftwerk-influenced dance music a release from the burden of 'love', as it is also a release from the burden of 'being black'? Actually it is on this last point that Kowdo veers back towards reconnecting with Gilroy.

The logic of anti-essentialism is precisely to look forward to no longer being black (Gilroy 1999) and science fiction futurism provides a fantasy metaphor for the escape from racial categorization.

Come alive London!

Simon Reynolds briefly describes his introduction to second wave rave in 1991 as a kind of conversion. His writing as a music journalist until then had indicated a marked preference for white indie music, for Morrissey, The Birthday Party, Throwing Muses and the sort of pop music which tips towards the experimental. His conversion was to a 'psychedelic dance culture' whose parts comprised anthemic tracks, musical flow under the direction of the DJ, pirate radio, specialist music shops, drugs and 'radical anonymity' in music production. These are also the key characteristics of the black dance subcultures which earlier emerged from the three points in Reynolds' compass, Detroit, Chicago and New York. The detail in this book is quite spectacular. On page after page every key track is logged, commented on and located within its wider cultural map. It is almost impossible to extract the most important moments in these intercon-necting naratives. However, the thumbnail, but nonetheless fascinating, sketch of lower-middle-class black youths growing up in Detroit in 1978 and having benefitted from the relative affluence of their parents who still enjoyed full-time incomes from the car factories, stands out. These boys embraced a combination of conspicuous consumption in the form of clothes and style, with a taste for white pop music including the British electro-pop icon, Gary Numan, the American art school band, the B52s, and, inevitably, Kraftwerk. Such fascina-tions led them to play a key role in the creation of what since has become known globally as 'techno', a style of music which virtually underwrote the birth of rave. Reynolds argues that this music actually described Detroit in transition from an industrial economy to a post-industrial urban dystopia. Techno is 'empty city' music.

From that starting point Reynolds moves to Chicago and charts the emer-gence of house (black, gay and 'upwardly mobile') and then to New York where both these trends undergo a further re-mix under the influence of the more avant-garde end of pop, including Laurie Anderson and Talking Heads. Back in the UK Reynolds gears up to confront the rave culture which so rapidly embraced not the minority but the majority of young people to the point that raving simply became a sign of being young in Britain in the late 1980s and through the 1990s. This section of the book provides by far the clearest guide so far, although the emphasis is on the music and the cultural activities which were closest to the production and dissemination of the music. Basically, through these chapters Reynolds writes a history of every main influence, every key track, and every connection linking tracks, musicians, producers and DJs. Inevitably his own preferences surface but the sheer depth of his knowledge and the high points which fire his enthusiasm actually make him a fairly trustworthy guide. The effect is similar to that in Eshun's book. The reader is left wondering how on earth anybody could listen to so much music and know every track, every re-mix, and still extrapolate from this to construct a convincing argument. Chapter three, for example, emphasizes the importance of the 'undulant groove and percussive foliage' of the first tracks by A Guy Called Gerald and Primal Scream's *Higher than the Sun*, another turning point in the creation of dub-oriented dance culture, and a forerunner to the work of Massive Attack. Reynolds' excursions into the more ambient, chill out music of The Orb and the later KLF also point to the crux of the argument which is that dance music becomes a creative resource, a frame of reference for musicians. As one producer and DJ says to Reynolds, 'the fact you can dance to it is irrelevant to us'. This 'new soundscape' and the technology which accelerates its growth also encourages an obsession with musical history. Sampling becomes synonomous with archival research and a new mutant genre, like a rogue gene, appears from week to week, from 'pastoral techno' to 'breakbeat hardcore'.

Like Eshun, Reynolds is fascinated by the futuristic impulses in the Detroit and post-Detroit techno sounds. He links this back to the Sun Ra and Herbie Hancock and traces its newer impulses in the work of DJ Spooky (Paul Miller) and others. In some of its most recent permutations 'dance music is a vehicle for lofty intellectualism'. This too becomes a central part of the argument. The contentious core to Reynolds' analysis is that dance music is now capable of containing and encouraging complexity and experimentation. Which of course is exactly what he looked for as a critic in his earlier musical tastes. Critics more tuned in to the historical elements and the complexity that was always present in different and earlier forms of 'dance music' (i.e. black music), including jazz, soul, disco and most of all reggae, would not of course need to undergo such a conversion. There is a sense in which he did not rate this music while it was still plain old dance or disco music. It was only when it became a thing of the mind as well as of the body that Reynolds sat up and began to listen. This discovery then lead him back to discover the bodily pleasures which he had previously discounted.

The two best chapters in the book are both focused on London in the mid-1990s. Reynolds' commentary on the almost verbatim transcript taken off a pirate radio station and reprinted is actually a fantastic piece of sociological analysis. The 'sublime nonsense' of the teenage jungle MCs and DJs is, Reynolds proclaims, one of the 'cultural artefacts of the twentieth century'. Who could disagree? He describes it as a kind of Dada speech, a 'doggerel of druggy buzzwords'. Full of insider lingo, and prattling along at the speed of light, it is completely mysterious to parents and those who don't participate. The exhortations, testimonies, the invocation of community, the invitations to come to tonight's party, the commentaries on last night's party, create the effect of a world which has completely abandoned itself to this as a way of life (and AWOL was the name of the earliest jungle club night held in Islington). Reynolds remarks on the enormous influence on this style of radio DJ-ing of reggae MCs, and the toasting tradition. But in my mind he underplays how this Jamaican connection continues to shape and energize the distinctive London element in this cultural phenomena. Why exactly did this happen in London and what socio-cultural interactions back and forwards between black and white youth provided the foundation for these chants and Blakeian cries, 'Come Alive London!'?

But these 'lines of communication across the city' as they gather in around the 'sub-bass frequencies' of drum 'n' bass which is, according to Reynolds, a 'raved up, digitalised offshoot of reggae', also tell a less euphoric story. This 'truly indigenous black UK music' comes into being through a 'genuine unity of black and white'. Drum 'n' bass is a working-class and a black cultural form built on the virtual non existence of an alternative labour market for young unqualified males in London. As jungle DJ Andy Garcia said in the *Guardian* newspaper, 'I have to make a go of this. If I don't there is only the prospect of a job in a warehouse.' Reynolds does not engage with this particular 'hardcore' reality, only signals it, but there is a sense in which economic desperation for the good things that everybody else in London seems to have, fuels the breakneck speed of this sound. The social connects with the symbolic and the technological with the desire to be 'far ahead', pushing the junglists like Goldie into an imagined dystopia, and along with 4Hero and A Guy Called Gerald he also is drawn by the 'Afro-futuristic imagination'. Reynolds adheres to the kind of populist purism which celebrates underground authenticity ('rave as psychedelic disco'). He likes the sheer volume and the technological complexity of hardcore techno, but dislikes when dance music strays into jazz, and delves into the history of bebop, reintegrating it with samples, as Roni Size has recently done. With echoes of that post-structuralist disdain for 'the human' as nothing more than a set of instructions and normativities which in musical terms require sensuality, lyricism and 'soul', Reynolds prefers the sublimely technological. When dance becomes less 'hardcore' and more jazz-influenced, when LTJ Bukem and Goldie explore the field of 'modern classical', he loses interest. This is not cerebral in the right way. Nor does he have any sympathy for the kind of collaborations which involve having Maya Angelou read over a dance beat backing track, as Branford Marsalis has done. This 'twittering' (as he puts it) reeks too much of heart and soul. But where Eshun does at least engage with what he sees as the limits of Gilroy's invocation of black community, Reynolds avoids any direct debate. His distance from Gilroy's socio-historical account can only be gleaned through a methodology and a playlist which opts for documenting the shuddering thrills of techno. This is, after all, the milieu in which he discovered what James Brown knew all along – that it wasn't unmanly to dance.

References

Bourdieu, P. (1984) *Distinction: Towards a Critical Judgement of Taste*, London: Routledge.

Eshun, K. (1998) *More Brilliant Than the Sun: Adventures in Sonic Fiction*, London: Quartet.

Frith, S. and McRobbie, A. (1978) Rock and Sexuality in *Screen Education*. Winter 78–79, No. 29.

Gilroy, P. (1987) *There Ain't No Black In the Union Jack*, London: Hutchinson.

—— (1993) *The Black Atlantic*, London: Verso.

—— (1999) *Between Camps*, Boston: Harvard University Press.

hooks, b. (1992) 'Representing Whiteness in the Black Imagination', Grossberg, I., Nelson, C. and Treichler, P. (eds) *Cultural Studies*, New York, London: Routledge, pp. 338–47.

Housee, S. and Dar, M. (1996) 'Remixing Identities: 'Off the Turntable', Sharma, S., Hutnyk, J. and Sharma A., *Dis-Orienting Rhythms: The Politics of the New Asian Dance Music*, London: Zed Books, pp. 81–105.

McRobbie, A. (2000) *Feminism and Youth Culture*, Basingstoke: Macmillan, Edn. 2.

Pini, M. (1997) 'Women and the Early British Rave Scene', A. McRobbie (ed.), *Back to Reality? Social Experience and Cultural Studies*, Manchester: MUP, pp. 152–70.

—— (forthcoming) *From Home to House: Dance Cultures and Changing Modes of Femininity*.

Penman, I. (1998) *Vital Signs: Music, Movies and Other Manias*, London: Serpents Tail.

Reynolds, S. (1998) *Energy Flash: A Journey Through Rave Music and Dance Culture*, London: Picador.

Sharma, S., Hutnyk, J. and Sharma A. (1996) *Dis-Orienting Rhythms: The Politics of the New Asian Dance Music*, London: Zed Books.

Thornton, S. (1996) *Club Cultures*, Cambridge: Polity Press.

INDEX

Page numbers in *italics* denote illustrations